RELIGION IN INDIA
Past and Present

Lawrence A. Babb

Willem Schupf Professor of Asian Languages and Civilizations and Professor of
Anthropology, Emeritus, Amherst College, Massachusetts

EDINBURGH ◆ LONDON

First published in 2020 by
Dunedin Academic Press Ltd
Hudson House
8 Albany Street
Edinburgh EH1 3QB

London Office: 352 Cromwell Tower
Barbican
London EC2Y 8NB

www.dunedinacademicpress.co.uk

ISBNs
Paperback: 978-178046-074-1
PDF: 978-1-78046-623-1
ePub: 978-178046-618-7
Amazon Kindle: 978-178046-619-4

British Library Cataloguing in Publication Data
A catalogue record for this book is available from the British Library

Typeset by Makar Publishing Production, Edinburgh
Printed by Hussar Books, Poland

Table of Contents

List of Illustrations

Note on Usage

Key terms from Indic languages that are not proper nouns are italicised on first occurrence and are unitalicised thereafter. Plurals of italicised terms are indicated by the addition of a non-italic 's'. In the interest of readability, these terms are given without diacritical marks in the text, but the most important among them are present in the glossary where – if diacritics are required for proper romanisation, which is not always the case – they are given both with and without diacritics. Proper nouns are unitalicised and given without diacritics in the text. Among proper nouns, those with a mainly modern context (e.g., Vishva Hindu Parishad) are given in the glossary without diacritics; others are presented with diacritics if needed for romanisation. In general, terms and names that have an important context in ancient languages are given with the medial and final short 'a', which is pronounced in Sanskrit and Prakrit but dropped in modern Hindi. Thus, I have written 'Digambara' rather than 'Digambar' and 'Rama' rather than 'Ram'. However, terms that have a mostly modern context – caste names, for example – are given in their modern form.

Acknowledgements

Due to this book's scope, my indebtedness to others is more diffuse than is usually the case. If only indirectly, the book bears the mark of several generations of Amherst students who did me the honour of enrolling in my classes on South Asian topics and whose interest and questions never failed to inspire and challenge me. I also owe much to Amherst College colleagues whose intellectual companionship has been a career-long liberal arts education. Among my Amherst colleagues, two deserve special thanks: Amrita Basu for reading a portion of the manuscript, and Maria Heim for good counsel and bibliographic advice. I am also very grateful indeed to Ophira Gamliel, outside reader for Dunedin Academic Press, whose good judgement and many excellent suggestions have greatly improved this book. But what knowledge and understanding I have gained of South Asian life is mainly due to Indian friends and academic colleagues – too many to be listed here – whom I have had the privilege of knowing, and from whom I have learnt so much, over the half century I have been travelling to India. Special mention, however, should be made of the Bothras of Jaipur who have been my family in India ever since my first visit to that city in 1990. Always welcoming, a refuge in times of stress, and ever the best of company, they have my everlasting thanks. For her patience with my projects and absences, and her constant support and love through life's ups and downs, my deepest gratitude is to Nancy.

Some Current and Former (British) Place Names

Current	Former
Bengaluru	Bangalore
Chennai	Madras
Dhaka	Dacca
Ganga	Ganges
Kochi	Cochin
Kolkata	Calcutta
Mumbai	Bombay
Mysuru	Mysore
Odisha	Orissa
Pune	Poona
Varanasi	Banaras
Yamuna	Jumna

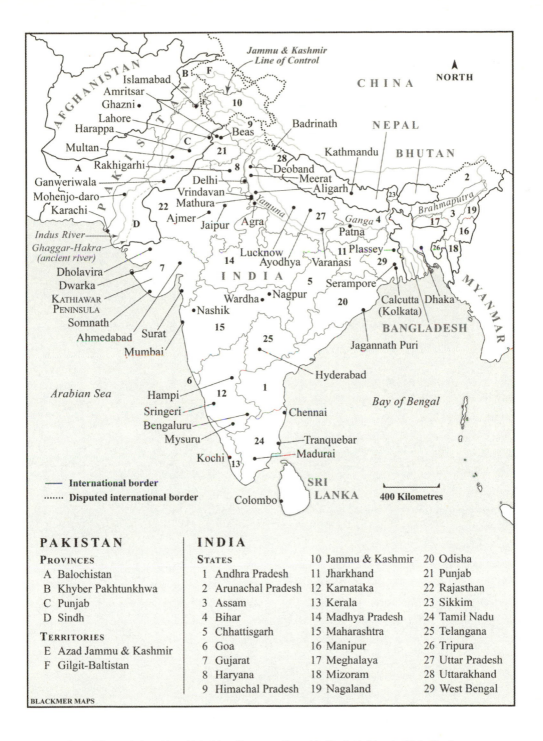

Map of South Asia with selected locations mentioned in the text. Map by Kate Blackmer.

PAKISTAN

PROVINCES
A Balochistan
B Khyber Pakhtunkhwa
C Punjab
D Sindh

TERRITORIES
E Azad Jammu & Kashmir
F Gilgit-Baltistan

INDIA

STATES
1 Andhra Pradesh
2 Arunachal Pradesh
3 Assam
4 Bihar
5 Chhattisgarh
6 Goa
7 Gujarat
8 Haryana
9 Himachal Pradesh

10 Jammu & Kashmir
11 Jharkhand
12 Karnataka
13 Kerala
14 Madhya Pradesh
15 Maharashtra
16 Manipur
17 Meghalaya
18 Mizoram
19 Nagaland

20 Odisha
21 Punjab
22 Rajasthan
23 Sikkim
24 Tamil Nadu
25 Telangana
26 Tripura
27 Uttar Pradesh
28 Uttarakhand
29 West Bengal

BLACKMER MAPS

Introduction

This book deals with Indian religions and does so in broad strokes. It covers major traditions and leading ideas, their origins and subsequent histories. It assumes a readership with no particular background knowledge of India other than the sort of general familiarity one might gain from a basic knowledge of world history and an alert reading of newspapers and periodicals. In the chapters to follow, I present an overview of the subcontinent's major religious traditions, past and present. These include the Vedic tradition, Buddhism, Jainism, Sikhism, the traditions that came to be known as Hinduism, and Islam. The book does not aspire to completeness. While the careers in India of such religions as Judaism, Zoroastrianism and Bahai are interesting and important, their followings are small, as is their overall histori-cal influence on India, and although Judaism is touched upon later in the book the others are not. Christianity is another matter; although its adherents constitute only a bit over 2% of India's total population, its historical importance and cultural impact have been great indeed.

There are other general works on Indian religion, but this one differs from most in one particular respect. Such surveys typically do not pursue the story into its modern political context. Here, however, I take the view that an account of religion in India can hardly be complete without considering religion's ever-tightening grip on politics in the Republic of India. Moreover, no full understanding of the republic's politics is possible without some knowledge of the religious traditions that are its historical background and contemporary context. The book, therefore, continues the story into the post-independence period with a focus on the migration of religion from the periphery to the centre of governance and political discourse in the modern Indian state. It does not follow the post-independence careers of South Asian religions in the region's other states, a matter best left to other, more specialised treatments.

My account is not only about religion; it is also about names. It has to be, because the issue of what nations, communities, places and religious traditions are called is particularly complex and fraught in this part of the world. In unpacking this, let us begin at the outside and work our way in. The region of the world in which this book is situated is South Asia. South Asia is the southernmost appendage of Eurasia and is the home of the Republic of India, Pakistan, Bangladesh, Nepal, Bhutan and Sri Lanka. (The Maldives and Afghanistan also belong to the South Asian Association for Regional Cooperation, but are to some extent outliers.) The South Asian subcontinent is roughly similar in cultural variegation to Europe. Its several linguistically and culturally distinctive regions are huge in extent and, were it not for the accidents of history, many of the entities that are states or provinces of South Asian countries today might well have become separate independent countries – South Asian equivalents of France, Germany, Spain and so on.

But what about 'India'? In reference to the civilisation that originated and evolved in South Asia, this term will be far more familiar than 'South Asia' to most readers of this book and is entrenched in English usage. The term 'India' and its variants derive from an ancient Persian term for the Indus River, and have been used by generations of outsiders to refer to South Asia and the civilisation to which it gave birth. It was not, however, the word used by the subcontinent's insiders to describe their world. That term was 'Bharata' or 'Bharatavarsha', terms derived from the name of an emperor described in Hindu scripture. To add to the confusion, insiders also use the term 'Hindustan' ('Land of the Hindus') to describe the subcontinent's northern region and sometimes in reference to South Asia generally.

To this must be added one point more. The equivalent of a tectonic terminological shift occurred in 1947 when a new nomenclature crystallised. This was the year of the British departure from their Indian Empire (which also included Myanmar [then Burma] and Sri Lanka [then Ceylon], both of which gained independence the next year). At that point, the subcontinent proper was divided between two independent republics: India and Pakistan (Pakistan itself splitting into Pakistan and Bangladesh at a later stage). The Republic of India was bequeathed the name 'India', an inheritance it seems glad enough to have, for Indians use 'India' constantly to refer to their republic, and the term is enshrined on currency notes, postage stamps and in innumerable official documents including the Constitution. The other official name is Bharat, which is also in ubiquitous use. But, obviously, the terms 'India' and 'Indian' cannot be used to describe the post-1947 South Asian world without qualification.

Throughout this book, I have employed the terms 'South Asia' and 'South Asian' in geographical contexts but have bowed to convention and employed the terms 'India' and 'Indian' in reference to the civilisation that grew and flourished in South Asia. I have done so because of its familiarity to most readers and because it is the terminology readers are likely to encounter in other books dealing with Indian religions. However, in chapters 6 and 7 the focus narrows to the Republic of India – as opposed to the other modern South Asian states – and in these chapters I am careful to be sure the political context is clear.

There is yet another problem of nomenclature that will never be quite set to rest in this book and that runs through its pages as a connecting thread. It might strike readers that, of all the labels deployed here, 'Hinduism' would be among the least problematic – after all, what could be more Indian than Hinduism? But, in fact, the existence of the entity denoted by this label is highly contested. And more, when Hinduism is declared to be the religion of a 'majority' – a claim that played key roles in both pre- and post-independence Indian politics – the dispute can become truly momentous. Arguably, as we shall see, the idea of Hinduism was an invention of the late eighteenth or early nineteenth century. But if the concept was invented, does that necessarily mean that there was never a reality behind it? And if that reality was itself a largely modern phenomenon, can we say that it is less real for all of that? These are matters to which I turn more than once and will be a major concern of the last chapter.

When our story begins, however, these disputes lie over four-thousand years in the future.

1

The Vedic Age and Its Legacies

From around the sixth century BCE, an ancient period by any reckoning, the Ganga valley was the scene of an extraordinary burst of city-building and state formation. However, it is an astonishing fact that this was not the first such epoch in South Asia, for another and even more ancient surge of city-building, South Asia's first, had already taken place roughly 2,000 years previously in the valley of the Indus River. These cities were the product of a brilliant urban civilisation that had arisen, reached an apogee, declined and – by the time cities began to rise again in South Asia – had been completely and utterly forgotten. And indeed, it would remain forgotten until the twentieth century.

The First Urbanisation

The story of its discovery – one that carries with it some of the romance of ancient-buried-city archaeology – begins in the nineteenth century with an activity typical of the period: the construction of railways. In the 1850s, British engineers were laying a track from Multan to Lahore (both cities in Punjab province in what is now Pakistan). Along the route, especially near a town named Harappa, were numerous ruins of brick-built structures, and the railway builders began using bricks from these ruins as ballast for the tracks. What nobody knew was that these bricks were about 4,000 years old. In due course, the ruins attracted the attention of the then-director of the Archaeological Survey of India, Alexander Cunningham. In search of ancient Buddhist materials, he conducted some desultory excavations there during which he unearthed a steatite seal with what appeared to be writing in an unknown script. Similar seals had already been found by others, but neither Cunningham nor anyone else had any notion of their true significance. It was not until the 1920s that the real nature of the ruins began to come to light. Investigations were then undertaken under the supervision of John Marshall, Director of the Archaeological Survey of India, at Harappa and Mohenjo-daro, some 400 miles downriver from Harappa. These excavations revealed that the brick ruins were, in fact, the physical remains of an apparently literate South Asian civilisation arguably comparable in importance to Mesopotamia, the Nile valley, China, Mexico and Peru.

Cities

This civilisation, generally known as the Indus civilisation (or the Harappan civilisation), is now far better understood than it was in those days. We now know that the sites at Mohenjo-daro and Harappa were two of what appear to have been five major urban centres (the others are Rakhigarhi, Ganweriwala and Dholavira), but there are many smaller known sites and doubtless many others yet to be discovered. The civilisation's total area of occupation was huge, extending along the coast from the Kathiawar Peninsula to coastal Balochistan and north-eastward up the Indus valley through Punjab (the region defined by the upper Indus tributaries, now divided between India and Pakistan) to the Himalayan foothills. While there were numerous towns and villages scattered throughout this region, the main areas of settlement were concentrated in two river valleys. One was the Indus and its northern tributaries; the other was a river known as the Ghaggar (in India) and Hakra (in Pakistan) that once ran parallel to the Indus to its east and is now mostly a dead riverbed.

The large urban centres of the Indus valley flourished from roughly 2600 to 1900 BCE, but this was preceded by a long period of cultural evolution that had taken place in the same region. The cultural continuities between the pre-urban and urban phases show clearly that the Indus valley civilisation was an indigenous product, not a transplant from some other civilisational centre. But it must also be emphasised that, if it was indigenous, the Indus civilisation was certainly not isolated, for it had

1.1 Harappan ruins at Dholavira, Gujarat (© Shutterstock by CRS PHOTO).

been exposed to cultural influences from West Asia even in its pre-urban phases, and the mature civilisation was linked to Mesopotamia (roughly correlating to modern Iraq) and elsewhere by extensive networks of trade. It was a grain-based civilisation, with barley and wheat, especially barley, providing its principal subsistence base. Domestic animals included humped zebu cattle (as well as a non-humped variety), water buffaloes, sheep, goats and dogs. Zebu cattle and water buffalo are among the most ubiquitous domestic animals today in the Indus region and throughout the subcontinent. There were apparently no or few horses, a significant fact when one considers the cultural and military importance of horses in later periods of South Asian history. Metal items were made from copper or bronze – they had no iron – and the cities were built mainly of burnt brick.

In the absence of decipherable written materials, we have no idea how political control was organised or exercised in the Indus valley and its subregions, but some reasonable deductions can be made. One authority (Kenoyer, 1998, p. 81) has drawn attention to the striking absence of military symbolism in the artefacts so far recovered and the apparent non-existence of monuments or palaces exalting the power of rulers. Because of this, Kenoyer suggests that political authority – shared, he believes, by political, trading and sacerdotal elites – was not supported primarily by force of arms and was most likely exercised through control of trade and religion. Another theorist (Possehl, 2002, pp. 5–6) takes matters even further by claiming that the Indus valley polity was an example of social and economic complexity without the state. This seems unlikely, but there is more than one way to organise state power, and the question of how this was done in the Indus valley remains open. But by whatever manner it was constituted – in councils, first-among-equals chieftains or by some other means – the exercise of authority seems to have been quite efficient, at least in some domains. The cities were clearly planned, with streets laid out in a grid-like pattern. The health and well-being of the inhabitants were greatly enhanced by the existence of well-designed and efficient drainage systems. Remarkably, a single, standardised system of weights was used throughout the Indus region for the entire period of urban maturity, and the bricks used in construction were of a standard size.

We would know far more about the life of these people were their writing system to be deciphered. The samples we have of their script are somewhat limited in type, consisting mainly of inscriptions on pottery and stamp seals (probably, but not certainly, of the sort that mark ownership), and we may suppose that writing was more extensively employed on perishable materials. However, it seems to be generally agreed that the writing system was logo syllabic (i.e., a system in which characters represent either meanings or sounds), and something over 400 characters have been identified. The lack of anything comparable to the Rosetta Stone for the Indus civilisation has defeated all attempts at decipherment so far.

Given our inability to read their writing, we cannot know for certain what kind of language the Indus people spoke, but is very likely (though not certainly) to have belonged to the Dravidian language family, the language family to which the principal present-day languages of South India belong. The most compelling evidence in favour of this conclusion is the fact that the Brahui people of Balochistan (a province in south-western Pakistan) speak a Dravidian language today. The Brahui language would thus appear to be a remnant of what was once a belt of Dravidian languages in western South Asia that included the Indus region and that was mostly submerged or pushed southward by the Indo-Aryans, whom I shall discuss anon. It is also indicated by the fact that early Sanskrit (see The End of the First Urbanisation, below), which is a non-Dravidian language but took shape in the northern Indus region, contains Dravidian vocabulary and bears the imprint of Dravidian phonology and syntax.

Indus Valley Religion

Our inability to read the Indus script is also a major handicap in trying to understand their religion. But even if we have no direct access into the subjectivity of the Indus peoples, the material remains of their culture give us some clues about their beliefs and some possible hints of continuity with later South Asian religions. This evidence, however, is not primarily architectural; the Indus peoples left no remains of temples or mortuary monuments that have yet been identified as such. It is, therefore, from their artistic imagery, especially as seen on pottery, terracotta figurines, children's toys and the stamp seals (and their impressions) that we know what little we do.

Bearing always in mind the speculative nature of the endeavour, there is a reasonable case to be made for some threads of continuity between Indus valley religion and elements of that congeries of beliefs and practices that we know as Hinduism. As an example, the omnipresence of the pipal leaf as a motif in Indus art in many different contexts quite likely presages the importance of the pipal and banyan trees as objects of worship and as religious symbols in later Hinduism (Kenoyer, 1998, pp. 105–6). And more generally, the ubiquity of vegetative and animal symbolism in Indus art suggests a possible attribution of sacred qualities to some trees and animals that is, indeed, characteristic of later popular Hinduism. More consequential is the fact that large numbers of Indus figurines have been found that almost certainly have specifically religious significance. They depict female human figures, quite possibly goddesses, and various male animals including and most notably male buffaloes. Because of the association of some of them with what seem to be household shrines, theorist Asko Parpola concludes that they were physical objects of worship (Parpola, 2015, pp. 173–4). If true, this is an important point, because although image worship is a core ritual in later Hinduism it was not practised by the Indo-Aryans (historically later than the Indus valley civilisation, and to be discussed shortly). The Indus materials might thus suggest that image worship is a practice that entered Hinduism from indigenous South Asian sources.

Along the same lines, Parpola suggests that the female figurines represent a non-Indo-Aryan earth-goddess cult symbolically linked with bulls and associated not only with fertility, growth and protection but also with disease and death (Parpola, 2015, pp. 236–54). The worship of such goddesses is widespread in Indian villages today, and Parpola believes that the goddess/bull cult, as specifically seen in the Indus materials, originally derived from a cultic complex that had diffused to the Indus valley from West Asian sources. In this ancient cult, the goddess is Mother-Earth and the bull or buffalo is Sky-Father, whose rainfall quickens the potential for life that the goddess carries. But this relationship is ambiguous, because the goddess who gives life also takes life away, and this destructive aspect of her nature is enacted by the sacrifice of the bull to the goddess. If, as Parpola argues, such sacrifice was an Indus practice, then it seems quite possible that it was a paradigm for the Hindu practice of sacrificing buffaloes to the goddess and its charter myth telling of the goddess Durga's vanquishing of the Buffalo Demon Mahishasura (on this point, see Hiltebeitel, 1978, pp. 773–92).

There is another point to be made about the bulls. Depictions of humanoid buffalo-horned figures in yogic-looking postures have been found on some stamp seals, and they are probably deities of some sort. The most famous example of these is a representation of a buffalo-horned figure displaying an erect penis. This figure has been interpreted as an early prototype of the Hindu deity Shiva, whom Hindu tradition portrays as a Great Yogi (*mahayogi*) and who is commonly worshipped in the form of a phallus-shaped object known as a *linga*. While the proto-Shiva hypothesis might be tenuous, the yogic posture, seen in other images as well, could possibly indicate an Indus continuity with the much later system of contemplative technology known as *yoga*.

Finally, many observers have noted the importance of water to the Indus peoples, which is understandable considering the importance of rivers in their lives, and this might well have had a religious dimension. The presence of bathing facilities in Indus cities (such as Mohenjo-daro's 'Great Bath') and the general attention paid to water supplies and drainage suggest that the Hindu emphasis on ritual bathing and purity could have been, perhaps in part, a later echo of Indus valley religious culture.

The End of the First Urbanisation

As all things do, the era of great Indus valley cities came to an end. A convenient dating-peg on which to hang this fact is roughly 1900 BCE, but the end did not come suddenly, and it was arguably not an 'end' at all but a transformation. However, in this matter we find ourselves confronting a much debated scholarly issue and an important zone of confluence between the findings of archaeology and the methods and motives of colonial historiography.

It was long thought that the Indus valley cities were destroyed because of military conquest. This theory found its basis in the indisputable fact that a people bearing a culture very different from that of the Indus valley were present in north-west South Asia by roughly the middle of the second millennium BCE. They called themselves Arya (noble). Generally known to historians as Indo-Aryans, they were a chariot-driving, semi-nomadic, cattle-keeping people, who spoke languages belonging to the Indo-European language family. The earliest strata of the Indo-Aryans' oral literature, the Vedas, were composed in an archaic variety of the language known as Sanskrit, and they contain verses that have been interpreted as describing an Indo-Aryan conquest of an ethnically distinct and apparently urban people. The king of the Vedic gods, Indra, is described as a destroyer of fortifications, and his enemies are called *dasa*, a term that later comes to mean 'slave.' These points and others led early theorists to the conclusion that the Indus valley civilisation was brought down by an 'invasion' of Indo-Aryans coming from somewhere in southern central Eurasia and who entered South Asia thorough the mountains of the North-West Frontier (see, e.g., Basham, 1968, pp. 27–33).

But while the Indo-Aryans definitely came from outside South Asia (although some historians believe otherwise, a matter addressed below), the invasion scenario cannot possibly be correct. In fact, without impugning the good faith of Mortimer Wheeler (a major excavator at Harappa) and other promoters of this idea, it must be said that this narrative possesses all the earmarks of a colonial charter myth, with the Indo-Aryans portrayed as a wholesome, hardy, light-complexioned warrior race who were early precursors to the British and other outsiders who came to South Asia as conquerors and rulers. But, in fact, the fortifications described in the Vedic verses bear little resemblance to the Indus cities, and the mountainous terrain described in these verses resembles the Indus valley not at all. Parpola (2015, pp. 97–106) argues, plausibly I think, that the battles against the dasas describe events that probably took place in what is now northern Afghanistan while the Vedic Indo-Aryans were still on the way to South Asia. Also, the Indus de-urbanisation began around 1900 BCE, but the main entry of the Vedic Indo-Aryans into South Asia is pretty securely dated at around 1400 BCE, at which point the mature urban phase of Indus culture was long in the past.

Finally, the imagery of an actual 'invasion' is highly misleading. The Indo-Aryans were a tribal people who lacked the organisational capacity to orchestrate the conquest of the great walled cities of a wealthy, urban civilisation or even to organise the military formations necessary to besiege and overpower such cities. Instead, the coming of the Vedic Indo-Aryans must have been a slow movement in which clan-based communities sifted their way into South Asia in successive waves through the rough country of the subcontinent's North-West Frontier. It is probable that some early-coming Indo-Aryan speakers (not the Vedic Indo-Aryans, who came mid-millennium) were present in Indus cities as early as 2000 BCE. These probably originated among a then-urban and flourishing people in what is now northern Afghanistan and southern Turkmenistan (known to archaeologists as the Bactria and Magiana Archaeological Complex), while the Vedic Indo-Aryans came later (Parpola, 2015, pp. 70–1, 79–82). But whenever they came, early or late, the Indo-Aryans must have found various ways of developing relationships – no doubt sometimes peaceful, sometimes not – with local populations. One result was linguistic fusion, which is attested by the fact that the earliest examples of Vedic Sanskrit (the language [or languages] of texts believed to represent the Vedic Indo-Aryans) bear phonological features that, as noted earlier, suggest Dravidian influence.

Further, we must also challenge the idea that there was ever an actual 'demise' of the Indus civilisation. De-urbanisation certainly occurred, but the Indus people and their cultural heritage remained, albeit in new and different social and political moulds (Kenoyer, 1998, pp. 174–9). The older urban order hollowed out, and the focus of Indus culture shifted from the centre to the peripheries of the core Indus region, specifically to Punjab and the areas corresponding to the present-day Indian states of Gujarat and Haryana. Here, increasingly divergent variants of Indus culture began to evolve. This concatenation of changes seems to have resulted mainly from environmental factors that resulted in flooding, the shifting of river courses, and crop failures, all of which disrupted the delicate networks of trade and political control that once held the centre (or centres) together, and these trends were probably gradual enough to have been hardly noticeable to individuals living during this period. These were the Indus valley peoples who were met by the later incoming migrations of Indo-Aryans

Indo-Aryans

One of the most interesting and enlightening areas of historical study is historical linguistics, also known as comparative linguistics. This is the analysis of the relationships between languages in historical perspective, with the purpose of tracing the evolution and differentiation of languages and dialects as they emerge from previously existing speech communities. This field, more in vogue in the eighteenth and nineteenth centuries than today, retains its value as a means of understanding the movements of peoples unrecorded in written history.

One of the true key moments in the development of historical linguistics was when Sir William Jones, a British jurist, arrived in Calcutta in 1783 (the same year in which he was knighted) to serve as a judge on the High Court of Bengal. As a highly educated Englishman of the era, he was well versed in Latin and Greek, but he was also a language-learning paragon who knew multiple languages and never tired of learning more. Once in India, his ceaseless scholarly activity led him to the study of Sanskrit, the language of the Hindu tradition's most sacred texts, a portion of the sacred literature of Buddhism and Jainism, as well as an enormous secular literature. This led to a major revelation, which was that Sanskrit was related to ancient Greek and Latin, a list that was later to expand to other languages of Europe and Asia. He announced his discovery in a lecture delivered to the Asiatic Society of Calcutta in 1786, and although he was not actually the first European to tumble to this truth he is generally credited with the discovery of what came to be called the Indo-European language family.

A language family is a group languages related to each other by common descent from some original speech community as shown by shared lexical and syntactical features. We have already met the Dravidian language family, to which the ancient Indus language is thought to have belonged. The Indo-European family includes most of the languages spoken – at the time of the discovery of the New World – in a vast belt extending from western Europe through Russia, and thence southward through Iran and Afghanistan to northern and central India, terminating at the Bay of Bengal (but also including Sri Lanka). Its easternmost branch is known as Indo-Iranian, and the Indo-Aryan languages of South Asia – Sanskrit and the languages descended from Sanskrit – comprise a subgroup of that. These are the major languages of the subcontinent's north; the principal languages of the south (the modern Indian states of Telangana, Andhra Pradesh, Karnataka, Kerala and Tamil Nadu) are Dravidian. This was not only a discovery with momentous implications for western historiography, but it was also a serious challenge to traditional views in South Asia that regard Sanskrit as an eternal and uncreated language, and as the mother of all other languages, not a linguistic sibling or cousin.

In that connection, it should be noted that, while most historians believe that there once existed a speech community ancestral to the entire family of Indo-European languages and that the language immediately ancestral to Sanskrit was carried into South Asia from outside the subcontinent, there exists a nationalist narrative favoured by some historians that insists that the Indus valley people were Aryans, and that the Indo-European languages spread outward from South Asia. The available evidence, however, overwhelmingly supports the view that the Indo-Aryans were incoming migrants. (For an account of this debate, see Trautmann, 2005.)

The language ancestral to the entire Indo-European family was spoken by peoples living somewhere in the southern Russian and Ukrainian steppes, perhaps as early as around 4000 BCE. Their language, dubbed 'Proto-Indo-European' by linguists, has been partially reconstructed, and on the basis of vocabulary items supplemented by archaeology it seems clear that the early Indo-Europeans lived in a temperate climate, cultivated wheat and barley, and kept various domesticated animals including dogs, sheep, cattle and horses. Their subsistence base was likely to have been a mixture of herding and agriculture. Given their pastoral bent, cattle and horses were undoubtedly a major cultural focus for them, and this is an aspect of their culture they retained when they reached northern South Asia. They also possessed wheeled vehicles, and the horse-drawn chariot became a trademark feature of their mode of warfare.

For reasons not clearly understood, these peoples dispersed from their homeland beginning about 3400 BCE, ultimately spreading to the places where Indo-European languages later emerged into historical visibility. As already noted, the first migrations of Indo-Europeans quite possibly arrived in South Asia during the late urban phase of the Indus civilisation, but the Indo-Aryans who composed the *Rig Veda* (the oldest body of Sanskrit material, to be discussed below) were probably not in South Asia before 1400 BCE or so. Semi-nomadic pastoralists at first, with horses and spoked-wheeled chariots, they settled in Punjab where they began to adopt a more sedentary agricultural mode of life. They spoke an archaic variety (or varieties) of Sanskrit.

It is often said that the social order that evolved as the migrants settled was 'racially' divided between the Indo-Aryans and the indigenes (supposedly the dasa 'slaves'), a division that ultimately gave rise to the later class and caste systems. But, as mentioned earlier, it is quite possible that the dasas of the *Rig Veda* are actually a people the Indo-Aryans encountered before their arrival in Punjab, and, in any case, the relationship between the Indo-Aryans and local populations in South Asia was more likely a complex mixture of alliance and conflict rather than conquest and subjugation. It must be remembered that the indigenes were probably highly stratified socially and, even at this late stage of the Indus valley civilisation, possessed a social order more complex than that of the migrants. As the Indo-Aryans mingled and intermarried with local populations, the local and in-migrating social systems must have mutually influenced, reinforced and ultimately merged with each other, the result being the social formations of which we have some glimpses in the Vedic materials.

Vedas and the Vedic Age

We know far more about the religious beliefs and practices of the Indo-Aryans than we do about the Indus valley peoples. This is because we have their religious literature, a portion of which bears the distinction of being the oldest known collection of religious texts. As Wendy Doniger (2009, p. 86) points out, our sources of information on the Indus valley peoples and the Indo-Aryans are mirror opposites: for the Indus valley we have an abundance of things but no words; for the early Indo-Aryans we have only a few things, for the archaeology is thin, but words are plentiful. The overall body of texts in question are known as the Vedas, and the era that produced them is often called the Vedic Age. By this is usually meant the period from roughly 1500–1400 BCE to 500 BCE or so, and it is so named because this is regarded as the era during which the Vedas were composed. This is obviously a very long period of time in which immense cultural, social and political change occurred, and this is reflected in the evolution of the Vedic materials over time. The earliest strata of the Vedas, however, appear to have been composed by the Indo-Aryan migrants while they were still confined to Punjab.

But what are the Vedas? This turns out to be a complex matter. It is beyond the scope of this book to go into serious detail about the structure of the Vedic corpus, but some awareness of this structure is necessary if readers are to understand how Vedic religious thought and practice developed.

Let us start by saying that the term 'Veda', meaning 'knowledge', possesses both a wide and a narrow denotation. In its widest sense, the term refers to a large and variegated body of material composed in early forms of Sanskrit and regarded as the authorising heritage of the various religious traditions known collectively (in modern times) as Hinduism. Indeed, it is sometimes said that belief in the sanctity of the Vedas is the defining criterion of being a Hindu. However, although the Vedic materials are certainly a key element of Hindu tradition, they are far from the whole story, as will be seen. Hindu orthodoxy regards these materials as uncreated and eternal. They were revealed to certain ancient sages who then passed them on, and, because of their status as revelation, they are collectively referred to as *shruti*, meaning 'heard'. This term distinguishes them from a much larger body of material called *smriti*, meaning 'remembered', which is regarded as authored, not revealed; it, too, is sacred to Hindus, but not at the same highest level as the Vedas.

The Vedic material was composed, not written, which is to say that this was a totally oral textual tradition. In fact, there is no evidence of any writing at all in India after the decline of the Indus civilisation until the mid-first millennium BCE, but even after the advent of writing the Vedic texts remained an oral tradition, and the ancient convention of oral learning and recitation of Veda is still practised by some Brahmans today. During the period of their composition, they were committed to memory and transmitted orally by priests, presumably within priestly clans or lineages. Because of their sacred character, great emphasis was placed on absolute accuracy of transmission, and extreme accuracy was guaranteed by mnemonic aids built into the prescribed modes of recitation. As a result, the Vedic material we have today is generally assumed to be a faithful reproduction of the texts as they existed at the time of their creation.

But although the term 'Veda' (or 'Vedic') can be used to refer to this entire textual tradition, it is also commonly used to denote its four principal subdivisions, the 'four Vedas'. These are the *Rig Veda*, *Yajur Veda*, *Sama Veda* and *Atharva Veda*. This fourfold division probably reflects the fact that each was to be used for a different purpose by a different type of priest in sacrificial rites (Witzel, 1997, pp. 284–7).

Each of these divisions is subdivided, in turn, into bodies of material originating in successively later eras in the evolution of Vedic tradition. These are the Samhitas, Brahmanas, Aranyakas and Upanishads. There is an inner logic to this temporal stratification, having to do with the principal concern of the Vedas generally, which was sacrificial ritual. The successive textual layers reflected a shifting of the focus of interest from performance of the rites, to interpretation and, ultimately, to issues of their deeper meaning. These changes occurred roughly in step with the social and cultural changes taking place during the long Vedic period, and from this evolution emerged certain concepts and values that became paradigmatic for Indic religion and provided the context for assent and dissent alike in the subsequent development of religion in India.

To begin with the earliest stratum, the word *samhita* means 'collection', and the Samhitas – consisting of collections of hymns, verses, prayers and ritual formulas – are the oldest part of each of the four Vedas. Of these four, the oldest and most important is the *Rig Veda Samhita*, which consists of 1,028 hymns composed in an ancient form of Sanskrit and is divided into ten books, each apparently once linked to a specific ancient priestly lineage. Most of this material was probably composed around 1200 BCE.

Less well known are the remaining three Samhitas. One, the *Sama Veda Samhita*, is basically a collection of stanzas from the *Rig Veda* arranged for chanting at sacrificial rites and is often said to be our earliest evidence of ancient Indic musical tradition. The *Yajur Veda Samhita* consists of prose and verse ritual formulas to be recited at sacrifices. The *Atharva Veda Samhita* is usually said to be the latest of the four collections, dating from perhaps 900 BCE, but much of its contents is probably older than that. It contains ritual formulas and magical incantations sometimes said to be drawn from a substratum of folk tradition. Pointing out that the dialect of the *Atharva Veda* seems to predate that of the hymns of the *Rig Veda*, one authority (Parpola, 2015, pp. 130–44) theorises that it was the creation of the earlier wave of Indo-Aryans who were present in the Indus valley before the urban decline .

As noted above, each of the four Vedas also includes material other than the four Samhitas. These sections are later additions and may be seen as appendices to the earlier material. The Brahmanas, huge in extent, consist of prose explanations of sacrificial rites and instructions on how to perform them. The Aranyakas, meaning 'forest treatises', are mainly prose reflections on the symbolism and meaning of the sacrifice. The Upanishads (the term means 'sitting down near', presumably referring to disciples gathered with a preceptor) are a subdivision of the Aranyakas; they are prose texts, highly philosophical and abstract. The oldest of them date from roughly 600 to 300 BCE, but many texts calling themselves Upanishads are far later than that. Of all these bodies of material, the Upanishads will be the most familiar to Western

11

readers, and their renown is well justified. Their content is various, but they contain deeply considered speculations about the human condition and the nature of the relationship between the inner human spirit and the cosmos.

With these basics in mind, let us now look more closely at the evolution of Indo-Aryan religious belief and practice as reflected in the Vedas. I begin with the social context.

Early Indo-Aryan Society

The subsistence base of the people who created the Vedic hymns was a mixture of herding and agriculture, and their principal crops were barley and wheat. However, it is clear that cattle were essential to their sustenance, a source of meat as well as milk and its products, and a powerful cultural symbol. Their mode of warfare made use of horse-drawn chariots with spoked wheels, and the horse also served as an important cultural symbol. Their metallurgy was copper and bronze based; iron was present in India during this period, but the extent to which it was utilised by the early Vedic peoples is unclear.

During the earliest years of the Vedic era, Indo-Aryan social organisation was largely based on ties of kinship and descent; out-marrying patrilineages were probably bound together in larger communities by a weave of marital connections. At first, Indo-Aryan polities were 'tribal' in character: leadership was diffuse and possibly situational (i.e., different leaders in different contexts), and probably exercised by chieftains who, at least in the earliest period, were seen as 'first among equals'. The further centralisation of these structures into proto-kingdoms occurred only later as the Indo-Aryans expanded south-eastward into the Gangetic valley.

The Indo-Aryans idealised their society as stratified according to a very simple scheme, and although this scheme described social reality only imperfectly it was probably an accurate reflection of some important features of social life as it evolved during the Vedic era. The overall social order consisted of four hereditary classes, each with its own specialised function: priests (Brahmans), rulers and warriors (Rajanyas, later called Kshatriyas), ordinary tribespersons (Vish, later Vaishya) and a lower labouring class (Shudras), whose function is described as 'serving' the higher classes.

The Sanskrit term denoting these classes is *varna*; hence, the system is often called the 'varna system' in writings about India. The fact that varna can be rendered as 'colour' in English has suggested to many that this system was racial in character, with the upper-class Aryans subjugating the racially distinct indigenes, whose social location was the Shudra class. However, by the time this scheme swims into historical visibility the descendants of Indo-Aryan migrants and indigenes were probably thoroughly mixed and present alike in all four classes. Although this system is often thought to be the same thing as the caste system, it is not; it is, however, certainly related to caste. The relationship between varna and the system of castes extant today will be addressed in Chapter 5.

The Sacrifice

The focus of early Indo-Aryan religion was not abstract beliefs; rather, it was all about rituals, and belief – as such – was closely tied to rituals as their explanation and justification. The core ritual was a rite of sacrifice that was a kind of hospitality rite for deities. The deities, it was hoped, would receive the sacrificial offering and respond with boons. There were two types of sacrifice: a relatively simple domestic version that could be performed by a householder on his own and a far more complex public version that was performed by specialist Brahman priests.

I have already alluded to the fact that the Vedic sacrifice was quite unlike the principal ritual form characteristic of the Hinduism of later eras. Hindu tradition emphasises the worship of images in shrines and temples, but, as far as we know, the Vedic gods were never worshipped in the form of images, and there were certainly no temples. Rather, as one might expect of a people with a pastoral background, their altars were constructed in the moment, centring on an elevated firepit. Offerings were conveyed to the gods by means of burning on a sacrificial fire, the offering's essence then rising to the gods above. The presentation of the offerings was accompanied by the singing and recitation of hymns and ritual formulas, which was the purpose of the hymns of the *Rig Veda*. The rite was premised on the idea that the gods were nourished by sacrificial offerings, and that they, indeed, required such nourishment. The offerings often consisted of milk products, especially butter or *ghi* (clarified butter, which burns well), but probably included all other components of the Indo-Aryan diet. Animals were offered, and this included cattle; at this point in South Asian history, the Hindu sacralisation of the cow and prohibition of beef were far in the future (Jha, 2002). The meat of bovine offerings was eaten in the sacrificial aftermath, but the meat of sacrificed horses was apparently not eaten (Doniger, 2009, p. 116). The offerings also included the Soma beverage, of which more below.

In its more complex form, the rite was performed by ritual specialists, Brahman priests, on behalf of a sponsor who was the primary beneficiary of the rite. The reasons for performing the rite had nothing to do with the elaborate soteriologies of liberation that emerge in a later era. Sacrifices were, to some extent, simply conventional and were performed to mark calendrical transitions, departures and arrivals, life-cycle changes of individuals and in connection with major public events such as consecrations of leaders. They were also organised to achieve specific results such as relief from illness, successful crops, the birth of sons, victory in battle or even post-death existence in heaven. Sponsorship also was a source of social honour.

The objects of worship were called *devas* (the Shining Ones). They were mostly male, in contrast to the Greek pantheon, and frequently personified forces of nature or natural phenomena; thus, the sun (Surya) was a deity, as was dawn (Ushas, a goddess), wind (Vayu) and fire (Agni). Dyaus personified heaven; Prithvi, a goddess, was the earth. Rudra, the 'Howler', was associated with storms and disease and lived in the mountains; he later became an element of the persona of the major Hindu deity Shiva. Death was Yama, said to have been the first human to die; he judged the dead and determined their future destination. Occupying a special position was Indra, the King of the Gods, who was associated with both warfare (as noted earlier, he was a destroyer of fortifications) and rain. As befits the association with rain, his principal weapon was the thunderbolt. This he used in performing his most celebrated deed, which was the slaying of a great serpent named Vritra; when the serpent expired, the waters of creation, which had been held in his coils, were released. Also of great importance was Varuna, associated with bodies of water but also seen (along with Mitra, another Vedic deity) as the guardian of an overarching principle of cosmic and ethical order known as *rita*. This ordering principle, to which even the gods had to conform, was a likely precursor to the later idea of *dharma* as an all-embracing moral code.

It must be borne in mind, however, that the importance of the Vedic deities lay not simply in their character as independent entities but also – and perhaps especially – in the role they played in sacrificial ritual. From this standpoint, the god Agni stands out from the crowd. He was the divine embodiment of fire and closely linked with the sacrificial fire. He was known as the Tongue of the Gods, or Bearer of Oblations, so named because of his role as the sacrificial fire by means of which offerings to the gods were conveyed to their divine destinations; he was, therefore, a crucial intermediary between humanity and the divine world.

Another standout was Soma, to whom numerous hymns are dedicated. Soma was not only a deity but also identified as personifying a substance offered in the sacrifice. We know that Soma was a plant of some kind from which a beverage was made, apparently hallucinogenic in its effects, as indicated by the fact that its consumers thought themselves to become gods under its influence. Indra was held to be great quaffer of Soma. Its actual identity, however, has been lost, quite possibly because the migrating Indo-Aryans left behind the climatic zone in which it grows. It could hardly have been opium or cannabis, for both have been long known and consumed in India and were never identified as Soma. One possibility, suggested by a distinguished amateur mycologist by the name of R. Gordon Wasson (1971), is that Soma was a mushroom, *Amanita muscaria* (fly agaric), that contains a hallucinogenic substance and seems to exhibit some of the physical features of Soma as described in Vedic hymns. Another suggestion is that Soma was a plant belonging to the genus

Ephedra (Flood, 1996, p. 43), a source of a powerful stimulant often employed as a weight-loss medication in modern times.

As to the belief system to which early Vedic ritualism was coupled and of which it was the foundation, we must remind ourselves again that we are not dealing with Hinduism. Perhaps best called Vedism, in its early phase it was a complex of beliefs expressing the world-view and values of a rural people whose main concerns were avoiding or ameliorating misfortunes and dealing with life's many practical hazards and difficulties. It was founded on the premise that there is a proper ordering of the cosmos and human affairs that is both natural and ethical, and its central idea was that humans are dependent on the gods, but that the gods will not come to our aid without sacrifices. Within this framework grew the rich body of lore and narrative about the gods and their characteristics and relationships with each other that we encounter in the Vedic hymns.

But of abstract theorising about the world there is not much in the *Rig Veda*. And yet there is something. One deservedly famous hymn (10.129) speculates about the creation of the cosmos in a manner striking for its philosophical maturity. The hymn (taken here from Doniger O'Flaherty, 1981, p. 25) begins by asserting: 'There was neither non-existence nor existence then; there was neither the realm of space nor the sky which is beyond.' After pondering the imponderable question of what 'neither non-existence nor existence' could possibly be, this extraordinary hymn concludes by saying:

> Whence this creation has arisen – perhaps it formed itself, or perhaps it
> did not – the one who looks down on it, in the highest heaven, only he
> knows – or perhaps he does not know.

We would do well to note that the creators of this hymn were totally illiterate, a reminder that literacy is not a prerequisite for deep reflection.

Along the same lines is another famous hymn in the *Rig Veda* (10.90), undateable but clearly a late addition (here taken from Doniger O'Flaherty, 1981, pp. 30–1). It is usually cited in relation to the *varna* system, of which it is the earliest known description, but it possesses a more general significance as a conceptual signpost pointing in the direction to which Vedic religious thought was tending. It is another creation hymn, but this time with an answer. The text proclaims that the cosmos arose from a Vedic-style sacrifice and dismemberment – performed by the gods who evidently already existed – of a gigantic cosmic 'man' (Purusha). Without lingering over details, the gist of what the hymn says is that from this cosmic sacrifice came the whole world. From it emerged 'those beasts who live in the air, in the forest, and in villages' and 'from it were also born [the Vedic] verses, chants, metres and formulas', as well as horses, cows, goats and sheep. And from the man's head, arms, thighs and feet emerged the four social classes of (respectively) Brahmans, Kshatriyas, Vaishyas and Shudras. And from his eye came the sun, and from his mind the moon, and so on.

Embedded in these words are some very important ideas. Leaving aside the obvious sacralisation of social hierarchy, it must be noted first that so central is the rite of sacrifice to Vedic religion that, in thinking about both the form of the creative act and the energies that powered it, the Vedic mind turned unhesitatingly to this all-important ritual. The hymn is really an account, in a sacrificial idiom, of how the distinctions between the things of this world came into being (Knipe, 1991, pp. 33–4); they arose because of the dismemberment of a sacrificial victim on a cosmic scale, with the implication that behind the diversity of the world is an original unity. And further, when performed on a human scale, the sacrifice was understood to reiterate that primordial creative act; indeed, the Vedic 'theory' of sacrificial efficacy maintained that the performance of the rite was necessary to keep the world extant and functioning.

And finally, the hymn establishes a crucial homology (Flood, 1996, pp. 48–9). On one side, there is the body (the 'man', human/cosmic), on the other the cosmos, with the opposition mediated and finally closed by the ritual. An implication is that the macrocosm of the cosmos is somehow present and available in the microcosm of the human body, an idea that had a big future in Indic religious thought.

The Second Urbanisation

It is in the Brahmanas that we begin to see the first stirrings of sustained religious theorising, and this trend continues to a fulfilment in the Aranyakas and Upanishads. The dating is uncertain, but these developments take place after Vedic civilisation had shifted its centre of gravity from the Punjab to the Upper Ganga and points further south and east. This was a period of extraordinary change in which the old Vedic tribalism became the foundation for the formation of states, and in which cites begin to reappear in northern South Asia after a hiatus of nearly a millennium.

In moving south-eastward, the Vedic peoples first found themselves in the area separating the Ganga and Yamuna rivers, a region known as the Ganga-Yamuna Doab, and from there they entered the lower Ganga valley. While this development is commonly described as a movement of peoples, this is probably only a partial truth. The Indo-Aryanisation of these regions must also have been a mixture of migration plus the diffusion of Indo-Aryan culture among indigenous peoples, fuelled perhaps by the prestige of Indo-Aryan ways. At the same time, however, there was certainly diffusion in the opposite direction, the result being a cultural synthesis. Coinciding with the shift were economic and social changes of great import. In the somewhat moister climatic regime of the Doab – as compared with Punjab – agriculture was more productive and became more productive still as Vedic civilisation made its way further eastward, especially when rice began to be cultivated around mid-millennium. Iron, invaluable in clearing land and tilling soil, probably also played a big role in productivity gains in agriculture. While the dating is not settled, iron is thought to have been used to some extent in India from before the end of the second millennium BCE, but it was apparently not in widespread use in farming until the middle of the first millennium.

Accompanying these developments, tribally-based nascent states emerged in the upper Ganga, and in time the centrality of kinship and descent to the organisation of these entities began to give way to the territorial ordering of full-fledged states. Perhaps in response to the defence requirements of such polities and the pressure of law-and-order issues arising from ever-higher population densities, authority became centralised either in the form of ruling councils or individual rulers. This was the context of the re-emergence of cities, of which the first archaeological traces are dated to about 600 BCE, and South Asia's 'second urbanisation' is usually dated from roughly 500 BCE.

Cities are venues for the flourishing of occupational specialties not directly engaged in food production – trade, government bureaucracy, professional soldiering, crafts and the like – and the caloric requirements of these non-food-producing segments of the population were met by the ever-increasing productivity of agriculture, especially in the mid- and lower Ganga region. These developments culminated in the Gangetic region corresponding to the present-day Indian state of Bihar. Here, in the fourth century BCE, an important state called Magadha became the centre of a rapidly expanding empire under the brief Nanda dynasty (345–321 BCE). Its capital was the city of Pataliputra (modern Patna). In the late fourth century, the Nandas were overthrown by a military adventurer named Chandragupta Maurya. His reign (321–298 BCE) marks the beginning of the Mauryan Empire – surely one of the greatest empires of the ancient world – which ultimately ruled (or at least nominally ruled) much of the subcontinent.

Religious Crystallisation

The Vedic tradition reached a new stage of philosophical maturity in the Aranyakas and Upanishads. Aranyaka means 'forest book', the implication being that the teachings given therein are esoteric and best transmitted outside the boundaries of cities and towns. The Aranyakas can be seen as transitional between the ritually oriented Brahmanas and the highly philosophical Upanishads. As noted earlier, the term 'Upanishad' means 'sitting down near', which would seem to refer to disciples gathered in the presence of a teacher or spiritual preceptor. Thirteen of them are considered the most important, and the earliest of these date from 600 BCE or so and predate the lifetime of the Buddha.

In turning to these late developments in Vedic tradition, I must first insert a caveat. The origin of the concepts I am about to discuss are conventionally attributed to trends in the Vedic tradition itself, but this is in large measure because the

Vedic tradition is most of what we know from the period in question. Although there are clearly points of evolutionary continuity connecting Upanishadic thought with earlier features of Vedic ritualism, that does not preclude the possibility – better, the probability – of important non-Vedic influences on what we see in the Upanishads. It must be remembered that the Upanishads were composed in a wide and varied religious world, much of which is historically invisible to us, and if the composers of the Upanishads were exploring the boundaries of the thought and knowledge of the day there were other similar explorers on the scene who operated *outside* the Vedic tradition. These were ascetics called Shramanas (meaning 'exerters' or 'strivers', derived from *shrama*, 'toil'), who were also in search of answers to the truly big questions. Although they challenged Brahmanical orthodoxy and found favour outside the Brahman fold, there must certainly have been Brahmans among them. Their mode of life stressed austerities and ascetic practices (hence their name), and they believed that the truths they sought could only be pursued while totally unhindered by the claims and distractions of society, which they abandoned. Although ascetic practices evolved within as well as outside the Vedic world, it is quite likely that the world-renouncing lifestyle was – to significant but undeterminable degree – non-Vedic in origin (Bronkhorst, 1998).

An additional factor to be considered is that, during this period, there was a distinct west-to-east cultural gradient in the Ganga valley, with Brahmanical influences much stronger in the west than in the east. It was in the eastern zone that Buddhism and Jainism arose, and it was likely that key elements of Upanishadic soteriology also developed here (Bronkhorst, 2011a). In any case, Vedic and non-Vedic traditions certainly exerted mutual influences, and Gavin Flood has put the matter well when he suggests the existence of a 'common heritage of meditation and mental discipline practiced by renouncers with varying affiliations to non-orthodox (Veda-rejecting) and orthodox (Veda-accepting) traditions' (Flood, 1996, p. 82). The Upanishads belong to the Veda-accepting, Brahmanical tradition.

As for why this stir of spiritual and philosophical speculation arose, it was almost certainly a by-product of social change. For city-dwellers, the easy flow of rural life with its slow rhythms and predictability was long in the past. Old beliefs and certainties were sharply challenged in this newer cosmopolitan social world in which culturally diverse groups were having to find new ways of dealing with each other while living cheek-by-jowl in crowded urban conditions. New occupations were coming into being, new social boundaries being drawn, and new forms of political control emerging. Amid all this disconcerting cultural and social flux, attaining spiritual repose must have been very difficult indeed, especially for those who were religiously sensitive. It is the voices of these spiritual virtuosi that we hear in the Upanishads and in the non-Vedic soteriological traditions to be discussed in the next chapter. There is every reason to believe that the cities were the basic sources of religious innovation, and the Upanishads were probably a product of the reflections of city-dwelling Brahmans who were left spiritually unfulfilled by the ritualistic ways of their country-cousin counterparts (Olivelle, 1993, pp. 58–63).

The religious evolution that led to the emergence of the Upanishads can be characterised as an abstraction and disentanglement of religious practice and thought from the physical rite of sacrifice in a manner that retained at least some elements of sacrificial symbolism. A key change was the emergence of the idea that the actual physical performance of the sacrifice was not always necessary to tap into its power; instead, this power could be mobilised by an ascetic adept who sublimated the rite's physical performance into mental images. Drawing upon the thermal imagery of the sacrificial fire, this power was understood as an inner heat called *tapas*, a term that later came to be a generic term for ascetic practice. The emergence of this idea had the effect of devaluing – though certainly not eliminating – the outer physical sacrifice and the priesthood that officiated it, and it helped pave the way to the non-ritual soteriologies that lay ahead. More generally, we also see a gradual refinement of the Vedic cosmology – to which sacrificial imagery was formative – into a systematic, rationalised world-view. The thrust of this development was *unification* – in effect, a running backwards of the sacrificial dismemberment that created the things and attributes of the experienced world. The result was a systematised vision in which the diversity of the experienced world was held to obscure a deeper unity rooted in a substance/principle called *brahman* that was immanent, if hidden, in the self of the individual as well as the cosmos at large.

Liberation

The religious innovation towards which late Vedic thought was moving was a doctrine – historically visible for the first time in the Upanishads – of radical liberation from the sufferings of worldly existence. At its heart were two linked concepts denoted by two terms, *samsara* and *karma*, and they are at the very heart not only of late Vedic soteriology but also of most if not all other systematised Indic religious traditions.

The term samsara means 'passage' or 'wandering' and refers to the transmigration of the self into a new body after death. The word can also be used to denote 'the world', that is, our world, to which transmigration is inherent and in which we are propelled from death to birth to death again in a world-career of ceaseless movement through the myriad forms of existence that living beings can take. The origin of the idea is uncertain. It is absent in the early Vedic materials, but it is anticipated in the Brahmanas, where it is held that one who offers sacrifice (apparently either as priest or sponsor) gains rebirth in heaven. This opens the door to an anxiety: will this new life be permanent, or will death still be a danger? And if one suffers a redeath, might there not be further redeaths and rebirths? Thus, the trials of old age and death might prove to be a permanent, repetitive condition. Such ponderings could well have been the germ of the concept of *samsara* as we see it in the Upanishads. But then it is also quite possible that it originated from non-Vedic sources (Bronkhorst, 1998), or that it was a joint product of ruminations in both non-Vedic and Vedic circles.

The other core concept surfacing in the Upanishads is that of karma. Whether the doctrine of karma originated within or outside the Vedic tradition is, again, a debatable issue. (For a lucid presentation of the 'external' view, see Bronkhorst, 1998; 2011b.) The word does not mean 'destiny', as is commonly supposed, although it certainly has destiny-related implications. Rather, its basic denotation is simply 'action', by which presumably any action could be meant, but which in Vedic times seems to have had a special connection with ritual action. Actions, and perhaps ritual acts more than others, have consequences – that is, they bear 'fruits' (*phala*). This idea ultimately became broadened and ethicised; karma came to signify ethically significant action, and the kind of fruit generated by action was held to depend on its moral nature. Good yields good, bad yields bad and, therefore, our present experiences are a product of good and evil acts in our past, and our current behaviour will determine our future experiences. This is not a matter of reward or punishment; it is simply the working of ineluctable laws of moral cause and effect.

Quite evidently, the ethicised concept of karmic causation fits perfectly with the idea of samsara. Because of the unfortunate and apparently pervasive mismatch between a person's moral deservingness and the experiences a typical life actually dishes out, deeds done in forgotten past lifetimes, or experiences yet to be had in future lifetimes, are needed to right the moral balance. Once fused, the doctrines of karma and samsara provide an airtight moral theory of our experiences, good and bad. This picture of the karmic world-career of the individual is the foundation of the idea of liberation or release that emerges in the Upanishads and, with important variations, of most other future Indic religious traditions.

In turning to Upanishadic soteriology, it must be clearly understood that the view of our situation in a world of transmigration presented in these materials is profoundly negative. It has nothing in common with, let us say, the Christian promise of eternal life. The accent is not on life but on death, which the Indic doctrine of transmigration eternalises and generalises. The eternalisation is self-evident: the self's wandering is without apparent end. The generalisation takes the form of the overall negative value placed on the whole process. The problem of life's misfortunes might be approached in a piecemeal fashion; every calamity, large or small, would then be *sui generis*, to be dealt with singly on its own terms. But in the Upanishads the problem of misfortune is abstracted away from particulars and is universalised into a harsh judgement on worldly existence itself – the endless cycle of birth, death, rebirth and redeath – which is seen as a kind of all-embracing calamity.

This is the 'from what' of the Upanishadic concept of liberation. Given the nature of our situation in samsara, nothing less than full liberation from its webs of cause and effect will do. The name given to such liberation is *moksha*.

On the premises given, however, liberation from samsara cannot possibly be achieved by means deployed *within* samsara – that is, by means of some sort of remedial action. This is because actions (i.e., karmas) bear fruit that must be consumed by the actor, and thus action itself is the cause of further entanglement in samsara's fatal noose. This was especially true of rituals, for ritual actions were the very paradigm of karma. Of course, by means of sacrifice one could gain heaven, but heaven, too, is part of samsara, and sojourns there are temporary and by no means constitute liberation from the cycle of rebirth and redeath. Given this predicament, the Upanishadic thinkers sought release from death's grip in an entirely different direction. It was not through 'doing' but through a special kind of 'knowing' that liberation was to be achieved.

But knowledge of what? It was knowledge of nothing less than a reality lying behind, and normally concealed by, the buzz and hum of existence in samsara. As we know, the concept of the sacrifice as a connecting point between cosmos and person suggested the presence of a unifying power, that of the rite itself, underlying the differentiation and variety of the sacrificially created world. This seems to have been the seed of the idea of a universal substrate, called *brahman* (not to be confused with the varna name, Brahman) underlying all things. In the speculations of the Upanishadic thinkers, this substrate came to be regarded as pure 'being' – that is, as existence as such, devoid of attributes. It could not be described in language because our words distort its reality by imputing qualities to it that it does not, in itself, possess. And if it is devoid of all attributes, it is changeless and eternal, and if this is so it is deathless. And if it underlies and unifies all things, it is present in a person's innermost self, even as it pervades the entire cosmos, and therein lies the secret of immortality.

In these materials, the word for one's true 'self' is *atman*. By this is not meant the empirical self, the transient personality that we normally suppose ourselves to be. Atman, rather, is ultimate, unchanging reality – pure being – normally concealed at the very core of the person, and it is necessarily the same as the ground of all being, which is brahman. Atman *is* brahman, the self of the cosmos. It is this reality that must be known.

One of the most famous and often-quoted passages on this point is found in Chapter 6 of the *Chandogya Upanishad*. Trying to teach his son the truth of our situation in the world, a father invites his boy to consider the bees and the nectar they convert into honey. Once converted, the father points out, there is no question of whether a given drop of nectar came from this tree or that. In the same way, when living things:

> merge into the existent, they are not aware that: 'We are merging into the existent [i.e., brahman].' No matter what they are in this world – whether it is a tiger, a lion, a wolf, a boar, a worm, a gnat or a mosquito – they all merge into that.

Later, in the same passage, he instructs his son to place some salt in water. It dissolves and disappears, but the water uniformly tastes of salt. Just so, says the father:

> This finest essence here – that constitutes the self of this whole world; that is the truth; that is the self (*atman*). And that's how you are ... (*Chandogya Upanishad*, Chapter 6. 9, 13; from Olivelle, 1996, pp. 153–5).

Worldly bondage, that is, turns out to hang on a question of identity. Who or what are you? is the question, and the answer to that question – the deepest and truest answer – is the liberating 'knowledge' (*jnana*) that is the road to liberation from samsara's snare. But obviously this kind of knowledge is different from what we normally consider knowledge to be. Here the *knowing* is an 'attainment' or 'realization' of the thing *known*. And what is known is one's true self that is uncreated, eternal and changeless, and thus beyond the reach of death's jaws. But it is not enough to be told or to assent to the proposition that the true self is brahman. Rather, one must turn one's mental gaze inward and grasp this truth directly by means of a physically and mentally disciplined form of introspection that came to be called *yoga* and that combined special postures with breath control and other specialised techniques. The goal was to pull the senses away from external stimuli, thus making possible highly focused states of inwardly directed concentration. The knowledge thus attained is a special sort of awareness, cultivated by casting off the reality-distorting categories of worldly knowledge, language and thought, with the object of achieving an unmediated apprehension of the true self within. One who succeeds in this will be liberated in life and will not be reborn when the physical body falls away.

To cultivate such self-knowledge required a special mode of life. One would have to turn away from the world and its blandishments, for these simply draw one outward through the organs of sense into further entanglement with ignorance and death. This was, therefore, a world-view bearing a deep affinity with world renunciation and ascetic practice. Whether the idea arose within Vedic or non-Vedic traditions, or both, the basic idea of escaping rebirth by means of ascetic practice became a powerful life model, both within and outside the Vedic fold (Olivelle, 1993, pp. 64–7). Previously, the ego-ideal was the householder, the family man who married, fathered children, did the work of the world and, above all, sponsored sacrifices, for which his marriage was a prerequisite. But now world-renouncing ascetics – not to be confused with priests, who were householders themselves – embodied a competing ideal. The renouncer shunned the attachments of marriage and family as fatal distractions from the pursuit of liberation. Still, even if the householder was pushed off his former pedestal, he remained a key figure in the spiritual equation, if for no other reason than the renouncer's dependence on him for the necessities of life. For this reason, a major dynamic in the future evolution of Indic religious traditions can be described as a dialogue between the renouncer and the householder-in-the-world concerning the goals to be pursued in life and how to pursue them, a conversation that has yet to be concluded (Dumont, 1970, 184–7).

Legacies

In considering the contributions of Vedic religious culture to the evolution of Indian religions, we would do well to distinguish between two related but separate domains, namely the wider 'Indic' religious world and the somewhat narrower 'Hindu' world. On the first point, the basic concepts that emerged in late Vedic times – whether from Vedic or non-Vedic sources, or both – became the fundamentals of later Indic religious traditions, whether orthodox or dissenting, Hindu or non-Hindu. The concepts of samsara, karmic causation and liberation from the transmigratory cycle of birth and death emerged as the unexamined premises of later systems, beyond the reach of doubt. And the linkage between world renunciation and serious spiritual attainment is likewise basic and rarely challenged, although the ideal of world renunciation was susceptible to innovation, as we shall see.

On the narrower question of Hinduism, I must start by saying that the Vedic tradition is, indeed, a core element of the Hindu heritage, a fact highlighted by the Vedas' status as the most sacred of the Hindu texts. But although veneration of the Veda is often said to be the defining criterion of who is a Hindu, Vedic religious culture, early or late, was never a form of 'Hinduism', which by any reasonable definition would not take shape until centuries later. Furthermore, many elements of the family of related traditions we call Hinduism are not 'Vedic' at all.

In expanding on this latter point, we should note first that, even in its heyday, Vedic religion was but one part of a far wider religious world, most of which is historically invisible because it left no texts. But we may be certain that numerous regional indigenous religious traditions existed in Vedic times, and these were in constant interaction with Vedic beliefs and practices. The Indo-Aryan component of this mix seems to have borne a social cachet that led to its widespread acceptance and domination of the religious scene, but, while maintaining its identity, it never ceased mingling with indigenous traditions, and this process left its mark on many aspects of Vedic tradition itself. However, we do not see these non-Indo-Aryan religious cultures clearly until a later era when elements of them swim into visibility in the post-Vedic sacred literatures that constitute the main body of Hindu texts.

All that said, many elements of the Vedic tradition were preserved in the Hinduism of later periods. For example, the deities of the Vedic pantheon survived the transition, although they lost most of their original importance and were eclipsed by other deities, becoming relatively minor figures in the throng of gods and goddesses venerated by Hindus. However, two Vedic deities grew in relative importance. One is Rudra, who prefigures the extremely important Hindu deity Shiva. Rudra's frightening Vedic persona is identified with the destructive and angry side of Shiva's nature, and 'Rudra' remains one of Shiva's names. There is every reason to believe, however, that the development of Shiva's mature character drew from indigenous traditions including, possibly, elements we have glimpsed in the Indus materials. The other exception is Vishnu. A relatively minor deity in the Vedic pantheon, Vishnu was associated with the sun among other things. In later Hindu tradition, he is a major deity indeed, and appears in the form of such marquee gods as Rama and Krishna. As in the case of Shiva, the evolution of his later traits and attributes – in his case, a very complex matter indeed – drew from many indigenous traditions, and the Vishnu we know bears scant resemblance to his Vedic counterpart.

There is, moreover, a deep continuity between Hinduism and Vedic tradition in the ritual sphere. As will be seen in a later chapter, the devotional worship of physical images of gods and goddesses – not a part of the Vedic ritual complex at all – is the central ritual act in Hindu traditions. However, the fire sacrifice, called *homa* or *havan* in Hindu contexts, is also a key ritual form in Hindu traditions, and is a direct descendant of the Vedic version (on homa and its relationship to the Vedic sacrifice, see Michaels, 2016, pp. 231–47). It is often performed in conjunction with image worship, but its format is quite different; it is centred on a fire altar, usually temporary, and involves offerings to the gods conveyed by fire, as in the ancient rite. Such a sacrifice is part of the array of rites in Hindu weddings, and the fire is said to be the 'witness' to the union. Also, the burning of the corpse in Hindu funerals is modelled on the Vedic sacrificial fire, and is said to be the 'last sacrifice' (Parry, 1994, pp. 188–90).

The Upanishadic doctrines as well as later schools of thought inspired by the Upanishads are generically called Vedanta meaning 'end of the Vedas'. The schools of thought bearing the Vedanta label are various, but one in particular, called Advaita Vedanta, is more famous than the others, and is often quite mistakenly thought to be the whole of the Vedanta. Advaita means 'non-dual', and this school brings philosophical rigour to the Upanishadic doctrine of brahman as the fundamental unity underlying the apparent diversity of the world. The creation of a southern thinker (born in what is the current state of Kerala) of the eighth century CE named Shankara, the Advaita Vedanta proposes a radical monism (i.e., the theory that reality consists of a single substance or principle) in which only brahman is fully real and all appearances are illusions resulting from the mistaken imposition on it of falsifying attributes. According to this view, there is no individual self at all, for all that exists is the unitary world-self that is brahman. Indeed, bondage itself is unreal, a by-product of ignorance and, therefore, liberation is also unreal, for it is simply the knowledge (in the special sense that I have outlined) that brahman, entirely devoid of qualities, is the only reality. We should note that these views share much with the teachings of the Buddha (next chapter), despite Shankara's hostility to Buddhism. Shankara's school has retained an extraordinary prestige from those days until now. Advaita Vedanta is generally the most familiar form of Hindu religious philosophy to Western readers, and was also much favoured by some Hindu reformers of the modern period.

2

Dissenters

The early history of Indic religions is often presented as a saga of 'orthodox' versus 'heterodox' religious movements of the late Vedic period. By orthodox is meant the Vedic tradition itself, including the Upanishads; by heterodox is meant schools of thought that rejected the authority of Vedas, and these are associated with the Shramanas (encountered in the previous chapter), who are usually portrayed as opposed to the Vedic Brahmans.

This picture is not entirely misleading, but there is an issue to be noted having to do with the supposed chasm underlying the heterodox/orthodox dichotomy. Although the Upanishadic teachings do appear to have been developed within a Vedic framework, it is important to remember that, as noted earlier, the conceptual foundation of Indic religions – most notably the concepts of samsara, karma and liberation from the cycle of rebirth (samsara) coupled with a high value placed on world renunciation – arose from complex interactions between spiritual seekers from both within and outside the Vedic fold, and we can be sure that some of the Shramanas were, in fact, Brahmans. Furthermore, it is far from clear that the Vedic/non-Vedic divide subsumes other distinctions. As will be seen, the two principal heterodoxies, Buddhism and Jainism, were arguably as different from each other in doctrine (though not in religious sociology) as either was from Upanishadic tradition. At the same time, both were overtly anti-Vedic, and in that sense, at least, can be considered 'dissenting' movements.

At least a part of the appeal of the religious innovations we call 'heterodox' was rooted in a profoundly changed social landscape. The social and economic infrastructure of sacrificial Vedism was a mostly rural way of life tightly bound to a simple socio-economic division of labour: priests, ruler-warriors, food producers, with a catch-all 'service' category added on. In cities, the advent of new occupations led to the rise of urban classes – traders and artisans, in particular – whose religious needs were different from those of the agricultural hinterlands and to whom Vedic-style ritualism had a limited appeal. The members of these classes must have been much less wedded to – if they accepted at all – the concept of social worth that was the foundation of the system of varnas. It is precisely these urbanites who appear to have been the primary supporters of the non-Vedic renouncers and the doctrines they created and promoted.

By now, the lifestyle of the wandering renouncer was well established, and these figures moved freely on the city streets and village lanes of the period, unencumbered by ties of family, occupation and polity. As noted in the previous chapter, their influence was greater in the eastern than the western Ganga basin because these were areas in which the reach of Vedic religious culture and the authority of its Brahmanical promoters were relatively weak. We know that the renouncers, Vedic and non-Vedic, contended with each other in debate, and the range of views they expressed was wide indeed. Unfortunately, what most of them had to say went unremembered and unrecorded, but from the standpoint of sheer intellectual adventure this must have been one of the most interesting of all places and times to be alive.

Only two of the non-Vedic schools are extant today. One is Buddhism, which was once a religion of empire in India. As will be seen, it ultimately largely disappeared from the subcontinent, but it persisted in the South Asian periphery and went on to a worldwide career. The other is Jainism. It was once a serious rival to Buddhism, but because of the severity of its monastic disciplines it never left the subcontinent until historically recently. Because of these same monastic disciplines, however, it persisted and retained its identity as a separate religion in India, and although its adherents are relatively few in number today, they constitute a very influential segment of the population of the Republic of India.

As readers will see, Buddhism and Jainism are quite different as far as their teachings are concerned, but they share two important traits that separate them as a pair from Vedic orthodoxy. The first is that both are associated with individual founding personalities, which is not true of Vedic religion. There are indeed individual and named voices heard in the Upanishadic materials, but there is no single commanding personality whose character is stamped on the tradition as a whole. Very different are Buddhism and Jainism, for the teachings of both are deeply intertwined with the biographies of particular individuals who exemplified these teachings in personal life. The other major difference is that these were (and Buddhism remains today) proselytising religions. So far as we know, the adherents of sacrificial Vedism never tried to 'convert' anyone, and it is hard imagine what such a conversion would actually be. Vedic religion simply 'came with the territory' of the Vedic social order, and even the latter-day soteriologies seem to have been restricted in social reach. The proselytising of the non-Vedic fits well with their internally coherent belief systems, to which I turn shortly, which were quite different from the more amorphous body of beliefs and practices of Vedic tradition. Furthermore, the vividness of the images of their founding personalities – embellished in rich charter mythologies – must have imbued these religions with special (and at the time, unprecedented) allure.

The Buddha and Buddhism

It must be clearly understood that 'Buddha' was never his name, for the word is not a name at all but a *title*, meaning 'Awakened One', and this was a title he came to merit – according to legend – only in his fourth decade of his life. His actual given name was Siddhartha, and his clan name Gautama. There is no firm agreement about his dates. Theravada tradition (the oldest branch of Buddhism) holds that he died at the age of eighty in 544–543 BCE, but the scholarly consensus seems to be that this is too early by 130 years or more. The earliest account of his life was not composed until roughly 150 years later, and the *Buddhacharita* ('Acts of the Buddha'), a major telling of the Buddha's legend and the source of the synopsis given below, was composed in Sanskrit by Ashvaghosha in the first or second century CE (Olivelle, 2008, p. xix). The basic story it tells has probably functioned as a narrative-style catechism for many millions of Buddhists, and it will serve as our entryway into the Buddha's teachings. While we cannot measure this tale against any objective historical standard, it conveys some of the crucial features of the Buddha's teachings in a highly appealing way.

The Buddha

The tale (abstracted here from Johnson, 1978; see Conze, 1959, pp. 34–66, for a condensed and highly readable translation) begins with the birth of a son, Siddhartha, to the ruler of the Shakyas. By convention described as a 'king', he was likely little more than a chieftain of some kind ruling a tribal polity in the foothills of the Himalayas in what is now Nepal. The Shakyas lived within the orbit of the great states of the Ganga basin, but were marginal to them.

Now, at the time of the prince's birth, the Brahmans of his father's court made the extraordinary prophecy that he would someday become either a universal king or an enlightened seer. This prophecy was later amplified by a visiting sage who predicted that the prince would one day give up the kingdom and all worldly pleasures, and would proclaim a great pathway to liberation from suffering. These predictions did not sit well with Siddhartha's father, who naturally hoped that his son would become his successor. To thwart the prophecy, therefore, the king confined Siddhartha to the palace where he could be shielded from all evidence of the world's miseries and would be prevented from reflecting on the question of suffering and its causes. In such circumstances, Siddhartha grew up, married and even had a son, all the while surrounded by worldly pleasures and in total ignorance of the existence of pain and loss. Arguably, his upbringing was rather like growing up in present-day Euro-America, where life's inevitable downsides are masked (at least, to some extent) by sequestering the ill in hospitals, parking the elderly in retirement communities, and consigning the dead to the ministrations of funerary technicians.

But this state of affairs was not to last, for a day came when the prince was seized by a desire to venture outside the palace grounds. The reluctant king allowed this, but to forestall any unpleasant encounters he arranged for anyone afflicted by injury, disease or old age to be removed from the roadway. But this the gods would not permit and, in order to inspire Siddhartha with a desire to renounce the world, they conjured up a vision of an old man on the road. Innocent that he was, for he knew nothing whatsoever about the facts of ageing and bodily decay, the astonished Siddhartha asked: 'What is this?' And when informed that he, too, would one day bear this same affliction, he was shocked to his core. There were two more such excursions. During the second, he learnt of the existence of disease, and on the third he saw a corpse, and with this came the realisation that extinction was his destination as well. Deeply shaken by these revelations, he lost all interest in his former pleasures. Then ensued another excursion, this time to the forest, and there he encountered an ascetic who had renounced the world. Siddhartha thereupon resolved to take up the life of renunciation himself, and so at the age of twenty-nine he fled his family and royal patrimony and joined the ranks of the mendicants and seekers who abounded in the Ganga valley of those days.

Theirs was a notably cosmopolitan style of life. Released from the ties of family and locality, these world-renouncers travelled across a vast landscape and did so with a degree of freedom perhaps matched only by that of the traders of the period (which might well have a bearing on the attractiveness of Shramanas' teachings to the trading class). Siddhartha must have met quite a cast of characters while among them. This included two famed spiritual adepts of the day, and he mastered their yogic techniques. He also met practitioners of the sort of extreme asceticism characteristic of Jain mendicants (to be discussed below). He and five companions adopted this latter way of life, but in the end he found it to be pointless self-torture. As a result of this experience, he later advocated a 'middle way', rejecting both worldly addiction to sense pleasures and also the fruitless painfulness of extreme asceticism.

In this way, six years passed in spiritual exploration, and in the process Siddhartha gained two key understandings. One was an appreciation of the *power* of the disciplines taught by the adepts of the period, and the other was a sense of the *limitations* of these self-same techniques. (For an especially good discussion of these points, see Carrithers, 1983, pp. 5–46.) As we know, these techniques were believed to enable the practitioner to attain higher levels of self-awareness, culminating in an apprehension, unmediated by any of the world's falsifying distinctions, of the undifferentiated and immutable self within. There is no reason to believe that Siddhartha was in the least sceptical about the general efficacy of these techniques – of which he must have been an able practitioner – except in one key respect. Although the practitioners of these disciplines did indeed achieve higher levels of awareness, he found that this was not the same thing as an attainment or realisation of an eternal and unchanging self. The essence of the matter was that the states achieved through disciplined introspection are clearly themselves a result of the skill and exertions of the practitioner and are thus dependent on these factors. The effects are real enough, but they are part of a chain of causation. As such, they come and they go, and if this is so, whatever they are, they can hardly be said to be attainments of an immutable state transcending the realm of decay, death and rebirth. This insight, in turn, gave rise to another. If the so-called true, immutable self is not actually 'known' in meditation, then on what basis can it be said to exist at all? Siddhartha's consistent approach to such matters was to insist that we can have certain knowledge only of things that we have personally experienced and, in the absence of such direct and personal experience of an immutable self, there is no basis for belief in its existence.

Siddhartha's Awakening (often rendered as 'Enlightenment') occurred just after his disillusionment with extreme asceticism. A well-known story tells of how a young woman, taking pity on his emaciated state, revived him with a bowl of milk and rice. Seeing this, his five companions left him in angry disappointment. He thereupon sat beneath a fig tree (the famed 'Bodhi Tree') and vowed not leave until he achieved Awakening. It is said that it came to him in the space of a single night, and with it he became a Buddha, a fully awakened being. In the vastness of cosmic time and space, here have been, are and will continue to be innumerable Buddhas, but he is the Buddha of our place and era, and to distinguish him from other Buddhas he is often called Shakyamuni Buddha, meaning 'Sage of the Shakyas'.

It is said that after his Awakening and following period of some weeks of reflection, he proceeded to Varanasi where, at a place called the Deer Park, he 'set in motion the wheel of the dharma' by delivering his first sermon to his first five disciples (who, in fact, had been his pre-Awakening companions in extreme asceticism). In this sermon, he enunciated four propositions usually called the 'Four Noble Truths' (but perhaps better rendered as 'Truths for the Nobles'; see Cantwell, 2010, p. 61) that encapsulated his understanding of our condition as sentient beings and outlined a method for the alleviation of suffering. In the manner of a physician, his analysis was a diagnosis of a problem and a prescription for a remedy. His focus on the problem (suffering) was laser-sharp, and his prescription was truly radical, as will be seen.

What He Told His First Five Disciples

The first of the Buddha's four truths is that of 'suffering' (*dukkha*), which is arguably the hardest to accept and the vital key to everything else. (See Rahula, 1974, pp. 16–50 for a particularly lucid account of the Four Noble Truths.) It is the simple proposition that suffering is inherent to our existence. This is very difficult for most people to accept because we tend not to look as carefully as we should at the way things go; rather, we see things as we wish them to be, not as they really are. To this point, I must add the qualification that, although the term dukkha is usually translated as 'suffering' or 'sorrow', these English words do not quite get to the kernel of what the Buddha was maintaining. It is not that life does not have its good moments, for we all know that it does. The point, rather, is that the good times *always* pass away for the simple reason that everything in samsara is impermanent. The result is not necessarily actual pain – although this is common enough – but a kind of pervasive dissatisfaction; we cannot get all that we want, and we cannot keep what we have and, as a result, life is pervaded by a sense of discontent, frustration, of never being quite fulfilled in the endless flux and flow of our lives. This is true even in the fine grains of life. You sit, and your ear itches; you give it a scratch. Now your hip complains; you shift position. And as you do, you find that you are thirsty. It goes on and on, in every time frame, micro to macro. Something itches, something hurts, something is missing, something or other must be done. So things go.

Moreover, it is not, let it be stressed, merely that we *experience* suffering. The Buddha, rather, made a more momentous claim. It is not that life has suffering *in* it, as we might normally say; it is that existence in samsara *is itself suffering* in the extended sense I have outlined, and this is so at every level, from the seemingly trivial itches and scratches of life to the great matters of illness, old age and death.

The second truth is that suffering has a cause. Its cause is thirst or craving, which seeks sense pleasures and the things that give rise to sense pleasures. It is a flame-like burning desire always to be in some condition that we are not. This is normally a completely unexamined habit of mind and emotion, never reflected upon, a deeply consequential fact of life that depends on our normal inability to see things as they really are. Related to this is one point more. In keeping with the second truth, the Buddha had a more complex and subtle idea of karma than that prevailing in other Indic systems. In the Upanishadic view, karma referred to the fruit-generating act itself. The Buddha, however, put the accent not on the act as such but on the intention behind the act, which is the real cause of its effects. This opens the door to a strong connection between morality and the problem of suffering, for it is precisely when, impelled by hate or greed, we choose to act in ways that harm others that we are most driven further onward in the cycle of rebirth.

The third truth follows closely from the second. It is that that suffering can be ended and the way to end it is to quell the craving that is its cause. Easy to say, but this is not an easy thing to do. Still, there is a way, and this is the fourth truth, which is the 'Eightfold Path', consisting of eight prescriptions and proscriptions for leading the kind of life that will extinguish suffering. The eight components of the Eightfold Path fall into three groupings. The first two components are 'right understanding' and 'right thought', and both are directly related to a proper understanding of how things truly are, which should be clear-eyed and realistic in a manner informed by the Buddha's teachings. The next three components are 'right speech', 'right action' and 'right livelihood'. These belong to the realm of ethics. One should refrain from falsehood, careless remarks and other forms of speech that harm others. One should refrain from dishonesty and theft, and act in ways that are helpful to others. And, finally, one should make one's living by means of honourable work and should avoid violent behaviour and occupations requiring violence. Refraining from violence is major theme in the Buddha's moral code. This tenet is called *ahimsa*, meaning 'non-harm', and it plays a major role in other Indic religions as well.

The final three components are 'right effort', 'right mindfulness' and 'right concentration'. These relate to the Buddhist system of meditation. One must control one's mental states and channel them in directions conducive to spiritual progress. One must cultivate a clear and immediate awareness of one's physical, emotional and cognitive states such that one becomes a dispassionate observer of these states as they arise and pass away. And one must follow the pathway opened up by these insights through successive states of concentration leading to a deep wisdom based on a direct apprehension of the true nature of existence, a process culminating in the cessation of thirst and suffering. This cessation is called *nirvana*.

Nirvana

It is sometimes supposed that nirvana is the annihilation of self. It is no such thing, and to explain why this is so will require us to turn to the Buddha's views about self.

Central to the Buddha's teachings was the idea that the constituents of any individual are five elements or aggregates (*skandhas*) that are in a constant state of flux and change. They are, as it is sometimes put, in a constant state of 'becoming', and behind the flux and flow there is no 'being' at all. One's sense of 'I' is simply a label that has been applied to the ever-changing concatenation of these elements looping in endless chains of cause and effect; like the flowing of a river, or the flickering of a candle flame, the supposed 'I' is never the same from one day, hour, minute, second, nanosecond, to another. Nothing, absolutely nothing, lasts and rebirth is, therefore, always going on. There is, as one can see, no place in this view of things for an unchanging experiencer, the immutable self, somehow lurking behind the scenes, for the flow is all there is. There is no experien*cer* – only experien*cing*. Although there is suffering – for this entire accretion of changings is itself what suffering is – there is no sufferer. This is the Buddha's famous doctrine of no-self (Sanskrit, *anatman*; Pali [explained below], *anatta*).

Nirvana, therefore, cannot be the annihilation of the self, for the self never existed; rather, it is the annihilation of the *delusion of the self's* existence that is the driver of the coherence of the aggregates that constitute an individual's identity. It is the fuel that feeds the flame of I-consciousness and, if it is removed, the flame dies and rebirth ceases, even in life and even in every moment in life. But as with the Upanishadic path, it is not enough simply to read or be told that there is no-self behind the flux and flow. What is needed is the actual removal of layer upon layer of misleading habits of mind acquired from one's earliest encounters with the world, a process leading finally to an understanding of our true nature as conscious beings. This requires nothing less than a radical reshaping of consciousness and approach to life, gained through a sincere application of the wisdom, morality and meditational system outlined in the Eightfold Path. A variety of expressions have arisen to describe nirvana, such as 'blown out' or 'extinction [of thirst]', but in truth it cannot be described. It will not even do to say that it is an experience unlike any other, for, in the absence of a subjectivity, it is not an experience at all. It is a state of things completely beyond the reach of our words.

Institutionalisation

With the Buddha's Deer Park sermon began a forty-five-year career of travel and teaching throughout the mid-Ganga region. The Buddha was on the move constantly, except during the four months of the monsoon season when it is customary for mendicants to stay in one place. He died at the age of eighty at a place called Kusinara (Kushinagar, in the current Indian state of Uttar Pradesh), apparently of some kind of food poisoning.

Although the proselytising impulse was foreign to Vedic orthodoxy, it became a major factor in religious traditions emerging from the Shramana movement. It was, therefore, certainly not unique to Buddhism, but it was the key to Buddhism's spectacular career as an Indian religion and, ultimately, as a world religion. A formula of conversion and commitment emerged – when is not quite clear – in which a convert 'takes refuge' in what is called the 'Triple Gems': 'I go for refuge to the Buddha, I go for refuge to the Dharma, I go for refuge to the Sangha.' These three things are the very core of Buddhism as a socially transmitted religious tradition (as opposed to a mere floating set of ideas). Let us look at them one at a time.

First, the Buddha. As has already said, the personalisation of a religious message in the image of a venerated founder was not part of the orthodox Vedic tradition but was central to the non-Vedic movements. As will be seen, this was true of Jainism as well as Buddhism, but the personality of the Buddha impressed itself with special power in Buddhist tradition. Recollection of the Buddha as a fully awakened or enlightened being was the source of religious authority, and the message was personalised and humanised through the powerful image of the Buddha's compassion for the sufferings of beings of the cosmos. It should be understood that the Buddha was not a deity, at least not as he was so seen by himself and his early followers; he was a very special human being, to be sure, but human, and he certainly did not teach that he was the source of some sort of saving grace. The Buddha himself must have believed in the existence of supernatural beings – gods and goddesses – but they

2.1   The Buddha teaching, from the wall of a rock-cut cave near Nashik dating 1st to 3rd century CE. Photo: courtesy of American Institute of Indian Studies.

had nothing essential to do with the central purpose of his teachings, which was the alleviation of suffering and nothing else.

When the Buddha passed away, he attained what is called *parinirvana*. This denotes a state in which there is a complete cessation of the continuity of the mental and physical processes that constituted one's existence in samsara. It is probably for this reason that, in its earliest days, the cultic side of his veneration – which inevitably arose and grew – focused on aniconic representations. The Buddha was no more; all that remained were signs of his departure. The *stupa*, therefore, became the focus of Buddha veneration, which at first was a sort of funerary cult. The Buddhist stupa represented an elaboration of a type of burial mound once used to bury great chieftains, and was often used to house physical relics (bone, teeth or objects used by, etc.) of the Buddha or his disciples. These objects came to be regarded as imbued with sacred power and were treated as objects of worship. By the first century CE, anthropomorphic images of the Buddha began to appear and function as objects of worship, and by the fourth century CE or so Buddha images were sometimes seen as manifesting the Buddha's actual presence in contradiction to the doctrine of his post-mortem absence (Berkwitz, 2010, p. 32).

Second, the Dharma (in Pali, Dhamma). Depending on the Indic tradition in which it is being used, the word dharma is rather elastic in meaning. In the present context, it refers primarily to the Buddha's teachings. The Buddha's insistence on the non-existence of an immutable self or atman marked his teachings off decisively from other religious traditions of the day, but we must be careful to note as well that the doctrine of no-self was not a stand-alone idea but was deeply imbedded in a complex and subtle understanding of the nature of reality. Readers must also bear in mind that the Buddha never thought of his teachings as a speculative 'philosophy' in the manner of a Descartes or Kant. His sole aim and object were the alleviation of suffering, not in answering questions unrelated to that single goal. He compared his teachings to a raft that one might find while seeking to cross a river. Having paddled across, would one carry it around on one's back? Hardly! It has done its job, and it is best left on the riverbank for some other traveller to use.

The Buddha's teachings were not put in writing during his lifetime. In fact, the Buddha himself was almost certainly illiterate (showing us once again that illiteracy is not incompatible with deep understanding). The first Buddhist written texts were the independent creations of monks residing in two very different locations: Sri Lanka and Gandhara (the latter corresponding to present-day eastern Afghanistan and northern Pakistan) (see Berkwitz, 2010, pp. 46–51). In Sri Lanka, elements of what became the Pali Canon (consisting of rules of monastic discipline, the Buddha's sermons and interpretive material, and known as the *Tipitaka*), the oldest material extant and the core scripture of Theravada Buddhism (below), were probably committed to writing in the late first century BCE. Pali was one of many regional languages of South Asia during this period, though where it was spoken is not exactly known, and the Buddha himself must have preached in a language native to Magadha. The Gandhara texts, less systematised than the Pali Canon, were also created by monks and were set in writing in the Gandhari language beginning in the first century CE; ultimately, these materials diffused widely into central Asia and thence to western China. Most of the texts belonging to the Mahayana school of Buddhism (below) are written in a type of Sanskrit known as Buddhist Sanskrit, or in Chinese or Tibetan.

Third, the Sangha. In the Buddhist context, this term refers to the body of monks and nuns who follow and put into practice the teachings of the Buddha. (In fact, the order of nuns disappeared around the end of the first millennium, not to be revived until the twentieth century.) When the Buddha first established the Sangha, it was basically a movement of true Shramanas, that is, of homeless world-renouncers. Crucial to the institutionalisation of Buddhism was the reshaping of this movement into monastic communities whose members mostly lived permanently in monasteries. In parallel with this development was the evolution of institutionalised relations between the monastic spiritual elite and a Buddhist laity who supported them.

At the heart of this relationship was (and remains today) a type of religious gift called *dana*. An obvious problem facing any religion centred on a large and economically inactive monastic core is that of providing reliable subsistence to the renouncers. This being so, laity must be given reasons to support the monastic elite with gifts. In Indic religions, in Buddhism but also others, the concept of dana (on which see especially Heim, 2004) supplies such reasons. The term denotes charitable gifts or donations – in this context to mendicants – that generate 'merit' for the donor. Although merit can be gained by any sort of virtuous act, gifting to mendicants is a particularly efficacious source of merit. Merit can generate worldly benefits in the here-and-now, favourable rebirth or enhanced prospects of future advancement towards the ultimate goal of nirvana.

With this concept as the foundation of lay-mendicant relations – and in common with other Indic religions – Buddhism developed a two-tiered structure. At the upper level was a monastic elite; they were understood to be on a more direct path towards the ultimate goal of liberation than laity, and they were the agency by which the Buddha's teachings were preserved and propagated. At a spiritually lower level was the much larger lay community whose members supported the monastic elite by means of gifting. Their religious interests were of a less transcendental sort, and their Buddhist practice was probably mainly motivated by the prospect of merit-generated good fortune in this or subsequent births. Lay duty centred on living by the tenets of Buddhist morality as embodied in the 'Five Precepts' (refraining from killing, theft, inappropriate sexual conduct, untruthfulness and intoxicants) and cultivating such Buddhist virtues as faith in the dharma, an active moral sense and generosity. Given the complete dependence of the monastic community on the laity, it cannot surprise us that special emphasis was given to generosity.

Sectarian Developments

A crucial development in the evolution of Buddhism was the emergence of a sectarian movement in the early centuries of the Common Era that came to be called Mahayana ('Great Vehicle'). The other major Buddhist sectarian tradition is known as Theravada ('Teachings of the Elders'), and it was a continuation of the older mainstream Buddhist traditions of the period. Although Mahayana is sometimes said to have arisen from lay dissatisfaction with the monastic elite, it seems more likely to have originated as a shift in spiritual orientation that developed within some elements of the monastic community itself. And although Mahayana was many things at once, at its heart was a shift in spiritual ideals reflecting an enhanced emphasis on the Buddha's compassion (Schmidt-Leukel, 2006, pp. 94–104). The ultimate result was the development of theological and philosophical systems of great complexity that are quite beyond the scope of this book. We can, however, glance at some essentials.

From the Mahayana perspective, the *arhat* (one who has attained Awakening and nirvana, and the beau ideal of early Buddhism and the Theravada tradition today) is less admirable than one who vows to become a Buddha and, while striving toward this goal, and out of compassion for all sentient beings, helps others along the path to liberation. Such an individual is called a Bodhisattva. This idea seems to have drawn its main inspiration from the *Jataka Tales*, which were Buddhist stories of the Buddha's marvellous doings in previous births while still on the way to Buddhahood. The pathway to becoming a Bodhisattva is open to anyone, even a layperson, and there are multitudes of Bodhisattvas in this wide cosmos.

While the Mahayana outlook probably did not originate among laity disgruntled with monastic elitism, it is also true that, ultimately, this was a movement considerably more hospitable to lay religiosity than the earlier mainstream traditions. The concept of many Buddhas and Bodhisattvas obviously opens a wide door to richly supernaturalistic renderings of Buddhist teachings. If, for example, Bodhisattvas have lengthy careers of rebirths while on their way to Buddhahood, then it is logical to assume that they acquired extranormal powers along the way and that they could deploy these powers not only to advance the spiritual interests of other beings but also to render assistance in more worldly matters as well. The historical result of this line of reasoning was the evolution of a Mahayana pantheon of Bodhisattvas who were objects of veneration and entreaty along the same lines as deities in other traditions, most notably Hindu traditions.

Diffusion and Decline

Although at first it must have been just one renouncer movement among many in ancient South Asia (mostly unknown to us), Buddhism was ultimately far more successful than others in propagating itself. There is no doubt that this had something to do with the Buddha's scepticism about the Brahmanical theory of social stratification and its ethical implications. Readers will recall that Brahmanical orthodoxy understood the system of hereditary varnas to be a built-in feature of the universe (as seen in the aforementioned hymn 10. 90 of the *Rig Veda*). Very different was the Buddha's view. What, he asked, was the foundation of the Brahman's claim to the highest status? It was the possession of certain virtues, but these virtues – the Buddha pointed out – can be possessed by anybody, and need not be conferred by birth. This assertion is of a piece with the ethical universalism of the Buddha's teachings that centred on such simple, powerful principles as truthfulness, harmlessness and loving kindness. These were the very moral precepts best suited to the increasingly cosmopolitan world in which the Buddha's teachings were in circulation.

Buddhist teachings appear to have found a particularly receptive audience among the growing merchant and artisan classes. These were groups that were most at home in towns and cities and shared little life-experiential common ground with rustic Brahman priests. Their networks of trade, moreover, would have constituted ideal pathways for the cultural diffusion of religious ideas and practices. But the most important factor facilitating Buddhism's spread was royal patronage. There seems to have been a natural affinity between Buddhism and the Kshatriya class (equally if not more true of Jainism, as will be seen). We can imagine that the old orthodoxy, linked as it was to the Brahman varna, might have had a diminishing appeal to an urbanising and reshaping Kshatriya class, especially in the mid-Ganga region, which was lightly Brahmanised in any case. The Buddha himself was a Kshatriya, and the *Buddhacharita* stresses a king-who-might-have-been theme; instead of worldly sovereignty, which he might have had, he becomes a spiritual king instead.

Buddhism found royal patronage most momentously in the kingdom of Magadha, which emerged as an imperial power under the rule of the Nandas in the fourth century BCE. As we learnt in the previous chapter, Magadha came under the rule of Chandragupta Maurya, founder of the Mauryan Empire, around 321 BCE. The empire expanded under his rule to stretch from the Bay of Bengal to the hills of Afghanistan, and there could hardly have been a more ideal medium than such an empire for the spatial diffusion of a religion. The teachings of the Shramanas flourished in the empire – not Buddhism alone, but also Jainism and Ajivikism (a rival to both Jainism and Buddhism that vanished around the fourteenth century CE). Chandragupta himself is said to have been a lay Jain and to have renounced his throne and become a Jain monk. It is even said that he ended his life by means of the Jain rite of self-starvation. But more important in religious terms was the reign of Chandragupta's grandson Ashoka (r. *c.*268–233 BCE), under whom the empire expanded to include almost the entire subcontinent and who was ancient India's most acclaimed ruler. It is said that, having felt remorse after seeing the carnage resulting from his defeat of the Kalinga kingdom (corresponding to the modern Indian state of Odisha), he renounced war and adopted Buddhist teachings. He caused stone pillars to be placed throughout his empire on which he had his ethical beliefs and theory of governance inscribed in the form of edicts. (An example of such a pillar – this one without edicts – can be seen on the cover of this book.) His policies of rule drew from the Buddha's teachings, and his edicts stressed such virtues as obedience to parents, truthfulness, compassion, kindness to others, generosity to both Brahmans and Shramanas, non-violence and moderation in consumption and accumulation.

Ashoka's benevolence as a ruler was clearly not inspired by Buddhism exclusively, and, in fact, he stressed the importance of giving respect to all religions and never actually made Buddhism into a state religion. But that said, it seems very likely that a big part of the appeal of Buddhism to Ashoka was precisely the usefulness of its ethical universalism in the context of imperial rule. The same qualities that made Buddhism a good fit for the cosmopolitanism of cities also seem to fit well with the requirements of life in a multi-religious, multicultural and polyglot empire.

Once established in India, Buddhism flourished there for many centuries and ultimately spread beyond the subcontinent to central, east and south-east Asia. It is said that Ashoka dispatched his own son to Sri Lanka to plant the seeds of the *dharma* there, and – whether this is true or not – Buddhism was well established on the island by the third century BCE. Sri Lanka became the South Asian redoubt of the oldest school of Buddhism, the Theravada branch (see Gombrich, 1998). From there Buddhism spread further to points east in south-east Asia, where the Theravada school prevails today. Buddhism also spread from northern India into central Asia and thence into China and Japan; in this zone, various forms of Mahayana tradition predominate. A late development was the emergence of a form of Buddhism called Vajrayana ('the Diamond Vehicle'). Sometimes considered a form of Mahayana, and closely linked with Hindu Tantra, it took root in Tibet, Nepal and Bhutan in the seventh or eighth centuries CE, where it remains today. Arguably, Buddhism became the travelling version of Indic civilisation, which it carried with it to the rest of Asia.

But while Buddhism was evolving into a world religion, by the late centuries of the first millennium CE it was declining in the subcontinent of its birth. Many reasons have been adduced for this and the causes of its weakening were probably multiple (Berkwitz, 2010, pp. 139–42). For one thing, it must be remembered that, even in Buddhism's heyday, the Brahmans, the Buddhists' greatest rivals, were never out of the picture. They continued to preside over and perform life-cycle rites and other rituals with which Buddhism had no connection, and the Buddhists, having relatively few ideas about statecraft of their own, were never fully able to supplant Brahmans as counsellors to kings, nor did they have command of rituals deemed essential to the protection of states (Bronkhorst, 2011a, pp. 230–7). The rise of Hindu devotional sects was also a major source of competition for both lay and royal supporters, and the similarity between Bodhisattva veneration and Hindu devotionalism in time blurred the distinction between some forms of Buddhism and Hindu traditions.

Into the mix of these and other problems came the Muslim incursions of the twelfth and thirteenth centuries CE and the sacking of great Buddhist universities and monasteries. This may well have been the lethal blow, but it should be remembered that, by the time Islam came into the picture, Buddhism was already sinking into the Hindu background, and we should bear in mind that many have found it all too easy to blame the Muslims for everything that goes wrong in South Asia. In any case, after the thirteenth century, Buddhism as such had largely vanished from the subcontinent. Still, it remained in the Himalayan periphery and in Sri Lanka, and in a few other pockets in the subcontinent. It also left a deep imprint on Hinduism. Examples include the psychologisation of bondage and liberation we find in the *Bhagavad Gita* (next chapter) and Shankara's contention that bondage itself is unreal.

Very different was the fate of Jainism. Once a major competitor of Buddhism, it never left the subcontinent until recently, to say nothing of reaching Buddhism's heights as a world religion. But neither did it disappear from South Asia, where it continues to prosper to the present day. It is to Jainism that we now turn.

Jainism

Although Jains constitute but a tiny fraction (about 4.2 million) of the modern Republic of India's population, their weight and influence in Indian society is great. Jains have traditionally been very prominent in trade and are a conspicuous presence at the topmost levels of Indian commerce and industry. Jains are noted for two emphases in their religious practice. One is the severity of their asceticism. Lay Jains as well as initiated mendicants engage in impressively severe austerities, especially various forms of fasting. In fact, death by means of ritualised self-starvation remains a Jain ideal to the present day. Jains are also well known for their strict adherence to the principle of ahimsa. A vegetarian diet is, therefore, a basic requirement of Jainism, and even certain vegetarian food items (such as vegetables that grow underground) are barred to mendicants and orthoprax laity on the theory that their consumption is unacceptably harmful to living things. (To harvest a potato, for example, requires killing living things in the soil as well as killing the entire plant, and the potato itself is seen as the home of multitudes of life forms.) When they move about the streets on their alms rounds, Jain mendicants are easily spotted because of the brooms they carry to sweep away minute living things before sitting or lying down; some also wear mouth cloths to prevent their breath from harming minute airborne forms of life.

As is Buddhism, Jainism is organised around the distinction between a monastic elite (both monks and nuns) and a larger laity who venerate and materially support the mendicants whom they regard as spiritual preceptors and assume to be more directly on the path to liberation than themselves. Fully initiated mendicants must subject themselves to a monastic discipline notorious for its severity. Among many other prohibitions, they are not allowed to stay in any single location for more than a few days (except during the rainy-season retreat), which inhibited the development of monasteries, although there were lapses into monasticism over the course of Jainism's long history. Liberation is seen as a distant goal for both mendicants and laity, but more distant for laity. While laity are enjoined to hold liberation always in mind as the ultimate goal of religious life, their practice is focused on a rich ceremonial life (on which see especially Cort, 2001; Kelting, 2001; and Laidlaw, 1995) and interactions with – and support of – the mendicant community. Such activities generate merit that brings about worldly well-being, favourable rebirth and progress along the road to liberation. Even lay Jains, however, undertake quite onerous forms of ascetic practice, especially in the area of fasting.

Jainism is often said to have been founded by a mendicant teacher called Mahavira ('Great Hero'), but this assertion requires qualification. Jains themselves do not view Mahavira as the founder of their religion, for they see Jainism as eternal and unfounded. (Buddhists have similar beliefs, but the Jains emphasise the issue more.) They maintain that Jain teachings have always existed and that they are simply periodically rediscovered by self-enlightened omniscient teachers known as Jinas ('victors', 'conquerors') or Tirthankaras ('establishers of fords', as in fords across a river). In all of time and space, these figures are uncountably many, with Mahavira being the last of twenty-four Jinas of our cosmic epoch and tiny corner of the cosmos. In this perspective, each Jina is less a founding figure than a re-establisher of teachings already extant. But, at the same time, there is no doubt that Mahavira's personality and example left an imprint on Jainism not unlike that of Siddhartha Gautama on Buddhism. An account of Jainism, therefore, can hardly begin without saying something about his career, and the ways in which the narrative of his career differs from that of the Buddha have an important bearing on differences between Jain and Buddhist teachings.

Mahavira

Mahavira's dating is somewhat uncertain. There are two main branches of Jainism, the Shvetambaras (whose monks and nuns wear white clothing) and the Digambaras (whose senior monks wear nothing). The Shvetambaras give 599–527 BCE as Mahavira's dates while the Digambaras favour 582–510 BCE (Wiley, 2004, p. 6). However, there is also a highly credible tradition that Mahavira and the Buddha were contemporaries, although, if so, they apparently never met personally. If this is true, then Mahavira's dates should probably be pushed forward by roughly a century (Dundas, 2002, pp. 24–5). His place of birth is said to have been a town corresponding to a village in present-day Bihar called Basukund. Tradition and text portray his father as a king named Siddhartha, but all we really know is that he was born into the Kshatriya class of rulers and soldiers.

The story of Mahavira's birth and career is in many ways very similar to the Buddha's, although there are conspicuous differences. Presented here is a summary of the account given in a text called the *Kalpasutra* (Vinayasagar, 1984). This text is said to have been composed by a monk named Bhadrabahu, who is believed to have died about 170 years after Mahavira's death. It belongs to the Shvetambara branch of Jainism, and we should note that the Digambaras tell the story somewhat differently but with the same essentials.

While the *Kalpasutra* describes the Mahavira's birth in terms generally similar to the account of the Buddha's birth, the text places much greater emphasis on the issue of Kshatriya status. According to the *Kalpasutra* narrative, Mahavira entered a Brahman woman's womb at the time of his conception. Apprehending this from his abode on high, Indra, the King of the Gods, intervened. He did so because of an eternal and universal law that a Jina should never under any circumstances be born outside the Kshatriya *varna*. On Indra's orders, his divine underlings shifted the foetus to the womb of a noble woman of Kshatriya status. She was wife of King Siddhartha and also pregnant at the time, so the gods were able to shift the foetus in her womb to that of the Brahman woman. Although the Digambaras do not accept this episode, they, too, maintain that a Jina must be a Kshatriya. On the night of Mahavira's conception, his mother had a series of dreamlike visions that, according to the king's interpreters of dreams, portended that he would be a great warrior and would rule the world as a universal emperor. But then they amended this by saying that the visions might also portend that he would become a spiritual warrior and universal teacher. This is, more or less, the same prophecy that was made at the time of the Buddha's birth, but it should be added that the warrior theme is more strongly emphasised in Jain tradition. According to the Jains, a Jina absolutely must be born in a Kshatriya family, whereas in Theravada tradition several of the twenty-seven Buddhas who preceded Gautama Buddha were Brahmans.

When Mahavira was born, huge celebrations broke out among the gods in their heavens and in his father's kingdom on earth. As was the Buddha, he was raised and came to adulthood as a prince and heir to a kingdom. But having spent thirty years of his life amid royal luxuries, he renounced the world and took up the mendicant life. In a year-long, massive vomiting up of the world and its pleasures and temptations, he gave up everything he possessed, great and small, and having shed his possessions, he went to an Ashoka tree in a nearby park where he discarded his remaining ornaments, pulled out his hair in five handfuls, and vowed henceforth to take only one waterless meal out of six. Wearing only a single piece of cloth, he became a homeless mendicant. The last vestige was the cloth, which he lost after a year by accident when it caught on a thorn. (The Digambaras say he was nude from the start.)

For twelve years, Mahavira wandered as a homeless mendicant. In its telling of this, the *Kalpasutra* greatly emphasises the extreme privations to which he subjected himself and that he bore with complete equanimity and detachment. In the thirteenth year of his homelessness, while taking only one waterless meal every three days and while meditating under a Sal tree and exposing himself to the relentless rays of the summer sun, he attained omniscience and became a Jina. As an omniscient being, he knew everything about all beings at all places and all times. Nothing was concealed from him.

This episode, too, is quite similar to the *Buddhacharita*'s account of the Buddha's Awakening, complete with tree (although of a different kind), but there are also important differences. An obvious difference is the extreme physicality of Mahavira's transformation. In the Jain narrative, there is a tight connection drawn between Mahavira's enlightenment and the preservation of equanimity in the context of extreme discomfort and privation. But, as we know, it was precisely Siddhartha's disillusionment with these same privations that opened the way to his Awakening. Furthermore, although the Buddha probably claimed omniscience and was certainly credited with omniscience by his later followers, the Jains place much greater importance on the issue than do the Buddhists (see Jaini, 1974; Heim, 2018 on the issue). This is because Mahavira's religious authority (and that of all Jinas) rests precisely on the strength of this claim. Mahavira is said to have possessed complete and permanent knowledge, entirely unmediated by the senses, of all knowable things – past, present and future – and to have known them all at once, the whole panorama in a single instant. The issue of the Buddha's omniscience is much contested in the Buddhist world, but the upshot seems to be that he certainly possessed the power to know anything at all, but only one thing at a time.

After his attainment of omniscience, Mahavira lived for nearly thirty more years, wandering from place to place (except during the monsoon season). We know that he was teaching during this period of his life, but the *Kalpasutra* has little say on this subject. He died, which is to say he shed his body and attained complete liberation from samsara, in a town called Papa in his seventy-second year. He left behind him a complete Jain community consisting of monks, nuns, laymen and laywomen.

What Mahavira Taught

In describing Jain teachings, one must begin with the fact that Mahavira shared the premise of transmigration with the Buddha and the orthodox Brahmans; this idea, at least in its essentials, appears to have been a totally unexamined conceptual starting point in all three of these traditions. But, beyond this basic agreement, Jain teachings diverged, and in some respects radically diverged, from Buddhism and the Upanishadic traditions alike.

To start with a matter of emphasis, the Jains take an even more negative view of transmigration than other Indic traditions, placing great stress both on the intensity of the suffering of transmigrating beings and also on its duration. The Jains accentuate the inherently dismal character of our worldly bondage by means of a fixation on infinities. They reject the idea of a creator deity or indeed a creation of the world in any sense and, although this is a view Jains share with the Buddhists, they put on it their own dark spin. Time has no beginning or end, and our journey through the world, with miseries at every stop along the way, has meandered through every corner of the vast cosmos. And more, by mathematical necessity the entire journey has already taken place infinite times, and our journey with its aggregate of sufferings will continue forever unless we find a pathway to liberation. Furthermore, in contrast to the Buddha's more psychologised understanding of suffering, the Jains emphasise the physical actuality of pain and its endless repetition unless brought to a stop.

But what entity, exactly, is to be liberated from pain and suffering? On this point, the Jain view is profoundly different from both the Buddha's and that of the composers of the Upanishads. The Jains denote the self by the term *jiva*, which carries the basic meaning of 'life'; it can be translated into English, as one author (Dundas, 2002, p. 93) suggests, as 'life-monad', but most translators render it as 'soul' or 'self'. However, because of the rather distinctive meaning of the term in Jainism, I shall use 'jiva' itself instead of an English substitute in what follows.

According to the Jains, reality is divided into two utterly different constituents: living beings (the immaterial jivas) and lifeless matter. Our bodies are made of matter, and matter is the prison of the jiva, for embodiment is the cause of rebirth. Physical bodies come and go – although the matter they are made of is uncreated and eternal – and the jivas move ever onward. The jivas in the cosmos are infinite in number and circulate through it unendingly. In contrast to the Upanishadic view, there is no question of an identity between the jiva and any sort of universal substrate on the order of brahman, for the jivas are irreducible in their individuality and plurality, and no such substrate exists. Obviously, too, this is a view completely at odds with the Buddha's doctrine of no-self. It does, however, have a parallel in the philosophical system known as Samkhya to be discussed in the next chapter.

According to Jain teachings, jivas are embodied in a multitude of different forms: as humans, deities, denizens of Hell, plants and even as such apparently non-living things as air, water, fire and earth. But whatever the nature of their embodiment, jivas are identical in the sense that they have the same defining qualities: consciousness, bliss and energy. Although these qualities are always present, they are occluded by embodiment, but in liberation, which is the shedding of all encumbering layers of matter, they can be fully manifested. Consciousness, fully realised, is omniscience and thus a liberated being fully activates the innate, though normally suppressed, ability to know all things.

But what accounts for the persistence and intractability of the jiva's embodiment and rebirth? It is because of karma. The Jain understanding of karma, however, is radically different from that of other Indic religious traditions. As we know, the term carries the basic meaning of 'action'; action generates fruit, and the nature of the fruit depends on the nature of the action, and if the results are not experienced in this lifetime then they will surely occur in another. As we also know, the Buddha stressed the element of intention; it is not just the action but the motivation behind it that matters most. According to the Jains, however, karma is actually a subtle type of *matter* that floats free in every corner of the cosmos. Whenever we act, our actions attract this matter and cause it to adhere to the jiva, thus holding it in material bondage. The influx of karmic matter is unavoidable, but the intensity to which it sticks to the jiva depends on the intentions and dispositions of the actor.

Liberation (moksha) is a condition that can be achieved only by a complete removal of karmic matter from the jiva, and the physicality of karma, as the Jains conceive it, has an important bearing on how this might be done. To the Jains, liberation cannot be attained merely by means of a special sort of knowledge or self-awareness. This is because the karmic deposits are physically real and cannot be thought away; they must be actually removed. Doing so is a two-stage process. First, the influx and adhesion of karma must be reduced and eliminated. This means regulating one's behaviour in such a way as to avoid the sorts of actions that encourage influx and eliminating the mental dispositions that cause it to stick. Violent actions, which by their very nature arise from and nourish the worst of our passions, top the list. Thus, the cessation of violence is a crucial step towards liberation. This is the soteriological root of the Jains' commitment to non-violence, although compassion for all living things is also an autonomous Jain virtue, quite apart from any instrumental value it might possess. And more, one must cultivate a state of mental and emotional equanimity in which passions of whatever kind are quelled. One should strive to remain always controlled and restrained in one's interactions with the world and with other beings.

But more is required than a mere abatement of karmic influence and adhesion, for it is also necessary to get rid of the karmic accumulations already there. The principal means of doing so is ascetic practice. The point of such practice, when done in the light of Jain teachings and in the spirit of indifference to pain and pleasure, is not self-punishment. Rather, ascetic practice brings about two desirable conditions. At one level, ascetic austerity is both a manifestation of equanimity and a factor in its further cultivation, which lessens karmic influx and adhesion. But ascetic practice also loosens the hold of existing karmic deposits directly. Jains frequently employ the metaphor of fire in this context; austerities are said to 'burn away' the soul's karmic burden. Asceticism is, therefore, central to mendicant life, but it is not solely a mendicant concern, for ascetic practice is very much a feature of lay life as well.

Liberation, when and if it comes, is the endpoint of an already infinitely long journey, and is held to be possible only in a human body. Its achievement involves a succession of stages of passion-suppression and karma-removal – fourteen in all – that begin with a stage of false views and end, after a long climb (with possible slips backwards), with the attainment of complete liberation from all passions, be they desires or aversions, and the attainment of omniscience (*kevalajnana*). When such an omniscient person dies, all karmic residues are shed; the jiva then rises to the top of the cosmos, where it will abide in omniscient bliss for all of infinite time to come.

It is important to note that despite the extreme emphasis on non-violence in Jainism, there is a distinctively martial theme in Jain religious culture. Mahavira was a Kshatriya, as are all Jinas. The birth of a Jina is heralded by dreams that portend that the child will either be a warrior and king or a great teacher (the same, of course, was true of the Buddha). The term Jina means 'victor' or 'conqueror'. Jainism is a warrior's path, but outer worldly conquest is deemed inferior to, and replaced by, the conquest of the body and its passions.

Diffusion

It is probable that Jain teachings were propagated by proselytising mendicant groups of some sort in the early days after Mahavira's departure. Jainism diffused outwards from Magadha in two directions. It travelled eastwards into Bengal, and thence down the eastern coast into the subcontinent's south. It travelled westwards to the city of Mathura (supposedly once visited by Mahavira himself) and then beyond. Legend proclaims that one Samprati, a grandson of the emperor Ashoka, was responsible for the Jain penetration of the south. Supposedly, the emperor first sent sham monks to teach the locals how to feed and support Jain mendicants, and then followed up with the real thing. Leaving this aside, it seems likely that Jainism was present in the extreme south as early as the third century BCE (Jain, 2010, Vol. 2, p. 440). Jainism's subsequent career in the south was very successful, largely because Jains were adroit at attracting patronage from southern warriors and kings, especially in what is now the Indian state of Karnataka. Part of the appeal to such figures might well have been the aforementioned martial theme in Jain religious culture.

Historian Smita Sahgal (1994) argues that Jainism's western movement occurred mainly in post-Mauryan times, c.200 BCE–300 CE. She suggests that in this region – and in contrast to the east and south – Jainism found little royal patronage, which was largely pre-empted by Buddhism and Brahmanical orthodoxy. Instead, Jainism's foothold was largely gained because of the economic development and expansion of trade that took place there, particularly under the Kushanas, whose empire greatly facilitated trade between northern South Asia and central Asia. Expanded commerce favoured the trading community, which rose in wealth and relative social status and became the social base of Jainism in this region. The city of Mathura had become a Jain epicentre by roughly the second century BCE, and when – in the fourth and fifth centuries – Jainism's centre of gravity shifted into what is now Rajasthan and Gujarat, it carried the strong association with trade with it, an association that has endured to the present day.

A result of Jainism's bidirectional diffusion was the emergence of significant differences between the religious cultures of northern and southern Jains, as manifested most dramatically in the sectarian fission between Shvetambaras (north and west) and Digambaras (south, but also present in the north). Doctrinal fundamentals are the same between these two branches, but other differences are many, and of these the most basic and definitive relates to a highly visible matter of monastic discipline. As noted earlier, Shvetambara means 'white-clad', and mendicants of this branch wear white clothing, whereas Digambara means 'space-clad', and advanced male mendicants of this branch are nude. These rules apply only to mendicants and have nothing to do with laity.

The Shvetambaras and Digambaras have widely different views of the causes of their split. There is general agreement that Mahavira and his disciples were nude. The Digambaras, however, maintain that, in roughly 360 BCE, a group of monks migrated to the south to escape a twelve-year famine. When they later returned to the north, they were met by an ugly surprise, which was that the northern mendicants had adopted a spurious canon and had backslid into the wearing of clothing. The horrified migrants then became the Digambara branch. A Shvetambara version blames a renegade monk; he abandoned clothing under the mistaken idea that he was at Mahavira's spiritual level, and then acquired a following of misled disciples. The most likely reason for the split, however, is the influence of regional isolation and the amplification of difference over time. The split began to crystallise around the fifth century CE, and the subcontinent's south (mainly in what is now Karnataka and southern Maharashtra) became the Digambara heartland, with some Digambaras in the north as well. The Shvetambaras became predominant in the north and west, especially in, contemporary, Gujarat, Rajasthan and Punjab.

The Shvetambaras and Digambaras also possess different canonical literatures. The Shvetambara canon is written in an ancient language called Ardhamagadhi (in

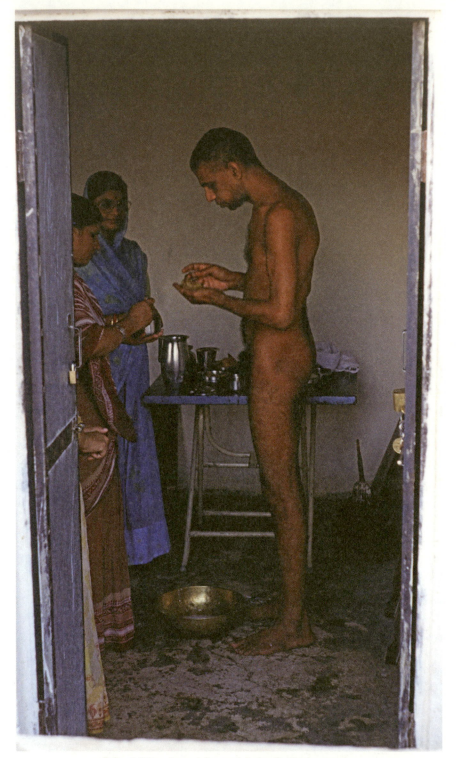

2.2 A Digambara Jain monk being fed by laywomen.

which Mahavira is said to have taught). It is an immense body of material consisting of forty-five texts (although this figure is not accepted by all subgroups). It is
said to have been reduced to an authoritative written version in the fifth century
CE, and Shvetambaras regard it as representing a significant portion of Mahavira's
original teachings. The Digambaras believe that almost all the original canon was
lost; they, therefore, reject the entire Shvetambara canon as bogus and accept as
valid only two texts of their own. In addition to the canonical texts, learned monks
in both Shvetambara and Digambara traditions have created an immense post-
canonical literature that has acquired semi-canonical status, and these two textual
traditions together constitute one of the glories of South Asian religious and philosophical literature.

In addition to the Shvetambara/Digambara split, there have been numerous
other fissures in the Jain community. On the Digambara side, a major development was the gradual disappearance of nude monks and the emergence of a class
of clothing-wearing religious functionaries from the early thirteenth century.
However, their supremacy was challenged from the seventeenth century onwards
by a reform movement known as Terapanth ('Path of Thirteen') and a revival of
mendicant nudity in the twentieth century. On the Shvetambara side, the major
sectarian dispute has to do with the legitimacy of the worship of Jina images in
temples, which was never more than a marginal issue among Digambaras. Shvetambara temple worship was challenged by reformers from the fifteenth century
onwards, and the Svetambara world today is divided between those who do and
do not worship Jina images in temples (see Cort, 2010).

Legacies

As we know, Buddhism, as an institutionalised religion and a religious identity,
disappeared from most of the South Asian subcontinent centuries ago. It lived on
mainly in Sri Lanka and the northern Himalayan zone, principally in Nepal and
Bhutan. Buddhism also left a profound impression on certain aspects of Hinduism, and a form of Buddhism has been revived recently in the Republic of India,
of which more below.

The Buddhism of Sri Lanka belongs to the Theravada school and is the religion
of about 70% of the population (the other major religions are Hinduism, Islam and
Christianity). Freedom of religion is guaranteed by the Sri Lankan Constitution,
but the state is deemed to have a special obligation to foster and protect Buddhism.
Buddhism's early spread in Sri Lanka occurred under the umbrella of royal support,
and a symbiotic relationship resulted in which the monastic orders depended on
kings for material support and kings depended on the monastic community for
the legitimacy of their rule (on these points, see Berkwitz, 2010, pp. 142–55). The

politicisation of Buddhism has expanded in the post-independence period and has become an extremely important factor in Sri Lanka's recent political history (see Seneviratne, 1999).

Although Nepal is generally regarded as the country of the Buddha's birth, most Nepalis are Hindus of one kind or another (about 80%). Buddhism, the religion of roughly 10%, is practised by a range of ethnic groups of which the Newar community, living mainly in the Kathmandu valley, is the most prominent (Berkwitz, 2010, pp. 156–62). Although the Newars are highly Hinduised, many practise a form of Buddhism to which Vajrayana teachings and the worship of Bodhisattvas and Tantric deities are central. The Buddhism of Bhutan is Tibetan Buddhism, and Bhutanese monastic communities have historically maintained close ties with Tibet.

The most important Buddhist presence in the Republic of India is the so-called 'neo-Buddhist' movement (Omvedt, 2003; Zelliot, 2001). It was initiated by Dr Bhimrao Ambedkar (1891–1956), who was born a member of the Mahar caste, a Dalit caste found mainly in the Indian state of Maharashtra. (The term 'Dalit' has replaced the term 'Untouchable' formerly used to denote castes of the lowest status.) A highly educated man, he was one of the leading authors of the Indian Constitution. He fought a lifelong war against the discrimination and humiliations suffered by the Mahars and other lower castes, and ultimately decided that amelioration of their status was not possible within Hinduism. Buddhism, he also concluded, could be an ideal alternative religion for the Mahars and others like them. On the one hand, it was certainly genuinely Indian, and conversion would thus not be a rejection of Indian heritage; on the other hand, Buddhism did not support caste discrimination. In 1956, he and thousands of his Mahar followers underwent a ceremony of conversion to a version of Buddhism. The Buddhism he promoted was highly idiosyncratic, uncanonical and refocused in the direction of social justice. The movement he started, now with an order of monks and nuns, continues to attract mostly lower-caste converts to the present day.

In turning to Jainism, we must first note the obvious fact that Jainism had a destiny totally different from Buddhism's – an exact inversion, in fact. If Buddhism disappeared from most of South Asia, it went on to Asia-wide and later worldwide dissemination. Jainism never left the subcontinent (except marginally and recently), but it remains deeply rooted in the Republic of India. The reason Jainism remained bottled up in South Asia was probably monastic discipline; Jain mendicants, who are the tradition's main social transmitters and propagators, are not allowed to employ artificial means of transportation for fear of inflicting harm on forms of life, and thus could not leave the subcontinent. As for the reason it survived in South Asia, Padmanabh Jaini (1979, pp. 286–7) is surely right when he points to the close relationship between mendicants and laity, strongly encouraged by the requirement of constant mendicant movement (which prevents mendicants from bunching up in monastic communities), as a key factor. Close and continuous contact meant that laity had sustained contact with Jain teachings, and the scattering of the mendicant communities meant that there were no great Jain monasteries and universities vulnerable to sack and plunder.

While Jain teachings, as such, have nothing whatsoever to do with the caste system, Jainism as a practised religion has become deeply entwined with caste (to be discussed in Chapter 5), which plays a major role in organising Jain communities as they exist on the ground (Babb, 1996, 2004; Sangave, 1980). Although Jainism was once a proselytising religion, this is no longer the case, and virtually all Jains are linked to the religion by birth in a Jain family and caste. Some castes consist entirely of Jains, some only partly so; some are Digambara, others Shvetambara. The Jains of South India are almost entirely Digambara, and most are farmers or small-time traders. The Jains of North India belong to castes traditionally associated with trade and banking. The prominence of Jains in commerce is often attributed to Jainism's strong commitment to non-violence; trade, the argument goes, is a suitable profession for Jains because it does not involve physical violence. However, the fact that many southern Jains are farmers would seem to problematise this argument. Because of the occupational difference between northern and southern Jains, northerners are, on average, far wealthier than their southern co-religionists.

It is true that the Jains today are but a tiny community when considered against the Indian population as a whole (there are very few in Bangladesh or Pakistan). The number given by the Indian census of 2011 – 4.2 million – is probably an undercount because many Jains return themselves as Hindu, but the total is still small. But even if Jains are few in number and sometimes identify as 'Hindu' (usually in political contexts), they have successfully maintained their identity as a distinct religious community. In fact, due to the importunities of some Jains, Jainism was granted legal 'minority religious status' in 2014, thus joining Muslims, Sikhs, Christians, Buddhists and Parsis as an official religious minority. The results of this change have yet to play out completely, but among the benefits is immunity of Jain temples and trusts from government meddling and potential takeover. It also has the effect of allowing Jain-run schools to reserve up to 50% of the seats for Jains and to teach Jainism in such schools. In the longer run, the change may enhance public awareness of the distinctiveness of Jainism and the nature of its contributions to South Asian civilisation.

But if Jains are few, they project a very big presence in the life of the modern Indian republic, especially in the area of commerce. Because the Jains, especially the Jains of the north, have specialised in business and business-related occupations, they are commonly stereotyped as wealthy merchants. Although the reality is more complex, this stereotype contains an important grain of truth. Jains are indeed major actors in India's business world, and they have played and continue to play a central role in India's commercial life. Many of India's most successful businessmen have been and are Jains, and the beauty and magnificence of many Jain temples give visible testimony to the wealth and piety of their businessman supporters. Jains are not only owners or top executives of many of India's leading corporations, but they can also be found nowadays in the higher echelons of major international firms. A good example of the international growth of a Jain-dominated business is India's diamond industry centred in Mumbai and Surat. Jains, most famously from the Gujarati town of Palanpur, dominate this industry, and its recent rapid development has pulled it from the margins of the world diamond business to a position close to its centre. Today, Jain diamantaires have taken their place among the industry's elites in such international centres as Antwerp and New York.

3

Hinduism

Does Hinduism exist? It seems like an odd sort of question when you consider that it is said to be the religion of roughly 80% of the Indian republic's enormous population. Of course, it exists. But there is still an issue. It has partly to do with names. We must start with the fact that 'Hinduism', the name, did not originate within the religious world that it names, but was imposed upon it. To add to the complexity, the very imposition of the name led to important changes in the religious world so named; in fact, it can be argued that the naming of 'Hinduism' led, in part, to its existence in its contemporary form, a matter to which I return later in this book.

The term 'Hinduism' conjoins the word 'Hindu' with the suffix 'ism'. However, the word 'Hindu' does not actually belong to Sanskrit, supposedly the foundational language of Hinduism. Rather, it originated from the Persian term *sindhu*, a name for the Indus River, and was applied by Muslims as an ethnographic term to describe the inhabitants of the subcontinent on the river's far side. In its turn, 'ism' is an English suffix, and the marriage of 'Hindu' and 'ism' – that is, the creation of the modern concept of Hinduism as a distinct 'religion', that of the 'Hindus' – was a product of British rule. Prior to this, the dominant religious identities of the Hindus were many, not one, and were largely focused on various sectarian traditions (but for a different point of view, see Lorenzen, 1999). In other historical or ethnographic contexts, these sects might well be considered 'religions' themselves, and in important ways this remains true today.

However, these issues of nomenclature and identity should not be allowed to become an unhelpful diversion from the fact that there is undeniably a religious reality behind the concept of Hinduism. Hindus will tell you so, and they ought to know. From a strictly content-oriented standpoint, Hinduism is best described as a bundle of related religious traditions. But though different, these traditions bear strong family resemblances consisting of shared concepts, values, mythologies, ritual forms and more, and the reality of Hinduism lies in these common features. Furthermore, we must suppose that the coming of Islam to the subcontinent accentuated the visibility of these commonalities, thus providing a foundation for an emerging 'Hindu' religious identity. Even so, Hinduism might be better described as a religious culture than as a clearly bounded and internally integrated religion. It was never, that is, a discrete system of beliefs and practices focused on certain core tenets, and that remains true today. But with this stipulation established, I shall bow to long-entrenched convention and continue to employ the term 'Hinduism' without embellishments in this and later chapters, and return to the question of its history and evolving meaning in Chapter 5.

Origins

If this much is granted, then we must address another difficult issue, that of when this rather amorphous reality came into existence – not the name, but the variegated religious culture that has been so named. To this question there is no obvious answer, but on one point let us be clear: the Vedic tradition is not at all the same thing as Hinduism. As I suggested in Chapter 1, the Vedic material is certainly a part of the overall Hindu mosaic and is arguably foundational to some Hindu traditions. It is also a source of legitimacy for beliefs or systems that, whether really Vedic or not, claim Vedic ancestry. But it must also be borne in mind that, as has already been stressed, many elements of what came to be Hinduism were assimilated from local cults and sects that we cannot see through the lens of Vedic texts and that coexisted with, and even predated, the Vedas. In that perspective, much that is 'Hindu' was present long before the Vedic Indo-Aryans even entered South Asia.

Still, a discussion of Hinduism has to begin somewhere and, if it is not in the Vedic Age, then a reasonable temporal benchmark at which to take up a continuing story is 320 CE. This date marks the beginning of the Gupta Empire, a return of mega imperium to the subcontinent after the demise of the Mauryan Empire nearly half a millennium before. Ruling from Pataliputra, as did the Mauryas centuries previously, the Guptas exercised varying degrees of authority over most of the north during their heyday in the late fourth and fifth centuries. The Gupta period (320–550 CE) is generally regarded as the Classical Age of Indian civilisation, and while Hinduism certainly cannot be said to have begun with Gupta rule this is the period when it began to coalesce in a generally recognised form. However, the crucial changes began during the post-Mauryan, pre-Gupta centuries and did so in competition with Buddhism and Jainism, which were both expanding during this period.

One element in the mix was Vedic beliefs and practices as maintained, ritually enacted and transmitted by the Brahman class. But although these traditions were preserved in the post-Vedic period, purely Vedic elements began to be pushed to the side by, or fused with, new deities and forms of worship with the passage of time. Many of these new features were drawn, recast or modified from the local, non-Indo-Aryan religious substrate that was always a part of the total religious context. The promoters of these new cultural formations were Brahmans who often held high positions in the courts of kings and nobles, and to this extent one can see their emergence as a 'restoration' of Brahmanical religious culture after the batterings inflicted on Brahmanism by Buddhism and Jainism (Michaels, 2004, p. 39). Significantly, the language of this newly re-emerging orthodoxy was Sanskrit (versus the Prakrits, the ancient vernacular languages of which the Buddhists' Pali and the Jains' Ardhamagadhi are examples); later, Tamil – the language of classical South Indian civilisation – and, to some extent, Telugu came to play a similar role in the south.

Among the many religious changes occurring during this period, two of the most significant were the emergence of new deities and new ritual procedures, and these trends were related. The major deities moving into the foreground during this period were not without a Vedic context – albeit tenuous – but they were essentially composites that blended some Vedic elements with traits drawn from the non-Indo-European substrate. If not totally new, they were more new than old, and they were invested with Brahmanical legitimacy by a process known as Sanskritisation.

This term was originally coined by anthropologist M. N. Srinivas (1965) in reference to a strategy of social mobility in which low castes emulate the customs and usages of high castes in seeking higher status. This useful concept can also be applied to the upward movements of elements of religious culture more generally. When, for example, an obscure local deity is elevated in status by being deemed to be a 'form' of a lofty and well-known deity whose attributes and history are described in Sanskrit texts, and when this new link is sanctioned in texts with the upgraded deity's new persona stabilised in writing, this is also a form of Sanskritisation. When it occurs in reverse, as it often does, the process can also be described as 'localisation' or 'parochialisation' (Marriott, 1955); that is, a 'higher' deity is pulled down from the realm of sacred literature and enters a local pantheon, taking on traits and attributes from local religious culture. This circulation of cultural elements between high culture and local cultures seems to have been a major factor in the growth and elaboration of the evolving Hindu pantheon.

Not only were the deities new, but the relationship between worshippers and the objects of worship was also undergoing a deep transformation. The name generally given to this new way of looking at the divine is *bhakti*, a word meaning 'devotion' in Indic languages. The basic idea conveyed by this term is that a particular deity (male or female, and for that matter any august or saintly personage) can respond to the heartfelt devotion of worshippers for whom the deity can be a source of grace and salvation. The seeds of bhakti can be seen in the Vedic materials, most notably the *Shvetasvatara Upanishad* (Lorenzen, 2004, pp. 187–8), but the concept does not truly take shape until the early centuries of the Common Era. The earliest text that presents a systematic delineation of bhakti is the *Bhagavad Gita*, which belongs to the smriti as opposed to the shruti (i.e., Vedic) category of texts.

Because of the emphasis on specific deities as objects of devotion, bhakti went hand in hand with sectarianism, and, speaking generally, three mainstream sectarian movements emerged during this period, each focused on its own favoured divinity. One centred on the worship of Vishnu – as we know, a minor figure in the Vedas – two of whose ten *avataras* ('descents'; the forms in which he manifested on earth), Rama and Krishna, later become major devotional foci. Together with his associated deities, Shiva, the Vedic Rudra, becomes another major devotional focus, especially in the south. The Great Goddess (generically, 'Devi'), a figure combining maternal and martial traits, also becomes the object of devotional traditions. Much later still, as shall be seen later in this book, various sectarian traditions celebrated devotion to a formless (*nirguna*) divine being.

Paralleling these changes, a critical development in the ritual sphere was the increasing importance of the worship of physical images of deities by means of a rite called *puja*. While the history of this development is far from clear, the puja rite quite possibly emerged in part from a Tantric milieu (explained later in this chapter), the image serving as a physical prompt and pattern for mental visualisations in which the human performer identifies with the image resulting in his or her own divinisation (Padoux, 2017, pp. 113–19). But the puja rite was also intertwined with the evolution of devotional traditions, and ultimately became the paradigmatic devotional rite. The Vedic fire-based sacrificial rite was still practised, but puja was a far more suitable ritual vehicle for the expression of devotional sentiment.

The focus of puja is normally some type of physical icon or symbol that is treated as the deity's actual presence. Worshippers treat the deity (as manifested in the image) an honoured personage with whom one can be interact as one might with a human other – who can be welcomed as a guest, entertained, washed, dressed and fed in ways that express such human emotions as respect, affection and love. A food offering is typically the central feature of the rite. The offering having been made, the deity then tastes, consumes or draws the essence from it. It is then retrieved from the altar and consumed by the offerer or offerers. The recovered offering is called *prasada*, meaning the deity's 'blessing' or 'grace', and its consumption signifies an incorporation or appropriation of the deity's sacred power and/or good will by the worshipper.

This exchange does share something with the Vedic sacrifice, but it occurs in a different affective context in which a personal – and in some cases even intimate – relationship between worshipper and object of worship is symbolised and felt by worshippers. (On the structure of puja and similarities and differences between puja and the Vedic sacrifice, see Michaels, 2016, pp. 247–58.) The difference between puja and the Vedic sacrifice thus goes beyond a mere difference in form; it is different in spirit. The Vedic idea of the divine-human relationship was basically transactional; in exchange for homage and offerings, the gods would favour the offerers and intervene in their affairs. It was a relatively narrow aperture for human-divine interaction, with offerings made and hymns of praise sung to invisible deities (the exception was Agni, the sacrificial fire). In devotional tradition, the basic idea is that there is a real encounter and – in the ideal case – emotional engagement between devotee and deity.

The focus on physical images means that the puja rite is highly suitable as a rite of worship in temples. Although similar structures made from perishable materials were made long before, the earliest stone Hindu temples date from the Gupta period, and temple worship then evolved as a modal form of Hindu ritual. Royal imagery is a conspicuous element in much Hindu temple ritual, with the principal deity playing the role of a sovereign who is served and entertained by priest-courtiers and, in parallel with this, temples were to become an important medium for the ritual legitimisation of political authority. Just as the sponsorship of great sacrifices legitimised the rule of chieftains in Vedic times, the construction and support of great temples and the sponsorship of temple rituals were to become ways in which sovereign authority was displayed and sanctified. The most famous temples also became pilgrimage destinations, and pilgrimage was to become one of the most characteristic features of devotional Hinduism. But despite the importance of temple worship, the puja rite is perfectly at home in more humble surroundings, and has been performed as a domestic rite, without priestly assistance, since its inception. The family shrine with pictures and images of deities – often in an eclectic mixture – is a ubiquitous feature of Hindu homes.

It should be added, however, that the puja rite never completely supplanted the Vedic sacrifice. As noted earlier, the Vedic sacrifice, in the form of what is called hom or *havan*, remains a very important element in Hindu ceremonial to the present day. Often major Hindu ceremonials are a blend of both.

Key Literature

Let us stipulate that only when the literary tradition known as smriti emerges can we legitimately speak of Hinduism. Readers will recall that the Vedic corpus is called shruti ('heard'), on the basis of the belief that these materials are eternal and unauthored, and are known by us only because they were revealed to certain ancient sages who passed them on. Smriti ('remembered') refers to a vast body of texts that are considered to be authored and sacred but not at the same level of sacredness as the Veda. In totality, the non-Vedic scriptures are truly huge in extent, and a detailed accounting of them is quite beyond the scope of a survey such as this book. Within this body of material, however, there are certain broad categories, and, of these, three stand out as particularly important: texts on law and morality (Dharmashastras), the

Epics (the *Mahabharata* and *Ramayana*) and a somewhat shapeless body of texts called Puranas. Let us look at these separately.

Law and Morality

The word 'dharma' is certainly one of the most pervasive and significant in Indic religious traditions. It can denote 'religion', 'morality', 'duty', 'teachings', 'attribute', 'law' and more; in general, it refers to the normative side of life, that which should and should not be done. Such concerns are systematised in the smriti texts, most notably in the Dharmashastras (meaning 'treatises on dharma'). Of these, the best known and arguably most important is the *Manava Dharmashastra* (*The Laws of Manu*, hereafter *Laws*), probably composed somewhere between the first century BCE and the second century CE, and closer to the latter than the former (Olivelle, 2004, pp. xxiii). According to Hindu tradition, Manu was the first human being, and the content of his *Laws* was transmitted to him by Brahma, the creator deity; Manu, in turn, passed it on to his pupils. This story can be seen as the charter myth of the *Laws*; as such myths typically do, the story establishes the authority of the text by connecting it with primordial beginnings, here not of the cosmos but, appropriately, of the human world to which laws and norms apply.

We do not know who actually composed the *Laws*, but it was probably but not certainly a single individual, certainly a learned Brahman (or Brahmans), who likely lived in the northern part of the subcontinent's south (Olivelle, 2004, pp. xxi–xxii). Henceforth, I shall refer to the author/s of *Laws* as simply 'Manu'.

The text covers an enormous variety of subjects and the extent of this variety is likely to come as a surprise to anyone who has studied the Upanishads. In dramatic contrast to the Upanishads' metaphysical emphasis on unity, in the *Laws* we find a driving spirit of differentiation and categorisation in which there seems to be a box for everything, and often boxes within boxes. Instead of reducing the world to an underlying unity, the text chops it up as if to come to terms with the pieces. However, in the midst of all the details concerning what should and should not be done in a huge range of circumstances, there is something more fundamental at work, for *Laws* can be read as a treatise on social theory. It presents us with a comprehensive account of the social order, how it is structured and how it fits into a wider cosmos. It tells us about the different categories of human beings, their differing traits and proclivities, and how their innate characteristics are properly realised in social conduct. This is definitely a biased social theory, for it is informed by the outlook and values of society's upper strata, the Brahmans in particular, and the *Laws* should never be read without bearing this in mind.

Of all the subjects addressed by the text, the most culturally significant is a complex of prescriptions and proscriptions called the *varnashrama dharma*. Its importance is suggested by the fact that adherence to its strictures is often said (inaccurately) to be an additional criterion of who is a Hindu, the other being veneration of the Veda. The term *varnashrama* combines varna and ashrama. We have already met varna; it is the system of four hereditary and ideally in-marrying classes into which ancient Indo-Aryan society was divided. In this context, the term ashrama refers to the stages of a man's life (not a woman's, nor of all men). In the text, *varna* is treated as the outermost category, with the rest of the normative system contained within, so let us begin with varna.

As portrayed in *Laws*, varna is a complete system, an integrated social order in which each class has a specific function in relation to the needs of the whole. That function is expressed as a dharma, a sacred 'duty', specific to each class. Brahmans are at the apex of the system (a judgement that does not go uncontested outside the realm of these texts); then come, in descending order, the Kshatriyas, Vaishyas and Shudras. In brief, the Brahmans' duty is studying and teaching the Veda and officiating at rites of worship; the Kshatriyas' is fighting and rule; the Vaishyas' is trade and agriculture; and the Shudras' is service rendered to the top three varnas. In addition, males belonging to the uppermost three varnas undergo a rite of initiation seen as a 'second birth'. They are thus known as 'twice-born', as opposed to the Shudras who are born only once. The mark of twice-born status is a cord consisting of three strands of cotton – sometimes called the 'sacred thread' in English – conferred at the time of initiation and worn over the left shoulder. Only twice-born men are permitted to study the Veda; Shudras may not. Finally, there is yet another category called Chandala. They have no varna status, for Manu insists that there are only four varnas. They exist, therefore, outside the social order altogether, and they are the ancient precursors of the Dalits of our era.

The ethic underlying this system is profoundly particularistic. What you should or should not do depends on the social category to which you belong, and that is a matter of birth. And furthermore, one's varna identity is not merely a label assigned as a matter of birth; rather, it seems to be part of one's inborn nature (Marriott, 1976). That is, one's social duty is not treated as an obligation imposed from without, but as an inborn 'biomoral' code, with the implication that to violate this code is to violate one's own nature.

In formulating this picture of the social order, Manu had to deal with some awkward facts, namely that there were many groups and subgroups in the Indian society of those days, not just four. These are the groups (mostly occupationally specialised) that have come to be called 'castes' in English (*jati* in Hindi and other Indian languages), and they are not the same thing as varnas. This presented a puzzle, which was that of how to explain the existence of these groups in a manner that was consistent with varna theory. Manu's main strategy was to regard them as the products of mixed unions between members of different varnas. It should be said this is basically a post-facto rationalisation and cannot stand as a valid theory of how castes actually originated. I shall return to the question of how caste 'works' in a later chapter.

One aspect of the miscegenation theory, however, touches on an extremely important principle that informs marriage choice in Hindu society to the present day. If there is to be a union across varna boundaries, then Manu much prefers the man to be of higher varna status than the woman rather than the other way around. Marriage with the man of higher status was said to be anuloma ('with the hairs') as opposed to pratiloma ('against the hairs'), and the distinction became a way of explaining the existence of the very lowest castes as products of pratiloma unions. The preference for marriages of lower-status women to higher-status men is known as hypergamy, and now, as then, match-making preference is notably hypergamous in Indian society (though not normally across caste or varna boundaries).

In *Laws*, the term ashrama refers to an institutionalised stage of life, of which there are four. The scheme applies only to males of twice-born rank – that is, not to Shudras and certainly not to Chandalas – and is loosely integrated with the concept of four 'ends' or 'goals' (purusharthas) of life, namely dharma, wealth, enjoyment and final liberation. The first ashrama is that of celibate studenthood (brahmacharya): after his initiation, a young man stays at his teacher's house learning Veda, pursuing dharma and supporting his teacher. The second stage is that of householdership (*grihastha*): having completed his education, a man returns to his parents' home, marries and takes upon himself all the responsibilities of worldly life. It should be added that in this strongly patrilineal social order it is simply assumed that a son will remain with his parents in marriage, whereas daughters will marry out. In the householder stage, a man pursues three of the four ends of life: dharma, wealth and enjoyment.

Now occurs a major transition. When he becomes old with wrinkled skin and sees his sons' sons, he enters the stage of forest reclusion (*vanaprastha*). He turns his householder duties over to his sons and leaves his home for the forest, although he may take his wife. There he performs rites of sacrifice and practises austerities, and in so doing begins the pursuit of the final end of life, which is moksha ('liberation'). This constitutes a transitional interlude leading to the final stage of life, which is that of world renunciation (*samnyasa*) and the direct and fully focused pursuit of liberation. By himself, with only a water pot and staff, he sleeps on the ground and travels continuously (except during the monsoon season). His sacred thread is burnt, which means he no longer has varna status. He attaches himself to no place and nobody. In effect, he leaves worldly society entirely.

The varnashrama dharma is an idealised scheme which we can be sure was only rarely reflected in actual biographical reality. It is best seen not as a road map for planning a life but as a theorisation of social identity. It imposes a grid on Hindu life. Who you are is defined by the social stratum into which you were born and the stage of life at which you find yourself. It can also be read as the solution to a serious problem. The problem, which had been lingering in the Indic religious world ever since the valorisation of world renunciation in the mid-first millennium BCE, was that of reconciling the contrary values embodied by the householder and the world renouncer. One solution we have already met. For the Buddhists and Jains, the resolution of this difficulty was monasticism. Renouncers lived outside the worldly social order. For their part, householders benefited from their teaching and supported the monastic community, for which they were rewarded in the coin of merit, allowing them to pursue the world's rewards while deferring the loftier goal of final liberation.

But for the Brahman class, to which class the author/s of Manu belonged, the difficulty took a different form. Their social identity as Brahmans, the sacerdotal and spiritual class par excellence, was supposed to incorporate in some manner the ideal of world renunciation, even if, in reality, most of them spent their lives as householders and professional priests (Biardeau, 1989, pp. 58–63). Although the ashrama system distinguishes four stages of life, the truly fundamental distinction it draws is between two modes of life – inside and outside the social world, householder versus renouncer – and it assigns positive value to both. But, and crucially, both values can be pursued by the same individual. Instead of sequestering renouncers as monks and nuns, the varnashrama dharma sequesters renunciation as a distinct phase of life. A difference between the more purely monastic traditions and the concept embodied in the varnashrama dharma is the strength of the claim of the householder's values. In the monastic traditions, this claim is light and may be rejected altogether. The varnashrama dharma, however, concedes a stronger claim to the world. It stipulates that although one may indeed abandon all social ties, there are obligations that should be discharged first.

Narrative Literature: The Epics and Puranas

A sacred literature composed in Sanskrit was the principal medium in which the evolution of sectarian Hinduism emerged into historical visibility. Along with Dharmashastra, these texts belong to the general category of smriti, but they are very different in character. If Dharmashastra is a normative genre, the texts to which I now turn are primarily a narrative literature (although they do contain plenty of normative material). It should be borne in mind that this discussion is focused on texts composed in Sanskrit, thus leaving out of consideration an ever-growing body of vernacular literature from early medieval times onward, and readers should also be aware of the existence of a vast and growing secular literature composed in Sanskrit and vernacular languages alike. The material considered here falls into two categories, the Epics and the Puranas.

I turn first to the earliest of these categories, the Epics. There are two: the *Mahabharata* and the *Ramayana*. Both are based on story lines that probably hearken back to the first half of the first millennium BCE, but the texts began to assume the form we know in the late centuries of the millennium. The 'Epic' label has become a well-established scholarly convention, but these two compositions technically belong to two quite different literary categories. Although both are commonly grouped together as 'history' (*itihasa*), the *Ramayana* is actually 'poetry' (*kavya*), which places it in the category of belles-lettres. But in any case, although not considered shruti, they represent a bridge between the Vedic and early Hindu periods. Both have also been reproduced in an abundance of regional versions, and both are woven deeply into the religious cultures of Hindus.

The *Mahabharata* is a very long account, in verse, of a very short war and consists of around 100,000 Sanskrit stanzas. Tradition attributes it to a sage named Vyasa, who is said to have lived when the war occurred. He is said to have dictated the entire composition to the elephant-headed god, Ganesha, who served as his scribe. The venue of the epic is the upper Ganga valley, and the war itself – said to have taken place at Kurukshetra near Delhi around the ninth century BCE – was the culmination of a dynastic struggle between two groups of brothers who were cousins to each other. After many tribulations, including an exile of thirteen years, the five Pandavas, the epic's heroes (polyandrously married to the same woman, Draupadi), ultimately prevailed over their cousins in an eighteen-day battle. In this endeavour, they were aided by a warrior named Krishna who is revealed to be the Supreme Being. This basic story (given as the barest summary here) provides a framework for what amounts to an immense library of theology, philosophy, folklore and much more that was added in layers over many centuries, a process that probably began in the late first millennium BCE and extended into the early centuries of the Common Era. Perhaps the best-known section of the *Mahabharata* is the Krishna's famous discourse on dharma and salvation known as the *Bhagavad Gita*. I return to this text at the end of this chapter.

The *Ramayana* is shorter and, at least judging from the expanded South Asian world in which it situates itself, its core narrative probably belongs to an era later than that of the *Mahabharata*. The story begins in the ancient city of Ayodhya, situated in what is now east-central Uttar Pradesh, but the narrative development ultimately expands to include much of the subcontinent. The text of the *Ramayana*, consisting of some 24,000 Sanskrit stanzas, is attributed to Valmiki, said to have been the first poet. As was the *Mahabharata*, the *Ramayana* has been recast and retold many times, in both north and south India, with versions written in various regional vernaculars. Among the most famous and influential of these in the north is the *Ramcharitmanas* ('*The Holy Lake of Rama's Deeds*') composed in the Awadhi dialect of Hindi by the poet Tulsidas in the sixteenth century CE. The most famous of the South Indian tellings is Kampan's (1180 BC) *Iramavataram* (*'The Avatara of Rama'*) composed in Tamil. (To gain an idea of the extraordinary multiplicity of versions of the *Ramayana*, see the essays in Richman, 1991.)

The basic story line of the *Ramayana* is almost universally known in the Hindu world (and widely known in south-east Asia beyond). It revolves around a marriage. Prince Rama was a son of King Dasharatha of Ayodhya; his wife was Sita, who was born from a ploughed furrow and was the daughter of King Janaka of Videha, to the east of Ayodhya. Owing to the scheming of the mother of one of Rama's brothers (a half-brother), who wished her own son to ascend the throne, Rama was banished from the city for fourteen years. Accompanied by Sita and his brother, Lakshmana, Rama then took up a life of forest exile. One day, while the brothers were out hunting, Sita was kidnapped by a ten-headed demon king named Ravana, who was the ruler of Lanka (generally thought to be present-day Sri Lanka). In their frantic search for Sita, Rama and Lakshmana gained the assistance of a monkey king named Sugriva and his army of monkeys. One of the monkeys, Hanuman by name, became Rama's valuable ally and companion, second only to Lakshmana. It was he who discovered that Sita had been taken to Lanka. Hanuman built a causeway to Lanka, allowing Rama and the monkey army to confront and defeat Ravana and recover Sita. After a joyous return to Ayodhya, Rama became king, but this happy situation was disturbed when Rama grew suspicious of Sita's conduct while she had been held in captivity. She submitted to a test of her virtue by fire, which she passed, but to satisfy the still-sceptical population Rama sent Sita into exile where, having taken shelter in Valmiki's hermitage, she bore him two sons. Much later she returned to Ayodhya with her sons, and then, having once again declared her total purity and devotion to Rama, she was taken back into the earth from which she was born.

Both Sita and Hanuman are probably examples of the Sankritisation of local deities. We know nothing of the antecedent godling who became Hanuman, but he must have been a monkey or monkey-like figure, elevated in the *Ramayana* by being recast as the principal ally and servant of Rama. In Sita's case, it seems very likely that she was originally a goddess associated with agriculture, ploughing and the earth (Flood, 1996, p. 109).

The composition of the Puranas (meaning 'Ancient Stories', 'Antiquities') began during the Gupta era and extended centuries beyond; in fact, texts self-identified as Puranas are undoubtedly being written at the present time. Some of the material in the older Puranas, however, must have been in circulation much earlier than the Gupta period. The most important Puranas are, by convention, eighteen in number. The material they contain is vast and highly variegated. In them we find dynastic histories, genealogies, ritual instructions, cosmological and cosmographic details and much, much more. Above all, the Puranas are the principal source (along with the Epics) of the innumerable narratives collectively labelled 'Hindu mythology'.

Together, they provide the foundations for what we can properly consider 'Hindu' as opposed to Vedic polytheism. The individual Puranas are not exclusively dedicated to specific deities, but there is a tendency for particular Puranas (such as the *Vishnu Purana* and *Shiva Purana*) to focus on specific deities, and this reflects the growing ramification of deity-focused sectarianism.

The Pantheon

The Hindu pantheon is an extraordinary treasure house of sacred symbols and linked mythology. It is true that the Buddhists and Jains also have their pantheons, but not on the same scale, level of complexity or sheer symbolic richness as the Hindu pantheon.

The Hindu pantheon is often presented in abstract (and is frequently so described to non-Hindus) as the Trimurti ('triform') consisting of three major deities held to represent the three primary aspects of divinity: creation, preservation and destruction. These three deities, often portrayed with their spouse/consorts, are Brahma (the creator of the cosmos), Vishnu (its preserver) and Shiva (who destroys the universe at the end of each cosmic cycle). Each of them has his own distinctive animal vehicle (*vahan*), as do all the major gods and goddesses of Hindu tradition; Brahma's is the swan, Vishnu's the eagle and Shiva's the bull.

However, to present the Trimurti as the basic framework of the Hindu pantheon is exceedingly misleading. To begin with, Brahma's inclusion in this august company is hard to justify. Brahma has little role in actual Hindu practice, certainly nothing to compare with the roles of Vishnu and Shiva. Although temples dedicated to his worship exist, they are very few. Furthermore, the abstract labels of preserver and destroyer greatly oversimplify the respective characters of Vishnu and Shiva. Vishnu sometimes destroys, and Shiva creates; in fact, the divine personalities of these great deities are complicated, filled with nuance and cannot possibly be caught in any sort of catchphrase. And more, the entire Hindu pantheon contains many more deities than the three gods of the Trimurti and their spouses. While it is true that Vishnu and Shiva are key Hindu deities with pan-Hindu followings, it is also true that there are other deities of pan-Hindu importance – many of them forms, family members or associates of these two. In addition, the pantheon includes, willy-nilly, a huge multitude of gods, goddesses and godlings of regional and local tradition.

But also, and perhaps most important of all, the Trimurti diminishes the importance of female divinity by representing the female side solely in the form of the consorts of the three male deities: Sarasvati (the goddess of learning and music; consort of Brahma), Lakshmi (the goddess of prosperity and auspiciousness; consort of Vishnu) and Parvati ('Daughter of the Mountain', a more polyvalent goddess;

consort of Shiva). These three consorts are actually different forms of a generic Great Goddess, Devi, who is an autonomous figure and fully co-equal with any or all of the gods.

Still, with these qualifications in mind, Vishnu, Shiva and the Great Goddess can be treated as entryways into Hindu polytheism, and so it is to them that I now turn.

Vishnu

Devotees of Vishnu are known as Vaishnavas, and they are distributed among many different sects and subsects. Such is Vishnu's importance, however, that his worship – and/or worship of deities associated with him – is part of the generic religious culture of Hindus. His beginnings were modest. In the *Rig Veda*, he is a minor figure, portrayed as benevolent and linked with Indra, but in the Brahmanas, Epics and Puranas he comes fully into his own as a composite figure whose complex attributes and character must have been the product of a succession of Sanskritising mergers.

Devotional traditions focused on Vishnu and his various manifestations probably began in the north in the region around the city of Mathura. From roughly the sixth to tenth centuries CE, Vaishnava devotionalism diffused southward and found a very hospitable environment in Tamil-speaking regions of the south. There it was recast and emotionally intensified by a group of poet-saints called Alvars. They were mostly non-Brahmans, a fact that lent impetus to the spread of Vaishnavism among all social strata of the region. In late medieval times, this more emotional Vaishnavism returned to the north, where it inspired the vernacular verse of northern poet-saints. This is a subject to which I return in the next chapter.

Vishnu's outstanding attribute is benevolence, a trait also manifested in the character of his spouse, Lakshmi, the goddess of prosperity and well-being. His goodwill is expressed in his periodic interventions into the doings of our world when things go wrong. These appearances are called Vishnu's avataras, his 'descents'. When the need is desperate, when dharma is threatened, he descends from his high heaven (called Vaikuntha) to our terrestrial plane to combat the forces of darkness and evil.

By most conventions, Vishnu's avataras are ten in number. (For fine retellings of their stories, see Doniger O'Flaherty, 1975, pp. 175–237.) He descended first as a fish, in which form he saved Manu, the first man, from a flood; he later came as a tortoise who served as the base of a churn with which the gods and their demon counterparts obtained the nectar of immortality. He then appeared as a boar, whose tusks saved the earth by raising it from the bottom of the ocean, and then as man-lion who killed a demon named Hiranyakashipu. He next came as a dwarf who bestrode the universe in three steps (a later version of a Vedic myth), and then as a Brahman warrior-ascetic who quelled a Kshatriya revolt. The seventh and eighth avataras are Rama and Krishna, to whom I return below. They are called the 'Epic' avataras because it is in the *Ramayana* and *Mahabharata* respectively that they step on stage (although the *Bhagavata Purana* [below]is actually by far the more important Krishnaite text). The ninth avatara is none other than the Shakyamuni Buddha. According to the Vaishnava version of the Buddha's story, his mission was to propagate false doctrines in order to lead demons and evil-doers to their destruction. The final avatara is named Kalkin; he will come at the end of the current cosmic era to rid the world of heretics and the wicked and usher in a golden age, at which point a new cosmic cycle will begin.

But of these ten, it is Rama and Krishna who are by far the ones who matter most.

The Epic Avataras: Rama and Krishna

The importance of Rama (full name, Ramachandra) in Hindu religious culture is difficult to exaggerate. In the Valmiki text of the *Ramayana*, he is mostly portrayed as a purely human prince and king, with his divinity asserted strongly only in the text's first and last books. By medieval times, however, he had become the centre of a widespread devotional cult that received a major boost from the formation of an ascetic order by a poet-saint named Ramananda in the fourteenth or fifteenth century. This group, known as the Ramanandis, was dedicated to Rama's worship and was headquartered in Ayodhya. Tulsidas's *Ramcharitmanas* was created in the sixteenth century, and was to become the basic text and charter of Rama devotion in the Hindi-speaking north as well as one of the most widely known and beloved of religious texts in this region. The influence of Rama devotion can be gauged by the fact that 'Ram' became a generic name for the Supreme Deity in Hindi-speaking areas.

Rama is usually portrayed in pictures and represented on temple altars with his faithful brother Lakshmana, his wife Sita and his monkey ally and devotee, Hanuman. He and the figures associated with him are sacred models of proper conduct, the presiding deities, if you will, of social roles. Rama himself is, above all else, associated with kingly virtues. He is idealised as a benevolent and just ruler, and his reign in Ayodhya, which has come to be called *ramrajya* ('rule of Rama'), stands as a powerful symbol of what a just political order ought to be. The *Ramayana* portrays Hanuman as a perfect example of devoted service to Rama. In consequence, he is always present in Rama temples where he is represented in an attitude of prayerful adoration of Rama's image and thus serving as a model for what his human devotees should be. Lakshmana, having never left Rama's side during the whole ordeal of Sita's abduction and recovery, serves as a model of fraternal love and fidelity, as does Rama's younger brother, Bharata, who instead of occupying Rama's throne in his

3.1 Temple images of Lakshmana, Rama and Sita.

absence (as his mother intended when she engineered Rama's banishment), placed a pair of Rama's sandals there instead. Sita stands for womanly purity, which she proved by passing the test of fire, but she is also seen as the ideal of wifely devotion and loyalty in an extended sense. A satisfied mother-in-law might say in praise of a daughter-in-law that she is a 'veritable Sita'.

Hanuman has also become the focus of a widespread cult of his own (on which see especially Lutgendorf, 2007), and his shrines and temples can be found in virtually every village and urban neighbourhood in the north. He is imaged as chaste (although he did enter an unconsummated marriage), with no room in his heart for anyone other than Rama and Sita. Because of his chastity (no wastage of vital energies), he is immensely strong and is the patron deity of wrestlers. Worshipping him can be seen as a way of gaining access to Rama; that is, just as one might take one's problem first to an office flunky to gain the attention of the lordly official sitting behind the desk, Hanuman can connect humble worshippers to the great god's power.

In turning to Krishna, we find that he is a deity with at least two quite distinct personalities. The Krishna of the *Mahabharata* is a warrior and a king, a hero figure in the Indo-Aryan mould. This is the Krishna who appears in the *Bhagavad Gita*, to which I return at the end of this chapter. The Krishna who is most beloved, however, is Krishna 'Gopala' ('Guardian of Cows'), an image that was grafted at some later stage on to the more regal Krishna of the *Mahabharata*. This is Krishna as he was while a child and youth, and the foundational text of this tradition of Krishna worship is the *Bhagavata Purana*, a text probably composed in the south at around the tenth century. The wicked king of Mathura had learnt of a prophecy that a son of his lady cousin would one day take his life. To avert this, he killed her children as they were born, one by one, until one night Vishnu himself was born as Krishna from her womb. To protect him from his uncle, Krishna's father switched the newborn boy with the infant daughter of the wife of a cowherd who lived in a rural village near Mathura. There Krishna spent his infancy, childhood and early adulthood; only later did he fulfil his destiny by killing his wicked uncle.

This Krishna, the son of a cowherd, is the version celebrated by the great devotional poets of both north and south, and has inspired some of the most moving and beloved religious poetry and song of Hindu tradition. His mischievous childhood ways are a favourite subject, as are the amours of his adolescence. A constant theme is that of the ordinariness of his growing up; although he was the author of many wonders and miracles – brief glimpses of his divine power – all the while he was to all outward appearances just an ordinary cowherd boy playing with his friends in the dusty village lanes. Later, in adolescence, Krishna becomes the lover of the cowherd girls. The miracle was this: there were many girls, but he was the lover of all at the same time; and, more, to each he was whole and complete, as

3.2 Street art depicting Hanuman demonstrating his devotion to Rama and Sita..

if he were each girl's lover alone. Just so, such is his divine infinitude that he will always be whole and complete to each and every one of his devotees.

This imagery of the highest divinity taking such earthly form to exist among us and to form human relationships exerts an extraordinary emotional power. The power lies, at least in part, in the conjunction of extremes: in the idea that the very Lord of the Universe has now chosen to be an infant in the cradle, a naughty child, a friend to the villagers one and all, and a lover. One can revere him from afar as the Lord of the Cosmos, or one can seek him within the innermost recesses of the self, but one can also respect him as a master and lord, and one can love him as a parent loves an infant or child, as a friend loves a friend, or as lover loves her beloved. This is a core idea of Krishna bhakti.

Timescape

Vishnu's sequence of avataras occurs against the background of a Puranic theory of history that merits separate discussion. It came together in its final form by about 400 CE and situates the passage of cosmic-historical time in an apparently infinite series of repeating cycles (*kalpa*s) that always begin well and always end badly (Church, 1971; see Zimmer, 1946, pp. 13–22, for a particularly vivid retelling). Whatever else it does, this is a theory that explains the miseries of the world of our experience as a product of the point in the cycle – the fag end – at which we now find ourselves.

Each cycle consists of four *yuga*s ('epochs') and as the cycle proceeds the *yuga*s pass, one by one, each both shorter and morally and physically inferior to the one before. (In what follows, I have omitted discussion of the *manvantara* system, an additional system of time division that intersects with the yuga system, as an unnecessary complication.) The first epoch was the *satya yuga* ('the age of truth'). In this age, the dharma was whole and complete, by which is meant that the denizens of the age adhered to the duties and behaviours appropriate to their station, religious divisions did not exist, there was no war, privation was unknown, and the human lifespan was immensely long. This was an era in which, by bovine analogy, the 'cow of the dharma' stood on four legs, which is to say was perfectly supported. But this could not last for, in accord with a sort of moral thermodynamics, dharma began to leach away with the passage of time, and after the elapse of 1,728,000 years it was but three-quarters of what it once was. This was the beginning of the *treta yuga*. Treta means 'three', which is to say that only three of the four quarters of the dharma were remaining. By comparison to what lay ahead, life was still reasonably good, but gone was the perfection of the previous age. Now humans were no longer naturally virtuous, their lifespan was shorter, there were disputes and wars, and the support of human life required hitherto unknown exertions. After the passage of 1,728,000 years, the dharma had further leached away, and now but half was left. With this, the *dvapara yuga* began. The term dvapara derives from a root meaning 'two'; the *dharma* was now but half of what it once was. Now there was privation, want, disease and perpetual conflict; humans had lost sight of virtue and pursued possessions and pleasures of the senses. And yet this sorry state of affairs was not the end of the story, because after the passage of 864,000 years half of what remained of the dharma had vanished, which ushered in the *kali yuga*, the miserable age in which we find ourselves. Now all is darkness; falsehood, greed, cruelty and strife reign supreme, and the average human lifespan is at its shortest. Our kali yuga began at the end of the *Mahabharata* war, which is reckoned to have been in the year 3102 BCE, which is also said to have been the year of Krishna's departure from the earth. The kali yuga will last a total of 432,000 years.

Perhaps the most remarkable feature of this scheme is the extent of the timescape against which it is set. Each cycle begins when a lotus emerges from the navel of reclining Vishnu, upon which Brahma appears, who then fulfils his divine role as creator of the world. The cycles, each lasting 4,320,000 years, are repeating and one thousand such cycles equal one day in the life of Brahma. During his night, the creative process stops but resumes at the break of his day. Brahma lives for one hundred years of his days, after which there is a total dissolution of all worlds. But then, after a lapse of another one hundred of his years, the cycle of cycles begins anew.

3.3 Temple image of reclining Vishnu with lotus-borne Brahma about to re-create the world.

In the wider Indic context, the vastness of this timescape is not unique to Hinduism. The Jains and Buddhists have similar schemes that also highlight cyclicality and infinitude. Of these two, it is the Jain system that really stands out, because the Jains place far more emphasis on their scheme than the Buddhists do on theirs (which seems to be because of the Buddha's advocacy of the doctrine of momentariness with its corollary that past and future are but imaginary constructs [Jaini, 1974, p. 103]). The contrast between the Hindu and Jain systems is dramatic indeed, and can be described as one of waveform. The Jain version is a sine-wave version of cosmic history; the Hindu version is a saw-tooth wave. For the Jains, there is no moment of creation; rather, the cosmos (or at least our small part of it) moves eternally (and slowly) from peaks to valleys that are always just the same. At the peaks, the world is a Paradise resembling the Hindu Age of Truth. Then ensues a gradual moral and physical decline that takes many aeons. During the course of this decline a total of twenty-four Jinas appear, and the last of these in our currently downward-moving cycle was Mahavira, which means we are approaching the cycle's lowest point. But when cosmic history reaches its nadir, there is no Kalkin to set matters instantly right. Rather, there then begins a gradual improvement – a mirror image of the decline – during which another twenty-four Jinas will appear. This process never ends.

The reason for the difference between the Hindus' saw-tooth version of cosmic time's passage, with its abrupt restarts, and the Jains' version is far from clear, but it is at least arguable that the two approaches emphasise two different things. The Hindu version puts the accent squarely on the problem of explaining the tribulations of the world we experience. The moral squalor of our world is what it is because of where we are in the cycle, and the forecast of messianic Kalkin's advent suggests the possibility of history's redemption. Of course, as Doniger O'Flaherty points out the yuga theory does not actually explain why evil exists; it merely states that it comes into existence over and over again (Doniger O'Flaherty, 1976, p. 19). While also addressing the evil of the present and in a similar way, the Jain versions widens the scope in a way that highlights the infinitude of the soul's predicament; the soul has been wandering and suffering from beginningless time and its sufferings will continue for infinite time to come unless the opportunity to achieve liberation is seized. A universe of this sort is, if nothing else, one in which the extremely onerous demands of orthoprax Jain life – particularly as these demands pertain to initiated Jain ascetics – make sense.

Shiva

Shiva's name means 'The Auspicious One'. As is true of Vishnu, Shiva's importance as a deity transcends sectarian differences, for he is thoroughly integrated into the religious culture of Hindus generally. His character as a deity, however, is profoundly different from that of Vishnu, and Shiva and Vishnu can be said to represent a fundamental divide in Hindu thought. Vishnu is a deity of action, which is why he comes among us again and again in the form of avataras. He is also a social god. He is involved; he interacts; and he and those around him exemplify social roles: Rama the ideal king, Sita the ideal woman and so on. Very different is Shiva. He is a perpetual outsider – an ascetic, a disrupter, dwelling in the mountains.

His outsiderhood is dramatised by the well-known myth of how he was excluded from the sacrifice. According to one version (Kramrisch, 1981, pp. 316–20), his father-in-law, Daksha – a Brahman sage, a son of Brahma and the father of Shiva's wife, Sati – refused to include him in a sacrifice to which all of the other gods and goddesses were invited. This was because Shiva had insulted him by not rising to greet him on a previous sacrificial occasion, and also because Daksha was offended by his appearance and demeanour. Shiva was:

> Darkness (*tamas*) embodied … naked, smeared all over with ashes
> of burnt corpses, wearing garlands of severed heads, and the bones of
> the dead as ornaments … [roaming] over cremation grounds like a
> madman, sometimes laughing, sometimes crying, a drunkard, riding
> a bull surrounded by ghastly hosts of ghouls, ghosts, and goblins,
> altogether impure (Kramrisch, 1981, p. 317).

Sati, who was in fact the Great Goddess, was enraged by the insult to her husband and consumed herself by means of her inner yogic fire at the scene of the sacrifice. Driven mad by grief, Shiva smeared his body with her ashes, took her burnt corpse on his shoulders, and began a dance that shook the very earth. To save the earth from this pummelling, Vishnu used his discus (his weapon and one of his iconographic symbols) to cut Sati's body apart, piece by piece, and where each piece landed became sacred to the goddess and a place of pilgrimage today.

Exemplary of another and equally dramatic facet of Shiva's character is a famous Puranic myth (excellently retold by Doniger O'Flaherty, 1975, pp. 154–9, the source of the version given here) concerning a demon named Taraka. By means of his ascetic practice, Taraka had created such an internal fiery heat as to endanger the entire universe, and in order avert a disaster Brahma had granted him the boon that he could not be killed by any of the gods. This was a big problem for the gods, for at this point they were about to be vanquished by Taraka. But as Brahma reminded them when they came to him to complain, Taraka's boon had been granted with a condition. Taraka might indeed be killed, but he could be killed only by one born when the gods become pregnant from drinking Shiva's seed.

At the time the boon was granted, this seemed like an unlikely circumstance, for Shiva was lost in meditation in a cave, with his seed 'drawn up' (the conservation of semen being a source of the special powers generated by austerities). So, the first thing that needed to be done would be to awaken Shiva's dormant sexual desire. To this end, Indra sent Kama, the Hindu god of lustful desire, who entered Shiva's cavern in the guise of a southern breeze. Kama then drew his sugar-cane bow and shot Shiva with his arrow of flowers. Shiva opened his eyes and saw his spouse-to-be, Parvati – a later incarnation of Sati – engaged in her own meditations in front of him and, in his anger, he burnt Kama to a cinder with the fire from his third eye (later restoring him to life – although without a body – at Parvati's behest). But Shiva's austerities were over, for his desire was now well and truly awakened. Now, with Shiva's lust in full spate, a different problem arose. So violent was his love-making with Parvati that its agitations were beginning to shake apart the cosmos. And worst, it was also ceaseless, because Shiva's ascetic proclivities enabled him to retain his seed indefinitely. The gods finally dealt with this problem by present-ing themselves to the amorous couple and interrupting their lovemaking. When Shiva stood, his seed was spilt and it was immediately snapped up and swallowed by Agni, the god of fire, who swooped down in the form of a dove.

As we know, Agni is 'the tongue of the gods', and so all the gods became preg-nant with Shiva's seed, but his seed was unbearably hot with the accumulated heat of his austerities, and it was more than the gods could endure. Taking pity on their predicament, Shiva then instructed the gods to vomit up the seed, which they did, and Shiva directed Agni to place it in the womb of a worthy woman. Agni assumed his natural state as a fire and stationed himself on the bank of a river in which the wives of the seven great sages (sons of Brahma) were bathing. Chilled by their bath, they warmed themselves by the fire, and six of them became pregnant (the seventh was rightly suspicious of the fire and did not come close). Shamed, they placed the seed in the high Himalayas, but the mountain, unable to bear its heat, threw the seed into the Ganga. When the river tossed out the seed on to some reeds, it became a handsome boy named Skanda. It was he who slew Taraka.

This myth throws into relief Shiva's contradictory nature (Doniger O'Flaherty, 1973). He is an ascetic, but his very asceticism concentrates and distils his boundless libido into the heat-power that flashes from his third eye to destroy Kama and that, when shed as seed, becomes the ultimate hot potato, too hot for anyone to handle. That same power, once unleashed, drives his epochal lovemaking, which will never cease unless the gods intervene. He is the greatest of all ascetics (one of his epithets is Mahayogi, meaning 'Great Yogi'), but he is also the greatest erotic; his nature, pendulum-like, swings back and forth throughout cyclical cosmic time. In his nature are only extremes, no middle ground.

It should also be pointed out that, in consistency with the ascetic side of Shiva's nature, the conception of his other son was likewise unusual. This son is elephant-headed Ganesha, who is an important autonomous deity in the popular Hinduism of most areas of India. He is celebrated as a remover of obstacles, and thus is a deity

3.4 Street art depicting Shiva and Parvati.

3.5 Gansha portrayed in an announcement of a wedding.

who presides over the beginnings of things. Rites, ceremonies and the inception of important enterprises typically begin with homage to Ganesha. He is also a patron deity of the literary arts (and the arts generally) and all things that have to do with writing, a role that comes naturally to him because – as noted earlier – he is held to have been the scribe to whom Vyasa dictated the *Mahabharata*. His animal vehicle is the rat.

According to a well-known myth, Ganesha's unusual birth occurred as follows (here drawn from Doniger O'Flaherty, 1975, pp. 262–9). One fine day, Parvati asked Shiva to unite with her so that they could have a son, but Shiva rebuffed her, explaining that he was a renouncer, not a householder. Entreat though Parvati might, Shiva was adamant at first, but because of her deep sorrow at being childless he relented in the end. He pulled a piece of red cloth from her body that Parvati then fashioned into a male child, and the cloth-child instantly came to life when she put him to her breast. But Shiva then took a closer look at the child and did not like what he saw. Because of the unusual manner of the child's conception, he declared, it was afflicted by the inauspicious influence of the planet Saturn. At this point, the boy's head, which was facing north, fell to the ground. Parvati was inconsolable, so Shiva

3.6 Two lingas in yoni bases.

had to do something. At the command of a voice from the sky, he sent Nandin, his bull-vehicle, in search of someone facing north whose head could be joined to the dead boy's body. This north-facing someone turned out to be Indra's elephant, and that is how Ganesha acquired his elephant head.

Devotees of Shiva and his ancillary deities are called Shaivas. The form in which Shiva is normally worshipped is an aniconic object known as a linga, a term of which one meaning is 'phallus'. It consists of a blunt column sitting in a base called *yoni* ('womb' or 'vulva'). In scholarly writing about Hinduism, the linga is usually said to be a phallic symbol, an interpretation certainly justified by Puranic narratives about Shiva. Adding to this the fact that yoni means 'vulva' would seem to settle the issue, at least as far as mythology is concerned. From this standpoint, the two components together become a representation of the fusion of male and female principles that in some accounts is the ultimate foundation of reality. It is far from clear, however, that most worshippers take this view; for them, rather, the linga seems to be accepted as no more than a conventional aniconic representation of the god.

As we learnt in Chapter 1, some theorists think that a proto-Shiva was worshipped by the Indus valley peoples. Whether that is true or not, a proto-Shiva is indeed

3.7 Shiva linga being lustrated by a Brahman priest.

present in the *Rig Veda*. This is Rudra, the 'Howler', who is associated with chaos and danger, and Rudra has remained one of Shiva's names ever since. Over the course of time, a composite image of Shiva evolved incorporating additional traits of character drawn from regional and local traditions throughout the subcontinent. The mature Shiva we encounter in the Puranas is seen by the Shaivas as the Supreme Deity, just as Vishnu is so regarded by the Vaishnavas. And as among the Vaishnavas, various subsectarian traditions developed among the Shaivas, including ascetic orders. Some Shaiva ascetics associated with Tantric traditions became famed for their transgressive and extravagant behaviour: for example, they were covered in ashes, had matted hair, ignored all standards of social deportment, used human skulls as begging bowls, and raved as if mad.

Although it originated in far-distant Kashmir, a form of Shaiva veneration particularly important in the south, especially in Tamil country, is known as Shaiva Siddhanta. Theologically, Shaiva Siddhanta bears a striking similarity to Jainism, with which it was in often bitter competition (see Davis, 1991). In parallel with Jainism, this tradition characterises the self and Shiva as completely distinct. A worshipper does not seek any sort of merger with Shiva; rather than seeking to *become* Shiva, a worshipper strives to become *a* Shiva by shedding the impurities that bind the self or soul to the world. As in Jainism, these impurities are seen as material in nature. Their removal, therefore, requires ritual action, not mere disciplined introspection. But it also ultimately requires Shiva's grace, and on this point, the need for a saviour deity, Shaiva Siddhanta departs from Jainism.

In the Tamil country, Saiva Siddhanta merged with an enthusiastic form of Shaiva devotionalism celebrated in the poetry of sixty-three figures known as Nayanars, the Shaiva equivalents and contemporaries of the Vaishnava Alvars. Their verse expresses in Tamil the ideal of a direct and loving relationship between a devotee and Shiva. As was true of enthusiastic devotion in other traditions, Shaiva devotionalism stressed the equality of devotees, which enhanced its appeal to lower social strata.

The Goddess

The Hindu pantheon is not just a collection of gods and goddesses; it is a complex structure that conveys meanings by means of symbols, and nowhere is this more apparent than in the place of female deities within it. The pantheon is obviously immensely diverse on various dimensions, but a basic organising principle is gender. There are gods and goddesses, and their respective roles in the pantheon – and in the cosmic economy that the pantheon can be said to represent – are quite different. In developing this point further, let us begin at the top.

As we know, according to an ancient Indic model, the qualities of the world of our normal experience emerge only in the differentiation of an ultimate reality, itself devoid of qualities. Just so, divinity acquires its variegation – one might say – in its refractions in the form of specific deities. And of all the pantheon's differentiations, the most fundamental is that of gender. The highest divinity manifests in both male and female forms, as gods and goddesses, and the goddesses play a crucial role in the economy of the cosmos. They are embodiments of 'energy' (*shakti*), which is feminine in its very essence and is the energy by which the world turns. This is the force behind birth, growth, nurturance and life itself. But when directed along different channels, it can be immensely destructive. Devotees of the goddess in her various manifestations are known as Shaktas.

As we move downward in the pantheon's structure, we find parallel differentiations on both sides of the gender divide. On the male side are many ramifying branches and tendrils – alternative forms of gods, forms of forms, ancillary deities, local manifestations, in an array of divinities seemingly limitless in extent – with the great pan-Hindu gods, most notably Vishnu and Shiva, at the apex. There is a similar ordering on the female side. At the very pinnacle is the Great Goddess, whose generic name is *devi* (meaning simply 'goddess'), of whom all goddesses are lesser forms. She is the energy that powers the cosmos. She is manifested separately as the consorts of the three gods of the Trimurti, each seen as embodying the vital energy, the shakti, of the god with whom she is paired. Of these, Parvati, Shiva's consort, is the most complex. She shares his ascetic proclivities, but is his erotic partner as well. She is also the main connecting point between the benign spouses of the pantheon's presiding gods and a multitude – itself stratified – of independent goddesses whose beneficence is sometimes quite ambivalent.

Presiding over this latter sector of the feminine pantheon is Durga, celebrated for her defeat of Mahishasura, the Buffalo Demon, a Puranic episode that might well be a later and much transformed version of an ancient Indus valley myth-model (as I suggested in Chapter 1). This demon had gained the upper hand in a war against the gods because of a boon that he could not be killed by a male. At the end of their resources, the gods assembled in a conclave and, by focusing the energies of their anger together, they created the goddess whose name was Durga. Riding into a succession of battles on the back of a lion, she ultimately defeated and killed the Buffalo Demon. This, however, was not her only battle, for she took other forms, the most ferocious of which was a goddess named Kali. Kali emerged from enraged Durga's forehead when, in a different battle, she was in combat with a pair of demons called Shumbha and Nishumbha. They, too, had been given the boon of invulnerability to male foes. Kali's appearance was horrifying: she was emaciated, roaring, with lolling tongue and a skull-topped staff and wearing a necklace of severed heads. She ground up the demon army with her teeth.

Although Durga is mentioned in the *Mahabharata*, and Kali briefly as well, she does not achieve literary prominence and a full Sanskritic pedigree until around the seventh century. This is the possible period of the appearance of her most important

3.8 Temple image of Durga with lion vehicle.

text, the *Devi Mahatmya*, which is a portion of the *Markandeya Purana*. It was during this period that she began to be identified with Parvati, who was her gateway into the Sanskritic pantheon with its pan-Indian spread and its superior social cachet. In the case of Kali, her association with Shiva (through Durga and Parvati) seems natural enough because both deities are marginal, often represented as social outsiders. It is likely, however, that local goddesses very much like Kali were already part of the religious culture of the entire subcontinent and had been so from Indus valley times and before. These local goddesses were and remain today associated with the fertility of the earth as well as malevolence, disease and misfortune, traits that also underlie Kali's unusual appearance and ferocious temper. An example of such a goddess is the Shitala, a goddess of north and central India with equivalents in other regions, who presides over and embodies smallpox (now, of course, extinct) and other pustular diseases.

The goddess as Durga or Kali is worshipped everywhere but is particularly important in the regional religious culture of Bengal. Bengali devotionalism constructs her as a loving mother, despite her fearsome attributes, but even as a loving mother she remains associated with death and destruction, and worshippers slake her thirst for blood with animal sacrifices (also commonly offered to fearsome or dangerous forms of the goddess in other regions). Why would anyone revere and love such a deity as 'mother'? As one writer (Kinsley, 2000) has pointed out, it is because she embodies a deep truth. She, and no one else, is the ultimate source of life, the energy behind the ceaseless movement, growth and beauty of nature. But where there is birth there is death, and Kali's ferocious visage reminds us of what the world looks like to those who see things as they really are. Clear vision strips away the disguise, and the world is revealed as untamed, disordered and filled with sorrow. Kali reminds us that birth is death, and destruction comes to all created things. One of the many names of the Great Goddess is Maya, which in one rendering means 'illusion'. To know and love Kali is – at least to the spiritually awakened – to know that with the best of the world comes the worst, and that one must see past these appearances to the higher reality they conceal.

Tantra

Shaiva and Shakta traditions are closely linked with each other, and as a pair are coupled with the religious movement known as Tantra, which emerged around the middle of the first millennium CE and began to expand rapidly from roughly the eighth century onwards. The word Tantra has two levels of meaning. It denotes a specific body of texts, huge in extent, but it also refers to a form of ascetic practice, a body of beliefs and a ritual culture closely associated with Shaivism and especially with the worship of goddesses. At its heart is a body of non-Vedic concepts and practices stressing powers in nature and in the human body that can be tapped into by the proper meditational and ritual techniques. These concepts and techniques had probably already existed from remote antiquity in cults involving magic and the worship of powerful goddesses. Tantra ultimately became a pervasive influence in the Hindu world and left a deep imprint on the Tibetan form of Buddhism.

It is notoriously difficult to characterise Tantra's beliefs and practices as a single system (but for a lucid introduction, see Padoux, 2017). There are, however, certain key features. The overall object of Tantric practice is to mobilise sacred power within the human body with the ultimate objective of self-divinisation and liberation. Such practice is authorised and made possible by initiation by a 'spiritual master' (*guru*). At the foundation of Tantric practice is the idea that the primordial differentiation of reality is between male and female principles represented by Shiva and his female consort. The goddess, however, is extolled as more than simply the power 'of' Shiva and the other gods; in the Tantric framework, she steps forward as autonomous and omnipresent. She is one but also many, for she generates dangerous and bloodthirsty emanations called Yoginis, themselves objects of worship. The energies she embodies pervade the cosmos at large but are also present in the microcosm of the human body. They are thus available within the body as a means of attaining certain magical powers (called *siddhi*s, 'accomplishments') and ultimately of achieving spiritual liberation. The Tantrics place great emphasis on power-charged utterances (*mantras*); they are considered deities in their own right, and their correct repetition in ritual, coordinated with certain prescribed 'hand gestures' (*mudras*), awakens their powers. Tantric practice also makes extensive use of 'sacred geometric patterns' (*mandalas*) as an aid in ritual and meditative visualisations of deities and the cosmic realms to which the practitioner hopes to ascend in a journey within the body itself.

This inward journey is, perhaps, the most distinctive trait of Tantra. An ascending series of *chakras* ('circles', 'power nodes'), often six in number, are held to be distributed along the body's vertical axis from behind the genitals to the top of the head, a pattern replicating Mount Meru, the axis of the world. In the simplest terms, the practitioner embarks on a journey upwards by means of ritual, breath control and disciplined meditation, with special focus on visualisations of the realms to be visited and the deities to be found there. Such practice awakens a she-serpent, called Kundalini, who normally lies coiled in slumber at the base of the Meru-spine. As she rises from one chakra to the next, energising each in turn as she ascends, the practitioner experiences the celestial realms associated with the chakras and acquires various magical powers; then, when (or if) Kundalini reaches the top, she unites with Shiva, bringing the practitioner to the highest state of consciousness and the attainment of union with the Absolute.

Tantra is also somewhat infamous for its transgressiveness and sexual rituals (Padoux, 2017, pp. 86–97). The basic purpose of such rites is to provide a way for the practitioner to acquire and assimilate feminine power, and all such practices are supposed to be undertaken only while the participants have already elevated themselves to a transcendent plane by means of rituals and deep meditation. In a highly ritualised scenario, the adept and his partner undertake complex purifications, invocations of deities and intense visualisations that result in state of profoundly altered consciousness. They then unite, after which they exchange the resulting mixture of vaginal and seminal fluids mouth-to-mouth; with this they enter a state of absorption and union with the Supreme.

It should be understood, however, that Tantra was more than a mode of practice for an ascetic elite. Its heyday was from 600 to 1200 CE or so, which some have labelled the Tantric Age (on which see Burchett, 2019, pp. 29–63). During this period, it was the core of a more diffuse religious culture, shaped by Tantric concepts and especially by Tantric ritual idioms, that overspread the entire subcontinent. This religious culture was manifested a great range of contexts. Tantric adepts – seen as possessing unique access to divine powers – were sought out to heal illnesses or to solve other mundane problems, and at a loftier level Tantric ritual idioms became integral to temple ceremonial and the state rituals that legitimised political authority. Although Tantra subsequently lost its commanding position in the Hindu world, largely to various bhakti traditions, it remains an important part of the Hindu mix to the present day.

A Devotional Synthesis: The Bhagavad Gita

The *Bhagavad Gita* ('Song of God') is deeply revered and beloved by Hindus and is probably also the best-known Hindu text in the West. Consisting of several hundred Sanskrit verses, the *Gita* (as it is often called) is but a small part of the *Mahabharata*, but it stands on its own as an autonomous text. Its putative creator is Vyasa, author of the epic of which it is a part, but its actual authorship, almost certainly multiple, is unknowable. The *Gita*'s dating has generated much scholarly disagreement, but somewhere around the beginning of the Common Era would probably be close to the mark. Its fame is fully deserved, for it presents a convincing synthesis of disparate elements in the religious mix of its era, most conspicuously the contradictory values represented by the world renouncer versus those who remain in the world, and it does so by placing both under the umbrella of devotionalism.

Before moving to the *Gita* itself, something should be said about its philosophical background. It is not, it should be stressed, the monistic metaphysic that took initial shape in the Upanishads and was refined and fulfilled by Shankara's Advaita Vedanta. Instead, the *Gita*'s philosophical foundation is a dualistic system called *Samkhya*, which left an imprint on a wide range of other Indic theologies. (For a lucid discussion of Samkhya, see Klostermaier, 1994, pp. 399–407.) Resembling Jainism to some extent, and quite possibly rooted in the Shramana traditions,

Samkhya considers reality to consist of two totally different constituents: 'material nature' (*prakriti*), considered female, versus 'spirit' or 'self' (*purusha*), considered male (the word purusha literally meaning 'man'). Consciousness is an attribute of spirit alone. Material nature is ceaselessly in motion. It comprises three qualities, or 'strands' (*gunas*) – purity (or intelligence), passion and dullness – and, in varied combinations and quantities, these strands account for the makeup of our bodies, personalities, even our thoughts and all the other things of our experience. Material nature is no illusion; and the spirit's bondage in samsara is thus not a mistaken belief in its reality, for it is indeed real, but rather a mistaken *sense of identity with it*, and this is the ignorance the removal of which liberation requires. Samkhya served as a basic framework for a famed system of the theory and practice of yoga outlined in the *Yogasutras*, which was focused precisely on the eradication of the spirit's ignorance of its true relationship with material nature. This text was authored by a scholar named Patanjali, whose dating is uncertain but who probably wrote in the early centuries of the Common Era.

The *Gita* recounts events taking place at the very beginning of the *Mahabharata* war when the two armies faced each other across the battlefield, poised to strike. There are but two characters in the *Gita*. One is Arjuna, the third of the five Pandava brothers and a renowned warrior and archer. The other is his charioteer, Krishna, who is revealed to be far more than just another combatant by the poem's end, for he turns out to be the highest reality in human form, come to offer counsel in person to fortunate Arjuna. As Arjuna and Krishna survey the battlefield at the *Gita*'s beginning, Arjuna is suddenly stricken with indecision. His foes are his cousins, and although the dharma (sacred duty) of a Kshatriya is to fight in wars, killing his close kin would be a serious sin. When he turns to Krishna for advice, Krishna responds and the rest of the *Gita* is his response. Krishna first appeals to his duty as Kshatriya and his self-respect as a warrior, but it soon becomes apparent that the issue is not just that of the killing of kin or whether there is such a thing as just war. It is, rather, the far more basic question of action in general, and of liberation from the bondage of its effects.

An account of Krishna's full response is quite beyond the scope of this summary. Let us simply say that, having escalated the issue to this higher level, Krishna makes three key points (although not exactly one by one, as summarised here). The question of the degree to which these three assertions are integrated into a single overall view is a matter of opinion. In what follows, I have favoured the 'integration' side of the issue (on which, see, e.g., Deutsch, 1968).

The first of the three points is that action (karma) simply *is*; it is a basic feature of the material reality in which the spirit or self finds itself entangled. The complete cessation of action as strategy for achieving release is impossible, for, as Krishna points out, you cannot even maintain your body without acting. And furthermore

– Krishna now speaks as the deity he is – *he himself acts*, for in age upon age he rescues the world from calamity. Action simply is; it goes on, willy-nilly and so one must act, although one should do so in accord with the dictates of *dharma*. But then Krishna adds a crucial point, which is that, although action goes on as it must, 'you' (Arjuna in the dialogue, who stands for all of us) must come to see that you are not really the actor. Here is the link with Samkhya and Patanjali's yoga system. The spirit *itself* does not act and cannot act, for it is the mere passive experiencer of action. The actual cause of action is material nature's three strands, and thus cannot be the spirit.

The second of Krishna's big points is that – in any case – it is not action as such that matters. It is, rather, the inner disposition of the actor that is the real cause of the bondage of action. There are obvious echoes of the Buddha's teachings (as well as Samkhya) in this psychologising of the problem. While one must act, the issue is not the act itself but the 'fruit' (*phala*) of the action, the *clinging* to which drags the self ever onward through births and deaths. And although one cannot cease acting, one can free oneself from action's bondage by acting in the spirit of complete detachment from action's fruits. To act in this way would be in imitation of the Lord himself, who is eternally active but without attachment to the results. Action of this sort would be 'desireless action' (*nishkama karma*), and in realising such a state of consciousness one would, in effect, become a mere witness to actions undertaken by the body alone.

This would be a form of yoga, a mode of disciplined introspection. The yoga recommended in the Upanishads (and in Patanjali's yoga system) is a *jnana yoga*, a discipline of knowledge, a method of *knowing* one's way to freedom. Krishna's approach, too, is a yoga, but it is a *karma yoga*, a discipline of action, an approach to the problem of liberation that commends itself to those – such as Arjuna – who must do the world's work. Here is the possibility of pursuing an ascetic vocation, not at the end of life as prescribed by the *varnashrama dharma*, but while remaining actively engaged in life.

However, Krishna's third assertion is the most important of all. It is that he, the Lord, will liberate those who act in devotion to him. Here Lord Krishna departs from the Samkhya system as such, to which devotionalism is completely foreign (although theism does have a role in Patanjali's yoga). Although the karma yoga is sometimes presented as a sort of 'easy road' to deliverance for the man of action, even a moment's reflection will reveal that this cannot be true. Krishna is not telling Arjuna not to exert himself in doing the things he must do in life, but rather to exert himself to the utmost *even while* renouncing the fruits of his action. There is absolutely nothing easy about this, but Krishna offers a 'work around'. If the fruits of action are hard to relinquish on one's own, they will slip away quite naturally if one acts in the spirit of devotion to God and offers one's acts and their fruits as a loving sacrifice to Him. He then takes on himself the burden of those actions, freeing the actor from action's (i.e., karma's) fruits. The idea of *sacrifice*, with us in this book since the Vedic Age, is central to this, albeit in a very different context. Says Lord Krishna:

> Those who choose gods
> go to the gods.
> Those who choose ancestors
> go to the ancestors.
> Those who honour the ghosts
> go to the ghosts.
> Those who sacrifice to me
> go to me.
> Leaf and blossom,
> fruit and water:
> from the one who offers
> these to me
> with devotion,
> the one whose self is pure,
> I take that offering
> of devotion.
> Son of Kunti [Arjuna, whose mother was Kunti],
> all that you do,
> all that you take,
> all that you offer,
> all that you give,
> all that you strive for,
> in heated discipline [ascetic meditation] –
> do that as an offering to me.
> (Chapter 9, verses 25–27; from Patton, 2008, p. 108)

Later in the same chapter, Lord Krishna says:

> With your mind on me,
> be devoted to me;
> sacrifice to me,
> and bow with reverence to me.
> Joined in this way,
> with me as the highest goal –
> you will come to
> me alone.
> (Chapter 9, verse 34; from Patton, 2008., p. 110)

This would be a discipline of devotion, of bhakti, which in the *Gita* emerges as the fulfilment of all yogas. Krishna both *is* but *is not* the impersonal brahman of the Upanishads; he is both the ultimate reality and also a divine personality whom devotees can engage in devotion and who can respond to their esteem and worship. He is the 'Supreme Person' (*purushottama*), who somehow transcends the world while pervading it at the same time. How this is possible is perhaps best seen as beside the point; what matters is devotion and the deliverance the Lord himself has promised his devotees.

4

Islam and After

Too often Islam is constructed as 'other' in South Asia. This tendency was deeply implicated in the creation of post-colonial South Asian states and is intertwined today with international relations on the subcontinent as well as the internal politics of the Indian republic. But the idea of Islam as a religion foreign to South Asia is very misleading, for although Islam was born elsewhere it has long since made itself at home in the region. Present on the subcontinent for over a millennium, it has become fully acclimatised to South Asian cultural environments, and even as it has been South Asianised it has had a profound effect on indigenous religious traditions. Islam is the religion of the overwhelming majority of populations of Pakistan and Bangladesh. It is also the religion of about 14% of the population of the Republic of India. India, in fact, has the third largest Muslim population of all the countries of the world – only Indonesia and Pakistan have more. About one-third of all Muslims live in South Asia. Seen in these terms, there is nothing 'foreign' about Islam in South Asia or the Republic of India.

However, if Islam is a South Asian religion and, to narrow the focus, certainly an 'Indian religion' as well, it is not an 'Indic' religion. In this book, that term is reserved for religions tracing ancestry – full or to a significant extent in part – from the traditions brought to the subcontinent by the Indo-Aryans. In this sense, Buddhism, Jainism, Sikhism and the traditions that have come to be called Hinduism are Indic. Zoroastrianism, with its Indo-Iranian roots, might be considered a distant cousin. Islam, Christianity and Judaism have by various avenues become part of the South Asian and Indian religious mosaic, but they are not Indic.

But before taking up the threads of the story of Islam's South Asian advent and career, we need to take a closer look at Islam itself.

Islam

Islam was founded by an Arab merchant named Muhammad, born c.570 CE, who lived in the city of Mecca. At the age of forty, he began to experience a series of divine revelations on the basis of which he proselytised the rigorously monotheistic creed that is Islam. His revelations continued in a series that lasted twenty-two years, and the divine messages were ultimately collected and written in Islam's holy book, the Qur'an. His success at attracting converts aroused fear and animosity among Mecca's powerful, so Muhammad and his band of followers vacated to the nearby town of Yathrib, later renamed Medina. This took place in the year 622, which marks the beginning of the Muslim calendar. It was there that Islam became the belief system of a community of adherents. Conflict between Muhammad's followers and the Meccans continued until, in 630, Mecca surrendered and Muhammad returned to the city of his birth. Except for one additional visit to Mecca, Muhammad spent the remainder of his life in Medina. He died in 632.

Muhammad designated no successor, nor was it even clear what it would mean to succeed him, for his was the highly individualised charismatic authority of a prophet. But the community had to be led, and the first of its leaders was Abu Bakr, one of Muhammad's closest disciples. He and his successors were called *khalifa* ('Caliph'), meaning 'steward' or 'delegate'. After his death two years later, Abu Bakr was succeeded by another disciple, Umar, who lived ten years more, and was in turn succeeded by Uthman, whose leadership lasted twelve years. In this short period of twenty-four years, Muhammad's revelations were consolidated into the Qur'an and the community of believers expanded into north Africa and central Asia. Following Uthman's death (by assassination), serious issues arose around the succession. Some backed 'Ali ibn Abi Talib, who was Muhammad's son-in-law, but others favoured Uthman's cousin named Mu'awiyah. This resulted in a military challenge that was ultimately won by Mu'awiyah after 'Ali's death by assassination. Mu'awiyah was the founder in 661 of the first actual Muslim dynasty, known as the Umayyads, who ruled from Damascus in Syria. It was under the Umayyads (who lasted until 750) that Islamic rule expanded into a vast empire extending from Spain to Sind in South Asia.

There was, however, a continuing dispute about the leadership of the Islamic community, for there were some who believed that 'Ali should have been proclaimed leader of the community after Muhammad's death, and that the leadership should have remained in Muhammad's lineage. They were called Shi'a, which means 'faction'. Husayn, son of the defeated and murdered 'Ali, refused to pledge allegiance to Mu'awiya's son Yazid, and in 680 was killed by Yazid's army at Karbala.

This event marked the beginning of the emergence of the Shi'as as a separate community within Islam, distinguished by its commitment to the belief that the leadership of the Islamic community should be confined to descendants of 'Ali and Muhammad's daughter Fatima. The other major division, and the majority of the Islamic world, is called Sunni (derived from Sunna, meaning 'tradition'); they reject the Shi'a claim that descent should determine the leadership of the Muslim community. We thus see that the major split in the Muslim community did not arise over doctrinal issue but was essentially a political matter. There were further sectarian splits among the Shi'as, also arising from succession disagreements.

Today, Shi'as constitute about 15% of all Muslims. They are a majority in Azerbaijan, Bahrain, Iran and Iraq, and they are a significant part of the Muslim populations of India and Pakistan (a very small minority in Bangladesh).

Basic Beliefs

At the foundation of Islamic teachings are certain core truths that are considered beyond the reach of doubt or dispute. A Muslim is someone who accepts, or submits to or commits to, these truths. The first and foremost truth is that of monotheism. God is singular, omniscient, all-powerful, eternal and the creator of the universe and humanity. He is transcendent but knowable through his word (in the Qur'an, as revealed to Muhammad) and other attributes (such as his justice, or compassion), but in his essence he is unknowable to us. God, however, wishes to communicate with us, to warn us against wrongdoing and to instruct us in righteousness, and the medium he uses is prophecy. And to humans he gave the power to choose to do good or evil.

The first prophet, or 'messenger', was Adam. God instructed him, but Adam was disobedient. (For an especially lucid presentation of these basics, see Smith, 1957, pp. 10–15.) Since then, God in his mercifulness has sent many messengers, now mostly long forgotten, who transmitted God's will to the communities in which they lived, but time and again the message was distorted or ignored. The prophets best remembered are those of the linked Jewish and Christian traditions, for they were able to communicate God's will effectively, though never perfectly. After Adam came Abraham, who established the all-important truth of monotheism, which has never been completely forgotten since then. Moses added God's law to the truth of his oneness. However, the followers of Abraham and Moses were guilty of a major error, for instead of understanding God's revelation as pertaining to all of humanity, they thought it applied only to them. Then came Jesus. His followers understood the universality of the message, but their error was that of deifying the messenger in defiance of the all-important truth of monotheism.

But then – after humanity's long history of error, distortion and moral confusion – God in his mercifulness intervened decisively by sending a messenger who disclosed God's truth with total clarity and finality. The message was conveyed in Muhammad's revelations as recorded in the Qur'an, regarded as perfect and unalterable. It is written in Arabic, which is the sacred language of the Islamic world, and its verses are recited in Arabic, regardless of whether the reciter actually knows the language. The messenger, Muhammad, not only conveyed God's truth and will, but also laid the foundations for a community that would enact that truth – as embodied in the laws with which its members were entrusted – in its ways of life. This community was to be universal, open to all of humanity, and although it began among Arabs it did indeed become dramatically multi-ethnic in short order. It should be noted that Islam accepts the basic teachings of the Torah and the Gospels, and regards the Jews and Christians as belonging with Muslims to a wider community of 'Peoples of the Book'. They, too, were receivers of revelations, even if they were unable fully to comprehend them. Therefore, if we take an Indic perspective, Judaism, Christianity and Islam are really three different branches of the same basic religion, differing mainly over the issue of who was the last prophet.

All three, but perhaps Islam most of all, are entwined with a particular under-standing of history, and this is a point on which they differ from the Indic tradi-tions we have thus far seen in this book. Though details vary, as we have seen, the Indic systems posit a cyclical view of history in which there is no beginning or end, although there may be restarts and re-ends as there are in Puranic cosmology. In contrast, Islam takes a non-cyclical view of universal history. (The Isma'ilis, a Shi'a subsect, represent a partial exception.) God created the world, and when he did so he ordained a certain pattern for the behaviour of nature and humanity. And he did so but once. Men and women must work out their relationship with this pattern, and must do so once and for all, not over and over again. And they are free to do this, but also free to fail.

For the individual, resurrection and judgement lie ahead at the end of time (although whether the resurrection is physical or spiritual is debated). When that time comes, everyone who ever lived will be judged before God. Those who were totally virtuous in life will enter Paradise directly. Sinners will be sent to Hell, but their damnation is not eternal, for they, too, will enter Paradise after a term of punishment determined by the weight of their sins.

The Five Pillars of Islam

Islam prescribes certain specific practices, five in number, that draw clear bound-aries around the community of believers.

The first and most important is the profession of faith: 'I bear witness that there is no god except God and I bear witness that Muhammad is the messenger of God.' The profession of faith also serves as a formula of conversion to Islam, and it contains two assertions that are the very bedrock of Islamic belief. The first is the truth of God's unity and uniqueness. This, however, does not necessarily distinguish a Muslim from other monotheists. The second part of the profession, asserting that God's messenger is Muhammad, does precisely that. The separation emphasises the fact that Muhammad is not deified; he is God's messenger, not God. This is why Islam should not be referred to as 'Muhammadanism'.

The second of the five is prayer, which is prescribed five times per day (daybreak, midday, mid-afternoon, sunset and evening), and consists of the recitation of verses from the Qur'an and a series of prostrations while facing Mecca. It need not be performed in a place of communal worship, although doing so is favoured. Wherever

4.1 At prayer at the Jama Masjid, Delhi (© Shutterstock by Zvonimir Atletic).

it is performed should be clean, and the individual offering prayer should be ritually purified by washing hands, face and feet.

The third practice is charitable giving. The amount required is given as a percentage of one's accumulated assets. Among Sunnis it is 2.5%, but can be as much as 10% in some Shi'a groups (Elias, 1999, p. 70). It is not seen as charity for, in fact, it is owed to the poor by the more fortunate, whose wealth is really given in trust by God.

The fourth practice is a month-long period of fasting undertaken during the ninth month, the month of Ramadan, of the Muslim calendar. One should not drink or eat during daylight hours, nor engage in sex or violent acts. The month of fasting is not only a period of religious seriousness but also has a festive dimension, and the evening meal, taken after darkness falls, tends to be more elaborate than at other times of year. Quite evidently, by requiring the same observances and changes of lifestyle of all, the month-long fast accentuates community solidarity and, in multi-religious societies, community boundaries.

The last of the five practices is the pilgrimage to Mecca known as *hajj*. Undertaking the hajj at least once in a lifetime is considered an obligation for every Muslim who has the means and requisite health to make the journey. It is modelled after Muhammad's final visit to Mecca and is performed at a definite time of year when certain rituals take place there. Ritually purified and dressed in special clothing for the three-day duration of the hajj, pilgrims first circumambulate the Ka'ba, a cube-shaped building that is the holiest site in Islam and the physical focus of worldwide Islam. It is said to have been built by Abraham and his son Isaac, and it contains a black stone which the angel Gabriel gave to Abraham as a token of God's covenant. Pilgrims on hajj circle the building seven times and then perform other rites at nearby sites in recollection of important events in the life of Abraham. Then, having visited the site of Muhammad's Farewell Sermon, they celebrate Eid al-Adha ('Feast of Sacrifice') by sacrificing animals (mainly sheep and goats, but also cattle or camels) in commemoration of Abraham's willingness to sacrifice his son at God's demand.

Islamic Mysticism

Islamic mysticism, known as Sufism, arose in Islam's early years and was started by world-renouncing ascetics who dedicated their lives to prayer, fasting and meditation on the verses of the Qur'an. Their withdrawal from society was modelled on Muhammad's own proclivity to leave the city and spend time meditating in a cave, which was indeed where and how he received his initial revelations. The term Sufi quite possibly derives from the Arabic term for 'wool' (*suf*), out of which their simple garments were made. In a manner very similar to Indic ascetics, they lived in poverty, practised austerities and engaged in disciplined meditation as methods of cultivating heightened and focused spiritual awareness. In time, the emphasis on asceticism became blended with devotional expressions of love for God, and it was only after this fusion with devotionalism that Sufism began to take off in the ninth and tenth centuries as a popular religious movement reaching every level of society.

The object of Sufi practice is direct experience of God's presence, or even union with God. The belief that such an experience is attainable is based on the idea that the divine is present in everyone, even if hidden somewhere below our normal traffic with the material world, and that it can be engaged by destroying the egoistic lower self and renouncing attachment to the impermanent, material world of our normal experience. Spiritual progress occurs in stages and can be achieved by a variety of means including voluntary poverty, other austerities and certain practices conducive to elevated states of consciousness. These include breath control and 'remembrance' of God by means of the repetition of God's names, and the use of music and dance to bring about feelings of love for God and a sense of his nearness. The Sufis also came to believe that Muhammad and certain 'saints' (*shaykhs*) could serve as intermediaries between worshippers and God. These figures are believed to continue in this role after their demise, and their tombs have become important sacred centres and pilgrimage destinations..

Sufism gained its principal institutional expression in the form of ascetic orders, a process that began in the eleventh century. These orders were based on the concept of disciplic lineages, comparable to similar structures (*paramparas*) in Hindu traditions. Among the Sufi orders that flourished in South Asia, the most prominent was the Chishti order, established in the town of Ajmer (in present-day Rajasthan) by Khaja Mu'in al-Din Chishti, who came from Chisht in Afghanistan and who died in 1236. His disciples, in turn, took his teachings to every part of the subcontinent with the result that the Chishtis became the dominant Sufi order in South Asia.

Islam in South Asia

Arab traders first brought Islam to western South Asia, and an Arab army conquered the region of Sindh in the eighth century, more or less at the same time that the Arabs reached Spain. The most consequential advent of Islam in South Asia, however, was both later and carried by a very different ethnic vector, namely Islamised speakers of Turkic languages from central Asia. It all began in 997 CE when Mahmud (971–1030), the Turkish ruler of a central Asian empire, began a series of very destructive raids from his capital at Ghazni (in present-day Afghanistan) into the Gangetic plain and Gujarat, which lasted some thirty years. The raids were nearly annual and their main motivation was a mixture of avarice for plunder and religious zeal, not the conquest of territory. His Gujarati excursions took him to the major Hindu temple and pilgrimage centre at Somnath, famed for its Shiva linga, where the slaughter was huge and the loot enormous; this was the raid perhaps best remembered – or mythologised – and most resented by Hindus. The linga was smashed to bits and its remains are said to have been taken to Ghazni, where they became part of the steps into a mosque. However, despite Mahmud's military prowess, his successors were left with only a portion of the Punjab.

The reasons for the rapidity of Turkish military success were several. A crucial factor was the superior horses and horsemanship of the invaders. Probably for reasons of climate, South Asia has never been a good place to raise horses, whereas the Turks had the advantage of a plentiful supply of first-rate horses from central Asia and beyond. And not only were the Turks highly accomplished cavalry tacticians, but also their skill as mounted warriors was unsurpassed. They, for example, could fight with bow and arrow while riding, which was evidently a skill lacking among their mounted South Asian opponents. Furthermore, their military formations were more unified and responsive to command than the South Asian armies. The Turks were professional soldiers who continually travelled and fought together, whereas the South Asian armies consisted mainly of separate local levies brought together when needed.

The next chapter of the story begins with a resumption of Turkish incursions into the north, this time resulting in major territorial conquests. These were begun by one Muhammad of Ghur (1149–1206) who, with Ghazni as his base of operation, embarked upon a series of expeditions into the subcontinent in 1175. Although his military adventures there had their ups and downs, the decisive event was his victory in 1192 over the forces of the young Rajput king Prithviraj Chauhan, whose kingdom was in what is now eastern Rajasthan. The battle, in which Prithviraj was killed, took place at Tarain, located 93 miles north of Delhi, and Prithviraj's defeat left the Turks with a more or less clear field for further conquests. Having other imperial business to attend to, Muhammad returned to Ghazni, leaving his forces to make further conquests under the command of one of his generals, Qutb al-din Aibek, who took Delhi in 1193. Muhammad later returned to India, but was assassinated in his encampment near the Jhelum River. The successor to the rule of his Indian conquests, ultimately stretching from Punjab to Bengal, was Aibek and, although he died in a polo accident just four years later, his reign is seen as the beginning of the five-dynasty period known as the Delhi Sultanate.

Perhaps the first thing that should be said about Muslim rule in South Asia is that it did not reach down very far socially. One set of rulers was replaced by another. Attacks on Hindu temples did occur, but often primarily for purposes of plunder rather than religious sentiment, for Hindu temples were often repositories of great wealth. In effect, the Muslims simply joined a fray already long underway among Hindu rulers. It is true that non-Muslims were required to pay a special per-head 'tax' (*jizya*). However, although there were definitely conversions of Hindus to Islam, there was no policy of mass conversion, and Hindus were generally allowed to practise their religion unhindered.

The sultanate can be visualised as a three-tiered sociopolitical order of Turks, Iranians and indigenous South Asians (Trautmann, 2011, pp. 149–53). The Turks were the ruling military aristocracy and, because they had no firm traditions of succession, internecine struggles resulting in turnover at the top were frequent. Indeed, it could be said that the Turks' principal foes were other Turks, and not primarily the indigenous rulers or population. The Iranians, fleeing from upheavals in their homeland, brought literacy and organisational acumen to the mix; they became prominent in the sultanate's officialdom, mediating between the Turkish rulers – themselves highly Persianised – and their indigenous subjects. This is why Persian became the language of government and high culture in the sultanate. As for the subject populations, their main niche in the social order was to farm the land and to pay land taxes to finance the extravagant state ceremonial and wars of their rulers. Even in the sultanate's central zone (essentially the Ganga-Yamuna Doab), revenue was extracted by lower-level indigenous feudatories under the supervision of state officials; outside this zone, extraction took the form of tribute from the still-ruling indigenous kings. Commerce appears to have largely remained in the hands of traditional trading communities. Islam and Hinduism became territorially differentiated, with Hinduism continuing to prevail in rural areas and Islam becoming largely urban in the central zone of Muslim rule.

The apogee of the Delhi Sultanate was the early fourteenth century when it expanded into the south, but predatory taxation policies began to take a toll on the agricultural productivity of sultanate territory, which led to a decline in the strength of the state. In 1398 the north was invaded by the Mongol Timur, who sacked Delhi, and by the fifteenth century all that was left of the sultanate was a group of regional kingdoms. This was also the period of the rise of a Hindu kingdom and empire in the south known by the name of its capital, Vijayanagar, the ruins of which surround present-day Hampi in what is now the Indian state of Karnatika. Founded in the 1330s, its kings were Hindus who actively promoted Shaivism, but the two brothers who established the kingdom had previously served the Muslim Tughluqs, then ruling at Delhi, and might well have been Muslims at that time. Moreover, the Vijayanagar kings utilised Muslim cavalrymen in their military, and some of them styled themselves 'Sultan among Hindus'.

Mughals

Much of the monumental architecture so admired by foreign visitors to India (such as the Taj Mahal in Agra) was built by the Mughals, a dynasty that enjoyed two centuries of extraordinary success and left a huge imprint on the subcontinent. Mughal means 'Mongol', and the founder of the Mughal dynasty, Babur (1483–1530), was a descendant of both Timur and Genghis Khan. One of the subcontinent's more attractive historical figures, he was a cultivated man who combined his military expertise with a serious interest in poetry. He came from central Asia. Having failed to make much progress as a military adventurer there, he established a kingdom in Afghanistan, from which he challenged and defeated the Delhi Sultan at a place called Panipat (north of Delhi in the present-day state of Haryana) in 1526. Babur ruled only for four years, and his son, Humayun (1508–1556), was driven from South Asia by rival powers. But after a fifteen-year exile, Humayun returned to South Asia and re-established Mughal rule. He was an enthusiastic astronomer/astrologer and died as a result of a stairway fall when he was descending from his observatory.

Humayun's son and successor, Akbar (1542–1605), is justly celebrated as one of South Asia's most brilliant rulers. His reign lasted almost fifty years, and it was he who consolidated the empire and expanded it to cover almost the entire north, from the Bay of Bengal to the Arabian Sea. He included Hindus in his military forces and state bureaucracy, and some Hindus rose to high offices and achieved great distinction in his administration. He abolished the jizya tax on non-Muslims and cemented his ties with the Rajputs – a Hindu military aristocracy ruling in various areas of north, central and western South Asia – by marrying Rajput brides. Although he was illiterate (possibly because of a learning disorder), he patronised the arts and learning, which flourished during his long reign. One of his most celebrated character traits was his religious eclecticism, which was also a wise strategy of rule. Though a Muslim (of Sufi persuasion), he was deeply interested in the teachings of other religions, and spent time discussing spiritual matters with holy men from a variety of religious backgrounds. These included Christians and Jains as well as Hindus. He also devised a syncretic religion of his own (Din-i-Ilahi, 'Divine Faith') that drew upon Sufism and other faiths and that was adopted by some members of his court.

With Akbar's death in 1605, the empire was one of the world's wealthiest and largest. Jahangir (1569–1627), Akbar's successor and son of one of Akbar's Rajput brides, possessed the religious curiosity and some of the religious eclecticism of his father, but apparently found little of value in Hindu beliefs and practice. Still, his approach to his Hindu subjects was largely hands-off. Like his father, he was also a patron of the arts and culture. It was during his reign that the British began commercial activity in South Asia, a momentous historical moment indeed. After a vicious war of succession, he was succeeded by Shah Jahan (1592–1666) in 1628, also the son of a Rajput princess. His reign marked the material zenith of the empire and left a legacy of extraordinary architecture. He built the Red Fort and Jama Masjid in Delhi, but his most glorious creation was the Taj Mahal at

Agra; it was built as a tomb for his favourite wife, Mumtaz Mahal, and they lie there together today.

Even before Shah Jahan's death, a war of succession had broken out among his four sons. The victor was his third son, Aurangzeb (1618–1707), who had his father imprisoned from 1658 until his death in 1666. Aurangzeb became emperor in 1658, and, if Akbar is remembered by many Hindus with genuine admiration and affection, Aurangzeb is the Mughal emperor the Hindus most love to hate. There is no doubt that he alienated many of his Hindu subjects because of his adherence to a strict version of Sunni Islam. He re-established the jizya tax on non-Muslims (in lapse since Akbar's time) and was a major demolisher of temples (although he also supported other temples, and even provided land grants to some). But his zealotry was not directed against Hindus alone, for he also persecuted Shi'as. Notwithstanding all of this, Aurangzeb was by many criteria a very successful ruler who led the empire for nearly fifty years. Furthermore, if he was religiously intolerant in some respects, his army and state bureaucracies were filled with Hindus.

Aurangzeb was the Mughal under whom the empire reached its greatest extent (at least nominally), covering the entire subcontinent save for the deepest south. It was, however, overextended, and it was this rather than Aurangzeb's religious policies that led to the empire's decline in the immediate aftermath of his reign. His campaigns in the south resulted in an enormous drain on the empire's resources. Complicating an already serious situation were two internal military challenges. One was in Punjab and involved the Sikhs. In 1675, and for reasons that are obscure, Aurangzeb ordered the public beheading of Tegh Bahadur, the ninth Sikh guru and successor to the founder of Sikhism. As a consequence of Tegh Bahadur's martyrdom, his son and successor, Guru Gobind Singh (1666–1708), militarised the Sikhs and converted them into a solidary martial community that was a source of constant hostility to the empire during Aurangzeb's last years. I return to the story of Sikhism later in this chapter.

In central India, the problem was the Marathas, who had become a centre of resistance to the Mughals even before Aurangzeb's time. The Marathas originated as a Hindu peasant class in what is now the Indian state of Maharashtra. Many of them fought in the armies of the central Indian sultans, and one, a very able leader named Shivaji (1627 or 1630–1680), established a Maratha kingdom in the 1660s by seizing a portion of the sultanate of Bijapur and was crowned in 1674. Although Shivaji was once an ally of Aurangzeb, he – and later his sons after his death, and later yet the widow of one of his sons – fought an insurgency against Aurangzeb that became a serious drain on the energies and treasure of the Mughal Empire and contributed to its weakening during the latter part of Aurangzeb's reign.

After Aurangzeb's death in 1707, the empire rapidly fragmented and soon one of the greatest empires ever known lay in ruins, although it continued in a shadowy existence in Delhi. The Marathas, in particular, flourished in the midst of Mughal decline, and ultimately created a large empire, but they were not the only contenders for power in post-Mughal times, a matter to which I return in the next chapter.

Religious Conversions

Significant numbers of conversions of Hindus to Islam began from around 1300 CE and, as reported in the 1901 Census (Lal, 1973, pp. 155–6), about a sixth of the population of British India was Muslim by the end of the nineteenth century. The question of how and why Hindus converted to Islam is much debated because of its political implications in the Republic of India. It is, nonetheless, possible to discuss this issue sensibly, and a good example of such a discussion is a study of conversion in eastern Bengal authored by Richard Eaton (1993). He describes four basic approaches that have been traditionally applied to the problem, each flawed in its own way, and then presents a fine-grained analysis of the conversion process as it actually unfolded in eastern Bengal.

The first conventional theory is the 'Immigration' theory, which circumvents the need for an actual concept of conversion by supposing that South Asia Muslims are all or mostly descended from Muslim immigrants. This argument has a political significance, for – if true – it would seem to vindicate the view that Muslims are really 'foreigners' in South Asia, an idea congenial to some Hindu nationalists. However, although it is true that some South Asian Muslims, especially in the far north-west and coastal areas adjoining the Arabian Sea, are descended from migrants, it is inconceivable that migration could ever have occurred on a scale vast enough to explain the actual numbers and distribution of the subcontinent's Muslim populations. It is a well-established fact that most South Asian Muslims are the descendants of converts.

Second is the 'Religion of the Sword' thesis, which places the emphasis on armed force as the method of conversion. But the image of forced conversion bears little relationship to the reality, as has already been noted. It may be that such conversion took place in recently conquered territories, but once the dust settled the Muslim rulers faced a problem of governance rather than armed resistance. Effective governance requires a population willing to be governed, and in deference to this principle the Muslim rulers generally allowed their subjects to continue to follow their own laws and customs. As Eaten (1993) points out, the lack of any sort of systematic policy of conversion by force or political intimidation is indicated by the fact that the subcontinent's Muslim populations were not concentrated in the central zone of Muslim rule, which was the upper Gangetic plain. Rather, the greatest number of conversions were in eastern Bengal and western Punjab (the areas that became Pakistan in 1947), which were least exposed to Muslim military or state power.

Eaton's third theory is what he calls the 'Religion of Patronage' thesis. This is the idea that subject populations convert to Islam as a means of ingratiating themselves with a Muslim ruling class, thereby gaining relief from taxes, employment, professional advancement, enhanced social standing and so on. This certainly did occur, but it does not (as is also true of theory number two) explain the mass conversions that occurred on the fringes of Islamic power in South Asia.

Eaton (1993) calls his fourth theory the 'Religion of Social Liberation' hypothesis. According to this scheme, because Islam carried with it an ethic of social equality – supposedly rooted in Sufi tradition – Hindu members of the lowest castes adopted Islam as a strategy for achieving upward social mobility by exiting the Hindu social order in which they were so oppressed. But, says Eaton, this version of history oversells the idea of Islamic egalitarianism (largely a recent idea propounded by nineteenth century Islamic reformers). And also, and more important, it ignores the fact that premodern promoters of Islam in South Asia did not contrast it with Hindu civilisation socially, but theologically; what was important was monotheism (against Hindu polytheism), not social justice. But perhaps, most tellingly of all, we confront again the fact that the locus of the most massive conversions to Islam were peripheral regions in which Hindu institutions, including the caste order, had a relatively weak hold on local populations. At the same time, however, it seems likely that, in urban settings in the Gangetic plain, individuals and clusters of families, often of the artisan class, did convert as a means of achieving upward social mobility. For example, the family of the Kabir, the great *nirguna sant* (to be discussed later in this chapter), in all probability belonged to a recently converted lower Hindu caste of weavers.

So where does that leave matters? With regard to eastern Bengal, Eaton (1993) points to certain very specific and contingent historical factors that must be considered in unravelling the reasons for mass conversions to Islam. This is the region that became the eastern wing of Pakistan after independence and later became the sovereign state of Bangladesh. Eaton's argument is too complex to be completely summarised here, and it might or might not be applicable, or exactly applicable, to other regions in any case. Still, it is worth noting its high points because it illustrates the need for nuance and receptivity to complexity in dealing with the issue of religious conversion in South Asia. First, the conversions in eastern Bengal were actually quite late, occurring mainly after the Mughal conquest of the region in the late sixteenth century (and the Mughals, it should be noted, had no policy of proselytising Islam). The process began with the granting of forested land to Muslim individuals and Sufi shrines – Sufism being a style of piety much favoured in Mughal circles – for clearing and development. Manpower was drawn from local populations who found themselves pulled into the orbit of an emerging Sufi-oriented 'religious gentry', whose shrines and mosques were the spiritual and physical nodes around which sedentary peasant communities coalesced. Conversion was part of this coalescence, and Islam (in its Sufi formulation) thus came as part of a package of agrarian development and concomitant social and cultural change.

That Sufism played a key role in conversion in eastern Bengal cannot come as a surprise, and this was certainly true in other regions, although the economic and social particulars would have been different. As we know, Sufism and Hindu devotionalism are neither conceptually nor emotionally that far apart. It is, therefore, logical that Sufis were major agents of conversion to Islam in South Asia. It is also important to acknowledge that Hindu and Islamic traditions were interacting with each other from the start of Islam's South Asian career. This means that over the course of many centuries Islamic and Hindu traditions co-evolved, each leaving at least some imprint on the other.

Religious Transformations

While it might be supposed that the centuries of Muslim domination would have been a period of Hindu decline, this is far from true. In fact, the entire period, especially the fifteenth and sixteenth centuries, saw an extraordinary efflorescence of devotional Hindu traditions. This was actually one of the most creative periods in the religious history of South Asia.

Southern Devotionalism

To take up the threads of this story, we must begin by travelling back in time to the south and a period before the Muslim incursions of the tenth century and after. As seen in the previous chapter, highly emotional forms of Vaishnava and Shaiva devotionalism were propagated in Tamil poetry by the Alvars and Nayanars, respectively. This was a development of roughly the sixth century CE and after. Many of these poets were non-Brahman, some were women, and the movement inspired by their poems had broad appeal among non-elite social strata. But at the same time, important changes were occurring in southern Brahmanical orthodoxy on both the Shaiva and Vaishnava sides.

On the Shaiva side, the influence of Shankara – often considered to be India's greatest philosopher – was crucial. As seen earlier, Shankara was the systematiser of the Advaita Vedanta, the non-dualist religious philosophy that held that bondage arises from ignorance alone and that stresses a path of pure knowledge to liberation. He is also said to have established ten mendicant orders, collectively known as the Dashanamis, devoted to pursuing this concept and to have founded monasteries in the four corners of India: Jagannath Puri (in Odisha), Badrinath (in the Himalayas), Dwarka (in Gujarat) and Sringeri (in Karnataka). The heads of these establishments are known as Shankaracharyas.

A corollary of Shankara's philosophy is that devotion to a deity with qualities cannot be, in itself, a path to liberation. However, there is certainly room in Shankara's system for worship and devotion as a means of advancing in the direction of a true understanding of brahman, even if devotion alone is insufficient. In the ninth century and onwards, Shankara's Advaita system became linked with an orthodox Brahmanical tradition known as Smarta ('followers of smriti'). The Smartas are not inclined to strong sectarian preferences, but Shiva tends to take pride of place in Smarta temples. South India is today the heartland of Smarta Brahmans and temples.

Rivalling Shankara's stature as a Hindu philosopher and theologian was Ramanuja (late eleventh to early twelfth centuries). He was born to a Tamil Brahman family who belonged to a Vishnu-worshipping sect strongly influenced by the songs of the Alvars and known as Shri Vaishnavas, and he became a strong defender of devotion as a path to liberation. Rejecting Shankara's strict monist position, Ramanuja advocated a Vishishtadvaita (a qualified monism). He, too, believed in the ultimate oneness of reality, but he also insisted that material reality is not an illusion but the body of brahman, and that individual selves are likewise real but as parts or emanations of brahman. Because bondage is real, liberation cannot be achieved by knowledge alone, although knowledge is a prerequisite. Rather, liberation comes as an act of grace resulting from rites of worship and personal devotion to the Highest Self who is Vishnu, and liberated selves retain their individuality and separateness from Vishnu.

By the early second millennium, the southern bhakti movement was thus coming into cultural equilibrium with the region's Brahmanical orthodoxies, and the result was a regional religious idiom – encompassing popular devotionalism, temple worship, literatures in both vernacular languages and Sanskrit, and philosophically rationalised soteriologies – that retains its distinctiveness to this day and also had a deep impact on Hindu traditions elsewhere on the subcontinent. From the south, this devotional movement spread northwards, and it was during the period of Muslim rule that it came into full flower in the north. Here, too, its vehicle was poetry composed in vernacular languages, and, as in the south, it had profound appeal to non-elite social groups. In both south and north, these devotional traditions, especially as carried in the songs of the great bhakti poets, became part of the fabric of the religious lives of ordinary Hindus.

Northern Devotionalism

A major question arising in relation to bhakti in the north has to do with its relationship with Sufi Islam, for there are indeed similarities between Sufism and Hindu bhakti, particularly in thematic similarities between Sufi and bhakti poetry, as seen, for example, in the mutual emphasis on the pain of passionate love-in-separation to describe the relationship between devotee and the divine (Lawrence, 1987, pp. 369–71). This has led to suggestions of mutual influence, which gain plausibility when one considers that bhakti in the north began to take on its characteristic features only during the late sultanate period and after. A recent suggestion along these lines comes from Patton Burchett (2019), who argues that the milieu out of which northern bhakti emerged was a vernacular performative culture that originated among Sufis and is reflected in the centrality of performance and song in bhakti traditions. The context in which this evolution occurred was a deep transformation of the sociopolitical order which led to an atrophy (though not the elimination) of medieval Tantra and its institutional supports, especially the ritual cultures of Hindu courts and the monasteries within which it was cultivated and transmitted. Tantrism and Shaivism became the 'other' against which the new bhakti – mostly Vaishnava – defined itself, even as it incorporated elements of Tantrism into its outlook and practices.

Bhakti took two different directions in the north, conventionally designated by the expressions *saguna bhakti* and *nirguna bhakti*. The term '*saguna*' means 'with attributes', and saguna bhakti refers to a type of devotionalism focused on God in a specific forms with specific attributes. The term '*nirguna*' means 'without attributes', and nirguna bhakti is a type of devotionalism emphasising a devotee's inward engagement with a formless divine being. Devotionalism in its saguna form is 'plain vanilla' bhakti that was, although varied, always subcontinental and not specifically northern. The nirguna tradition, however, is a northern phenomenon, associated especially with the Hindi-speaking north.

Northern saguna bhakti was generally a form of Vaishnavism, with Rama and Krishna as its main foci. The Krishnaite traditions, which were focused on Krishna Gopala, were embodied in the songs of some of the greatest poets of northern vernaculars. The two standouts in dialects of Hindi are Mirabai and Surdas.

Mirabai (1498–1546, but uncertain) is said to have been born a Rajput princess in the town of Merta in present-day Rajasthan. Her biography (Hawley, 2005, pp. 48–69, 89–178), or what is conventionally taken to be her biography, is a widely known story in the Hindu world. It is said that she became totally devoted to Krishna in her childhood, leaving no room in her heart for any other attachment. Although this attitude would hardly seem to be a very good foundation for a successful marriage, she was forced to marry a prince of Chittor. Unable to adjust to married life, she spent her time in temples and in the company of wandering ascetics. Because of these proclivities (and other transgressions, such as her refusal to bow to her mother-in-law and worship her husband's clan goddess), her husband's family tried to murder her by means of poison, which they presented to her as the foot-washings of an image of Krishna. The deadly brew had no effect. Quite fearless in the face of these tribulations, and disdainful of the ties of conventional marriage, she became a wandering devotee and holy woman and left this world when Krishna drew her into one of his images at Dwarka. Some of the most beloved Krishna-oriented song and poetry is attributed to her, although the accuracy of such attribution is never certain. A major theme in her poetry is her love as a woman for Krishna, whom she portrays as her lover and husband.

Surdas (sixteenth century; dating uncertain) is renowned especially for his poems on the theme of Krishna's childhood in Braj, the region around Mathura and Vrindavan where Krishna grew up (and on whom see Hawley, 1984). There is no doubt that he is one of the greatest Hindi poets, and perhaps the greatest of all. Sur (as he is often called) is said to have been blind from birth. His blindness led his family to abandon him in early childhood, and while living on the banks of the Yamuna River he met a famed Krishnaite religious leader named Vallabha, who inspired him to create songs about Krishna's life. His best-known composition is the *Sursagar* ('Ocean of Sur') which contains thousands of verses attributed to him, and his songs (as well as Mira's) have become deeply woven into the religious life of the Hindu north. (For a translation of the *Sursagar*, see Bryant and Hawley, 2015.)

Although he did not achieve distinction as a poet, something should also be said of a figure known as Chaitanya Mahaprabhu (1486–1534), who was Bengal's most famous exemplar and propagator of Krishna devotion. Chaitanya was a Brahman by birth, who was believed by his followers to be an incarnation of Krishna and Radha (Krishna's lover) in a single body. As a means of expressing devotion, he gave special emphasis to a practice known as *sankirtan*, the collective dancing and singing of Krishna-oriented songs. This emphasis on singing the names and deeds of Krishna was carried forward by his followers and became the core devotional practice of the tradition known as Gaudiya Vaishnavism. Gaudiya Vaishnavas are particularly well known for the singing of the Hare Krishna mantra: 'Hare Krishna Hare Krishna/ Krishna Krishna Hare Hare/ Hare Rama Hare Rama/ Rama Rama Hare Hare.' A late offshoot of the Gaudiya movement is the International Society for Krishna Consciousness, which was created by A. C. Bhaktivedanta Swami Prabhupada for the propagation of Krishna devotionalism in the West. His Western followers became famous for their chanting of the Hare Krishna mantra in airports and other public places.

The now nearly ubiquitous northern cult of Rama (and Hanuman) was given enormous impetus by Tulsidas (c.1532–1623), another of the great figures of Hindi devotional poetry and Rama's greatest poet-devotee in the north. A Brahman, he spent most of his life in Varanasi and, although he composed several works, he is best known as the creator of the *Ramcharitmanas*, a Hindi (in the Avadhi dialect) version of the *Ramayana* (on which see especially Lutgendorf, 1991). This is easily the best known and most beloved of religious texts of the Hindi-speaking region, and when Hindi-speakers mention the *Ramayana* it is normally to Tulsidas' work that they refer, not the Valmiki version, for this is the *Ramayana* most people actually know. As was true of many of the other regional *Ramayanas*, north and south, it is not a mere vernacular retelling of the Valmiki text; rather, it is a completely recast version of the Rama story, deeply infused with the spirit of bhakti. Public recitations of the *Ramcharitmanas* and re-enactments of episodes from it are an important feature of the religious culture of the north, and the imagery of Rama as an ideal king has found a very important niche in the political discourse of the Republic of India, as we shall see in a later chapter.

Nirguna Sants

Nirguna bhakti probably emerged first in what is now the Indian state of Maharashtra, but it was in the Hindi-speaking north that it took on some of its most distinctive characteristics. Its heyday was the fifteenth to the eighteenth centuries. The poets and spiritual innovators who created and propagated its various versions often belonged to lower social strata; some were from Muslim backgrounds, and some were Hindus from the lowest castes. They were not world-renouncers and wore no special symbols of sanctity. They were mostly householders who supported families, and they typically followed humble trades as determined by their caste or community tradition. Many were poorly educated and could express themselves only in regional languages.

The term by which these figures are usually designated is *sant*, and their teachings – various though they are – are known collectively as *sant mat* (the 'teachings' of the sants). The term 'sant' is usually translated as 'saint' in English, and the bhakti poets (including figures in the saguna traditions) are commonly known as 'poet-saints'. This rendering seems to have resulted from a purely fortuitous resemblance between the two words, 'saint' and 'sant', but the Indic term 'sant' is actually derived from *sat* ('truth'), and it might best be translated as a spiritually realised person. However, so entrenched has the 'poet-saint' usage become that there seems little point in departing from it here.

The nirguna sants were unconventional in the extreme. Given their social backgrounds, it is hardly surprising that they rejected the caste hierarchy and, especially, the superior social status, the alleged superior ritual purity and the supposed religious authority of the Brahmans. The northern sants also rejected Vedas and the Vedic heritage, and those of Islamic background rejected the Qur'an. Indeed, as Charlotte Vaudeville (1987, p. 23) points out, the objection was not just to particular texts, but the sants also took a dim view of the whole idea of scriptural authority. They also rejected the concept of Brahmanical priests as necessary mediators between worshippers and the divine, and they rejected polytheism and all forms of physical image worship.

The sants tended to understand the divine as a single, formless, all-pervasive entity, although the purity of the nirguna vision varied from one sant to another – purest, perhaps, in Kabir. They were inclined to understand the soul or self as distinct from that divine entity and liberation to consist of a union (short of actual merger) with it. They held that, because ultimate reality is inaccessible to the senses with which we engage the outer world, it must be sought on an internal landscape. There were three essentials of practice on which all the sants agreed (Vaudeville, 1987, pp. 31–5). The first was a focus on the divine name. If *saguna* devotionalism extols God's name and form, the option of form was by definition unavailable to the nirguna sants, whose object of veneration is formless. That leaves name alone. The repetition of the divine name is called 'remembrance' (*sumiran*) and was recommended as a means of achieving absorption into the Absolute. It could be done vocally or mentally. The sants preferred names drawn from Vaishnava tradition, especially Ram (Rama), but the 'Ram' of the nirguna sants had little to do with the Rama of the *Ramayana*; rather, it was simply a name for God.

The second essential of sant practice was the centrality of a 'spiritual guide' (*satguru*). The satguru, however, was and was not a human preceptor. In nirguna tradition, the question of whether a given sant had a human master is sometimes unresolved, but all the sants attached the highest importance to an interiorised master, who is the Ultimate understood as satguru, an internal presence encountered during meditation. The model for this relationship was the ancient guru-disciple relationship in which the guru initiates a disciple by imparting a secret power-charged utterance by whispering it in the disciple's ear. In parallel with the traditional guru's whispered initiation, the internal satguru initiates by imparting a liberating word (*shabd*, literally meaning 'word') that is said to have a spontaneous and electrifying revelatory effect on the devotee.

The third essential of sant practice is what is called *satsang* ('company of the true'). Devotees should seek each other's company, sit together and sing the names of God and the songs of the sants. Such assemblies are extolled as purifying in the same manner as bathing at a place of pilgrimage is for ordinary Hindus.

Sants and Naths

Although the sants advocated a radically distinctive spiritual path, their teachings were certainly not without traditional roots. For example, they owed much to the Vaishnavas, as seen in the tendency to use Vaishnava names for the formless divine and the idea of love of the divine as the essential precondition of spiritual progress. Also, the great importance given to joining in satsang has a parallel in the Vaishnava practice of assembling to sing devotional hymns. But it is at least arguable that their most important indebtedness was not to the Vaishnavas, but to the Tantric tradition. This was probably a result of contact with certain extraordinary figures known as Nath Yogis, who were renowned for their ascetic prowess and supernatural powers and who have deeply influenced the religious culture of western and northern India.

The Nath Yogis – Naths for short – were (and are today) a Hindu monastic order with numerous subdivisions established at some time between the tenth to twelfth centuries by an obscure figure named Gorakhnath. They are also known as Kanphat ('split-eared') Yogis because of their pierced ears. Although they professed neither Hindu nor Muslim identity, their teachings were shaped by Shaivism and the doctrines of Hindu Tantrics and Vajrayana Buddhists. The Naths practised a discipline known as hatha (the 'yoga of force'), which seeks spiritual development and immortality by means of certain difficult physical postures and modifications of bodily processes conducive to spiritual progress. The term *nath* means 'master', and Naths claim Shiva himself, whom they call Adi Nath ('the First Master'), as the original practitioner of this discipline.

The common ground between the Naths and the nirguna sants is extensive (Vaudeville, 1974, pp. 120–43). Because of their emphasis on the interiorised inward spiritual quest, the Naths rejected ceremonies and outward forms of worship, and to them distinctions of caste were irrelevant. They, too, rejected the authority of the Brahmans and the scriptures upon which this authority was based. This radically sceptical view of conventional religion, which was extended to Islam as well, became a central teaching of the nirguna sants. The sants, however, put little stock in the idea of achieving salvation through physical exertions, shifting the entire emphasis to the inwardness of the quest for the Ultimate instead; thus, the Naths' physical yoga had little appeal to them. Also, the nirguna sants believed in pursuing spiritual goals as householders, not as world-renouncers. But Nath practice emphasised the importance of cultivating an inward experience of unity understood as the culmination of an interior journey upward within the physical body. This was central to the teachings of the nirguna sants as well, and likely resulted from contact with the Naths. The Naths were probably also the source of the emphasis on the importance of the divine name and the idea of the internal satguru as the source of the salvific 'word'.

Sant Kabir

Of the sants, two figures tower over all the others. One is Kabir; the other is Nanak, the founder of Sikhism. In what follows, I look briefly at Kabir and some other sants who loom large in nirguna tradition. Such is the importance of Sikhism, however, that Nanak and the Sikhs will be treated separately in the closing section of the chapter.

Kabir's importance lies in the influence that his teachings and recalled charisma exert over the nirguna movement; he is, one might say, the seed from which the movement grew, because most of the later sants found inspiration in him. (For a wonderful essay on Kabir and translations of his verses, see Hess and Singh, 1983.) His exact dating is uncertain, but he lived in Varanasi in the fifteenth century. Although both Hindus and Muslims have claimed him, his name is a Muslim one and he was probably born into a family of weavers who had recently converted to Islam.

But whatever his religious background, his teachings were highly critical of both Islam and Hinduism as he understood them. Tradition avers that a throng of mixed Hindus and Muslims was present at Kabir's death. They quickly fell into fighting over his remains, but then noticed that the corpse had disappeared and in its place were two heaps of flowers. A voice from heaven then instructed the Muslims to bury their flowers and the Hindus to burn theirs in accord with the customs of the two communities. Kabir is said to have been a disciple of the famous Ramananda, but, in fact, his poetry shows far more familiarity with the teachings of the Nath Yogis than with Vaishnavism, and this despite his favouring of 'Ram' as the name of God.

Although Kabir is often characterised as a promoter of Hindu–Muslim unity, this seems to be more a politically convenient slogan (for some) than an accurate portrait of his views. In truth, he was disdainful of both Islam and Hinduism, or at least of Muslim and Hindu formalism, a contempt that he expressed with a very sharp tongue in verses famous for their terse directness. Of the Hindus he said:

> Pandit, how can you be so dumb?
> You're going to drown, along with all your kin,
> unless you start speaking of Ram.
> Vedas, Puranas – why read them?
> It's like loading an ass with sandalwood!
> Unless you catch on and learn how Ram's name goes,
> how will you reach the end of the road?
> (from Hawley and Juergensmeyer, 1988, p. 51)

And of both:

> Hindus, Muslims – where did they come from?
> Who got them started down this road?
> Search inside, search your heart and look:
> Who made heaven come to be?
> Fool,
> Throw away that book, and sing of Ram.
> What you're doing has nothing to do with him.
> Kabir has caught hold of Ram for his refrain,
> And the Qazi [Sharia jurist]
> He spends his life in vain. (from Hawley and Juergensmeyer, 1988, p. 52)

Sant Panths

Some of the nirguna sants continued to be venerated by sectarian followings after their departures. The best-known example of this is Sikhism, but there were others. Such an organisation is known as a *panth* ('path' to the divine).

The sect tracing direct spiritual descent to Kabir is known as the Kabirpanth. It is mainly patronised by lower castes and tribals, and has been estimated to number at least 2.5 million and probably more (Lorenzen, 1987, p. 292). But while the Kabirpanth is indeed significant as a legacy of Kabir, it should be borne in mind that the existence of such an organisation is hardly consistent with Kabir's own unruly and anti-institutional temperament. Also, the presence of an order of world-rejecting ascetics within its fold would seem to be a departure from nirguna ideals. Still, given its social locale and egalitarian ideology, it can certainly be seen as a sectarian expression of Kabir's opposition to caste hierarchy and the Brahmanical formalisms of his day.

Another important panth in nirguna tradition is the Dadupanth. This group venerates the memory of an important sixteenth-century sant named Dadu Dayal (1544–1603). Of Gujarati origin, and said to have been a cotton-carder by trade, Dadu ultimately settled in the town of Naraina – located close to Jaipur – where the sect's headquarters remain today. His poetic compositions were collected into a book (the *Dadubani*) by one of his followers, and the book itself has become an object of Hinduised worship by members of the panth. The panth flourished during the eighteenth and nineteenth centuries and maintained a close relationship with the rulers of Jaipur State.

Of special interest is the fact that an order of celibate warrior ascetics, called Nagas, developed within the Dadupanth. Armed ascetics were routine participants in the wars of northern India during the Mughal period and beyond, and some even fought in service of the British East India Company (Pinch, 2006). The Dadupanthi Nagas were a nirguna variation on this theme. The Sikhs, of course, were militarised by Gobind Singh, a matter to be discussed shortly, but the Khalsa (the martial fraternity of Sikhs) was not an order of world-renouncers. The Dadupanthi warrior ascetics collected taxes and served as soldiers for Jaipur State until their disbanding in 1938. Daniel Gold (1994) traces the emergence of Dadupanthi armed ascetics to the martial culture of the region as borne and propagated by Rajputs, and some members of the order were indeed recruited from Rajput backgrounds.

Another noteworthy sant sectarian legacy, later in origin than the foregoing, is a congeries of related sects bearing the name Radhasoami or Radhaswami that trace their spiritual genealogy to the teaching of a nineteenth-century figure named Shiv Dayal Singh (1818–1878) (Gold, 1994; Juergensmeyer, 1987, 1991; Babb, 1986). The movement he founded developed two major branches, one centred in Agra and the other in Punjab at Beas, and each of these, in turn, has ramified into many subdivisions. The recent vigorous growth of the movement's Punjab branch illustrates the continuing dynamism and attractiveness of nirguna teachings today.

Shiv Dayal Singh, known as Soamiji Maharaj (or Swamiji Maharaj) to his followers, was a Punjabi Khatri. This caste consists mainly of urban traders who claim the varna status of Kshatriyas (the meaning of the term 'Khatri'). He was clearly influenced by the poetry and teachings of the classical nirguna sants. These he probably imbibed from an important sant of his period called Tulsi Saheb, who lived in Hathras, about 30 miles east of Agra, and to whose congregation Soamiji Maharaj's family belonged. The extent to which Soamiji Maharaj's own teachings were actually transmitted to him by Tulsi Saheb is a rather arcane point of disagreement between different branches of the movement, but, whatever we make of that, his teachings, which he began to promulgate in 1861, were clearly his version of Nath-influenced *nirguna* tradition. Central to his teachings was the concept of an ascending internal journey in which every level of the cosmos is accessible within the human body. The journey begins by engaging with a current of sound/energy (called shabd, as in *nirguna* tradition generally) that flows from the Supreme Being and by means of which one can be drawn upward towards union with the Absolute. The Supreme Being is Radhasoami, a fact said to have been revealed for the first time to Soamiji Maharaj himself.

The Radhasoami movement has a clear appeal to modern and cosmopolitan spiritual sensibilities, as evidenced by the fact that it has developed a following of over a million adherents, mainly in northern India's urban middle classes, and especially in administrative and managerial circles. It has also acquired a significant international following.

Sikhism

But of all the nirguna traditions, the one with the strongest claim on our attention is Sikhism. This is so not merely from the standpoint of South Asia's religious ethnography and history but also because of the extraordinarily important role Sikhs have played in the history of the Republic of India.

The founder of Sikhism was Guru Nanak (1469–1539). He was born into a Hindu family near Lahore in what is now Pakistani Punjab, and his family belonged to the Khatri (merchant) caste. He was a married man with two sons, and in his younger days he worked for a living in the service of a regional ruler named Daulat Khan, but despite his early life as an ordinary householder Nanak clearly had religious leanings. It is said that while bathing in a river one day he experienced a revelation directing him to spread the word about the 'divine name'. He then became an itinerant holy man, eventually settling on the bank of the Ravi River in western Punjab. There he established a village called Kartarpur where he remained as a religious teacher for the rest of his life.

In time, his teachings and his poetic compositions began to draw followers into his orbit, apparently both Hindus and Muslims. His verses, which are famed for their beauty and poetic merit, were a particularly important attraction to potential followers. They were created to be sung communally, an activity that became an important focus of group identity and solidarity, and these early followers began to coalesce into a religious community under Nanak's guidance. They came to be known as Sikhs ('disciples' or 'learners'), and the community, still in its first stages of growth, was called the Nanak Panth (Path of Nanak).

Although Nanak might not have actually known of Kabir (McLeod, 1976, p. 7), his teachings fell squarely within the tradition of Kabir and the other nirguna sants. As was characteristic of the sants, Nanak rejected the idea that celibacy and ascetic withdrawal from ordinary life were necessary for liberation. His, rather, was a spiritual path for householders who support themselves and their families through hard work. He taught that there is but a single God, the formless, self-existent and timeless creator and sustainer of the universe who is immanent in his creation yet completely beyond the reach of human comprehension, and that this formless entity can be a source of saving grace to those who seek union with it. The bridge to this inner reality is guru, by which is meant the inner guru who is God, but who is also manifested in the living guru, a personal amalgam of formlessness and formed, who leads the aspirant on his inward journey. The blandishments of worldly life and our evil impulses bind us tightly to the cycle of transmigration, but not those who truly listen and hear God's voice within. Devotion to the divine name opens the way to ever-higher levels of perception of the divine, a journey that culminates in actual union with the formless Lord and complete release from worldly bondage.

It is often contended that Nanak's teachings were a synthesis of Hindu and Islamic ideas, a notion with considerable appeal to religious bridge-builders. But according to a leading authority on Sikhism, W. H. McLeod, similarities between the two traditions have been much overplayed (1968, pp. 158–63). Nanak's sources of spiritual inspiration were mainly the traditional sants. There are certainly features of sant teachings that resemble Islamic and Sufi tenets, but these ideas can be derived from bhakti sources and the doctrines of the Naths. There is no evidence, moreover, that Nanak actually ever encountered a 'classical Sufi', and there is a notable lack of Sufi vocabulary in his writings, in contrast with his extensive use of Hindu terminology and sant usages. These considerations, and others as well, suggest that Muslim influences on Nanak were 'relatively slight'. In McLeod's (1968) view, Nanak never thought of trying to blend Hindu religious culture and Islam, for in fact he saw neither of these two traditions as fundamentally right; to him, they were both, and equally, wrong.

The Panth's Evolution

The early success of the movement was rooted in several factors. One was the charismatic appeal of Nanak himself. Another was his stance towards caste. In common with the other nirguna sants, Nanak was opposed to caste discrimination. Although it was a custom already practised by some Sufis and Naths, one of Nanak's most important innovations was the custom of *langar* ('kitchen'), which is still observed by Sikhs today. In village India, a key manifestation of caste hierarchy consists of restrictions on interdining. The langar meal is prepared by volunteers and is served free to all comers in Sikh places of worship (*gurdwaras*) Members of all castes are required to share the meal while sitting in single lines without any acknowledgement of differences in caste status. Although one should not discount the purely spiritual motivation behind Nanak's hostility to caste, a downplaying of caste distinctions was highly advantageous from the standpoint of recruitment, and Nanak's opposition to caste discrimination was continued by the nine gurus who succeeded him as heads of the Panth.

But it must also be said that, although Nanak and his successors were adamant in their condemnation of caste discrimination, caste affiliation has played a surprisingly prominent role in the history and sociology of the Sikh community. Nanak and his successors all belonged to the Khatri caste, and to this day Khatris continue to constitute an elite group within the Sikh fold. However, the bulk of the converts to Sikhism (and the overwhelming majority of Sikhs today) belonged to a caste called Jat. The Jats are a rural caste of agriculturalists and landlords, renowned for their industriousness, toughness and strong sense of honour. During the sixteenth century, the Jats were acquiring greater control of land, but this rise in economic status was not matched by an increase in the caste's standing

4.2 Langar at the Golden Temple at Amritsar (© Shutterstock by Hari Mahidhar).

in local hierarchies. The uncompromising opposition to caste discrimination of Nanak and his successors, therefore, had an obvious appeal to the Jats and must have been an important factor in their recruitment (McLeod, 1976, pp. 11–12).

Nanak was clearly a highly charismatic figure whose personal force of intellect and character exerted a profound effect on his followers. However, no religious movement can last for long on such a foundation, for ways must be found to 'routinize' (as Max Weber, the pioneering German sociologist, famously put it) the founder's charisma – that is, the founder's idiosyncratic and revolutionary authority must be transmuted into traditional and/or bureaucratic forms (Weber, 1958). The routinisation of Nanak's authority was accomplished by his institutionalisation of the role of guru as the head of the community and his designation of a successor. His successor was Guru Angad, an associate of many years' standing, whom he chose instead of either of his sons. (Nanak's younger son became the founder of an alternative Panth built around an order of initiated ascetics. Known as Udasis, they exist to this day as a minority community in the Sikh world.)

Guru Angad's most significant contribution was the refinement of the Gurmukhi script for the purpose of recording Nanak's poetry in the Punjabi language. The name Gurmukhi means 'from the mouth of the guru'. As Pashaura Singh (2006, p. 133) points out, the importance of this contribution lies in the fact that it was neither the Perso-Arabic nor the Devanagari script in which Arabic, Persian and (in the case of Devanagari) Sanskrit were written. Thus, the cultivation of Gurmukhi represented a repudiation of the superiority of the literary and religious traditions transmitted in these languages, and created a further basis for the autonomous identity of the Sikh religious heritage.

During this period, the Panth was still devoid of any internal structure apart from the dyadic links between devotees and the guru himself. This began to change under the guruship of Amar Das, who succeeded Guru Angad after his death in 1552. He established the concept of a specifically Sikh sanctity for certain holy places, ceremonies and festival days. These innovations were a necessary ingredient in a fully organised and institutionalised – as opposed to a charismatically led – Sikh community, providing a necessary focus for community activity and identity. Guru Ram Das, who succeeded Amar Das in 1574, founded a village called Ramdaspur, where he seated his guruship; this village was ultimately to become the city of Amritsar, which is Sikhism's physical and ritual centre today. His successor and the fifth guru was Guru Arjan, who succeeded to the guruship in 1581. He was the source of innovations crucial to the further evolution of the Panth. He built the initial Gurdwara Harmandir Sahib (later also known as the 'Golden Temple') at Amritsar, which became the most important of all Sikh places of worship. It was also he who supervised the compiling of the holy book of the Sikhs known as the Adi Granth (the 'First Book', usually called the

Guru Granth Sahib today). It contained Guru Arjan's own poetic compositions and those of the other previous Sikh gurus as well as those of other sants, including Kabir. With this, the institutionalisation of the Panth as a religious community was approaching completion.

Guru Arjan's guruship also marked the beginning of the Panth's troubled relationship with the Mughal authorities, who viewed its extraordinary growth with increasing trepidation. Guru Arjan himself was detained by the Mughal administration in Lahore, where he was tortured and died while in custody in 1606. The exact manner of his demise is unclear, but his death came to be seen as a martyrdom and major milestone in the history of the Sikh movement.

The guruship of Guru Arjan's son and successor, Guru Hargobind, marked the beginning of a profound change in the culture of the Sikh community, for this was the beginning of open Sikh hostility to the Mughal Empire and Muslims more generally. It was during Hargobind's guruship that the Sikhs began to undertake armed resistance against the Mughal authorities. The conflict started during the reign of Shah Jahan, and Hargobind and his close followers sought safety from the Mughal authorities by moving to the hilly zone of northeastern Punjab. This conflict came to be seen by the Sikhs as a struggle against a powerful oppressor, which could only further consolidate the sense of common cause and shared destiny within the Sikh community.

One can think of the ensuing period as that of a smouldering fire that finally bursts into an open conflagration. The guruships of the seventh and eighth gurus were largely uneventful. Both were sequestered in the shelter of the northestern hills, where they could stay out of trouble with the Mughals. Very different was the guruship of the ninth guru, Guru Tegh Bahadur, who reignited open conflict with the Mughals by moving down from the hills to the plains. The exact circumstances are unclear, but Tegh Bahadur was beheaded in 1675 on the order of the Mughal emperor Aurangzeb. It seems probable that this was a result of the growth of the Panth and its increasing belligerence in the face of perceived Mughal intolerance. Tegh Bahadur was ordered to come to Delhi by the emperor where, it is said, he was offered, under torture, the choice of conversion to Islam or execution and chose execution. The execution was public and took place in Chandni Chawk in Delhi. Later, an important Sikh temple, Gurdwara Sis Ganj Sahib, was built on the site of his martyrdom.

Khalsa

The importance of the guruship of Tegh Bahadur's son and successor, Guru Gobind Singh, is second only to that of Nanak himself. He was proclaimed guru in 1676 under the name Gobind Rai at the age of nine. In time, he found himself in open conflict with Mughal forces, and this resulted in a fundamental alteration in the nature of the Sikh Panth. The change took some time to unfold completely but had fully crystallised by end of the eighteenth century. The key event was the formation of a religio-warrior community within the Sikh fold known as the Khalsa (Pure). According to tradition, this occurred in 1699 at a festival at Anandpur Sahib. Gobind Rai asked for volunteers among the Sikhs willing to undergo beheading. Brandishing a sword, the guru led the volunteers, one by one, into his tent, reappearing each time with bloody sword in hand. There were five volunteers in all and, after the fifth had entered the tent for his beheading, the guru revealed that all five were still alive, and that five goats had been beheaded in their place. These five, Sikhs of demonstrated total loyalty, became the nucleus of the Khalsa.

Having performed a rite of initiation involving the drinking of sweetened water that had been stirred in an iron bowl with a two-edged sword, the guru gave them all a new surname, Singh ('lion'). To this day, male Khalsa Sikhs bear this surname; females take the surname Kaur ('princess'). The five, in turn, initiated him in the same fashion, and he became Guru Gobind Singh. He required Khalsa members to carry or wear five symbols of their membership, often called the 'Five Ks': uncut hair (*kesh*), a wooden comb (*kanga*), a metal bracelet (*kara*), a steel sword (*kirpan*) and a special kind of undergarment (*kaccha*). He also imposed a code of discipline on the Khalsa that included the prohibition of tobacco and halal meat. In addition, he abolished a system of deputies (*masands*) that had been created by Guru Ram Das to collect tithes from the Sikh community and that had become corrupt; an effect of this was a strengthening of the bond between Sikhs and the guru.

The Khalsa is probably best described as a militarised social order resting on a religious foundation. The religious foundation was created by Nanak himself, but the origination of the militarisation was a somewhat more complex matter. The Khalsa came into existence in the context of persecution by, and struggle with, the Mughal authorities, and a commonly held view is that Gobind Singh created the Khalsa in the face of dangers and threats with the direct intention of militarising what would otherwise have continued as a quiescent, pacific and helpless spiritual community. However, it is also clear that internal forces were, in reaction to a prolonged period of Muslim persecution, pushing the Panth in the direction of militancy, in any case. Although the Panth's elite, including the gurus, were Khatris, the rural Jats and their caste culture had become a powerful force within the community. The Jats had strong martial traditions, and presumably then, as now, a reputation as a community not to be trifled with, and one reading of the evolution of the Khalsa is that it was a reflection of the increasing influence of the Jats within the Panth. But even so, Nanak's spirituality was not lost, for the martial values and code of conduct of the Khalsa were never allowed to push aside the ideals of inward devotion that were inherited from the Panth's earliest days.

Because of its predominance within the Sikh world, the Khalsa became, for all intents and purposes, 'the Sikh orthodoxy' (McLeod, 1987, p. 240). Still, it was never actually the entirety of the Sikh world, for a minority of Nanak-Panth membership continued in their old ways without seeking initiation into the Khalsa. Mostly non-Jats, they are seen as genuine Sikhs and are known as 'Sahajdhari Sikhs' (as opposed to Khalsa Sikhs, also known as 'Amritdhari', meaning those who have taken 'nectar' [amrit], i.e., have received initiation).

Guru Gobind Singh died at the hands of two Pathan assassins in 1708, and his death created a crisis of authority within the Khalsa. By normal expectation, the guruship would have passed to a son of the deceased guru, but Gobind Singh's sons all predeceased their father. According to Sikh tradition, Gobind Singh anticipated this difficulty by declaring the end of the institution of the personal guruship within the Panth. The guru's authority, he announced, would pass to the *Adi Granth*, the Sikh's most sacred scripture, which now became the *Guru Granth Sahib* – that is, the book itself became the guru (*granth* meaning 'Book'). Its authority would be shared by the Panth as a corporate body, now the 'Guru Panth'. The concept of Khalsa assemblies wielding political authority as Guru Panths was later shoved aside by Ranjit Singh (see below), which left the concept of the Guru Granth standing uncontested and on its own. From then until the present day, the *Guru Granth Sahib* has been treated as the actual guru and with the same degree of veneration. It is the focus of reverence in every Sikh temple. But more, the printed guru continues to provide counsel to the Sikhs, just as the living gurus once did. Many devout Sikhs guide their daily behaviour by opening the book at random pages and treating the text found there as a command for the day. The *Guru Granth Sahib* is also sometimes utilised as a guide to corporate decision-making in Sikh communities.

Sikh power in the Punjab reached its apogee in the late eighteenth and early nineteenth centuries during the era of Maharaja Ranjit Singh, the 'Lion of the Punjab' (Sher-e-Punjab). He was born in 1780, the only son of a local chieftain, at a time of incessant conflict between small Sikh principalities (known as *misl*s, and nominally all in alliance against outsiders) that emerged in Punjab in the aftermath of the collapse of Mughal power. Having suffered from smallpox in early childhood, Ranjit was blind in one eye and severely pockmarked, and he was also almost completely uneducated. Still, he proved to be an extraordinarily gifted military leader. He succeeded to his father's estates when he was only twelve years old, and became the leader of the Sukarchaklia Misl (in what is now Pakistani Punjab). In 1799, he succeeded in taking the city of Lahore, and in 1801 he was proclaimed the Maharaja of Punjab. By 1820, he was ruler of the entire Punjab between the Indus and Satlej Rivers. However, he was never able to expand his empire to the south of the Satlej because of a treaty he signed with the British in 1806. At its apex his empire comprised all of Punjab north of the Satlej up to the heights of the north-western

4.3 The Golden Temple at Amritsar (©Shutterstock by Aleksei Sarkisov).

Himalayas in Kashmir. He died in Lahore in 1839, and in his absence the Sikh Empire disintegrated soon after because of power struggles among his descendants. This left Punjab as easy prey for British conquest and annexation.

But however inglorious its ending, Ranjit's Sikh Empire is a vivid historical memory for the Sikh community, a recollection sustained by his architectural legacies. These include the beautiful Golden Temple at Amritsar, which Ranjit restored and expanded. He also built two of the Sikhs' most important temples at the sites of Gobind Singh's birth and death.

5

Religion and the Raj

I first encountered Indian civilisation as an undergraduate student in the early 1960s. The course I took was called 'Indian Philosophy', but it turned out to be one about Indian religion, a reflection of the fact that the boundary between religion and philosophy can be hazy in the Indic context. In any case, at the centre of it was something called 'Hinduism', which we were told was one of the world's oldest religions. If anyone in the room had problems with the notion of Hinduism as 'a religion', no one said so out loud. And yet there was a problem, if not fully acknowledged in that classroom in that era, and it amounted to more than an academic puzzle about abstract concepts. As will be seen in the next two chapters, the question of what exactly Hinduism is has shaped the destiny of nations.

This brings us to British rule, because the concept of 'Hinduism', if not the reality, came into existence during this period of the subcontinent's history, as did many of the forces that created the religiously rooted boundaries that currently mark the subcontinental map. An account of how India came under British rule is far beyond the scope of this book, which after all is about religion, not the history of the British Empire. But it may be useful to remind readers of a few essentials.

British Rule

Advent

The first significant European presence in South Asia was Portuguese, not British. The Portuguese interlude began with the landing of Vasco da Gama at Calicut in 1498, and for a century or so they dominated the subcontinent's overseas trade from a series of forts and bases scattered along the western and south-eastern coasts. They brought with them Catholic Christianity and their missionary efforts met with significant success. Goa became the capital of Portuguese India, and Goa retains to this day a strong Portuguese cultural mark in language, cuisine, architecture and religion. But soon the Portuguese were to be challenged in South Asia by other European powers. They were drawn, as were the Portuguese, by the prospects of lucrative trade. But instead of armed forces sent by governments, the method by which Europeans established their presence and influence in the subcontinent (and other areas of Asia) was joint-stock trading companies, themselves armed, that were granted monopolies in the Asian trade. Their modus operandi was to create coastal trading enclaves and, by establishing alliances with local powers, to extend their power into the interior.

The trading company that, after many struggles, came to dominate the South Asian subcontinent was the British East India Company (EIC). It was chartered by Elizabeth I in the year 1600, which fell within the waning days of Akbar's reign. The EIC at first aspired to the trade of the Spice Islands, but the trading opportunities there and in the rest of what is now Indonesia were pre-empted by the highly successful Dutch East India trading company. As a result, the British EIC had to fall back on India, which was then seen as definitely second best. They began by trading mostly in Indian fabrics instead of spices (which India did not possess in abundance), paid for mainly in precious metals. In 1617, the Mughal emperor Jahangir granted the company the right to established 'factories' – as trading posts were called – at Surat and elsewhere, and by the late seventeenth century the French and the Dutch had also established coastal trading enclaves. Because the Mughal Empire was then at the height of its power, there could be no question of inland conquest, and at this stage the Europeans were quite peripheral to the principal power rivalries in the subcontinental interior. All this was to change at century's end, when the Mughal hold began to loosen, and by the beginning of the eighteenth century various new indigenous and foreign contenders for serious subcontinental power began to emerge.

By the early eighteenth century, the EIC found itself in possession of three vital enclaves at Bombay (now Mumbai), Madras (now Chennai) and Calcutta (now Kolkata), and Calcutta was the base from which the British conquest of India began. The British were becoming ever more deeply involved in the subcontinent's power politics, and nowhere more consequentially than in Bengal. The Bengal trade was immensely profitable, and by the mid-eighteenth century the British had become well dug in at Calcutta. The Nawab of Bengal (nominally a subordinate governor of the Mughal Empire, but in truth exercising independent sovereignty) attacked and defeated the British there, but he in turn was attacked by the British in 1757, and EIC forces under the leadership of Robert Clive retook Calcutta. In that same year, Clive defeated the nawab's forces at Plassey, and, having installed a puppet nawab of his own choosing, he secured tax-collecting rights for the EIC over large areas of Bengal. This was the base from which the company rule was extended by military means over Bengal, Bihar and Orissa (now Odisha), and this resulted, in 1765, in the granting of formal tax-collecting privileges over this entire area by the hapless Mughal emperor. The immense profitability of this enterprise for the EIC was guaranteed by the availability of revenues (instead of payment from Britain) to purchase goods exported in trade.

Despite these successes, however, the British were still but one contender among several in the subcontinent. In the south, the kingdom of Mysore (now Mysuru), ruled by a highly competent military leader named Tipu Sultan, was a formidable rival. Tipu had already badly beaten the British at Polilur (near Kanchipuram in present-day Tamil Nadu) in 1780, but he was defeated by the British, in turn, in 1799. Next were the Marathas, who by this point had lost their one-time unity and had fragmented into several principalities. After a long series of military encounters with the Marathas, ending in 1818, the British established control over the Ganga valley and central India. By 1842, Sindh was under British rule. The Sikh Empire in Punjab, in serious disorder after Ranjit Singh's death in 1839, was defeated by the British in 1849 in the Second Sikh War. With this, British domination of the subcontinent was complete (except for Afghanistan, where the British, despite the three wars they fought there, were never able to gain a secure foothold).

Britain's wars in India were fought mostly by Indian soldiers with a smaller British military core, but perhaps the most important factor in British success was the network of alliances they created with the subcontinent's indigenous king-doms. A large number of these states continued to exist after the consolidation of British rule. Known as 'princely states', the British allowed their traditional rulers to govern with traditional pomp and display, but this was a façade. Although these kingdoms were nominally independent and separate from British India, they were, in fact, governed under the supervision of a British 'Resident', and were not allowed to conduct foreign relations or to interact with each other diplomatically. Still, it was a remarkably good deal for these ruling families; they continued to enjoy great wealth and other benefits of sovereignty without ever having to get on a horse to defend it. Something like a third of the subcontinent was controlled by the British through this system of 'indirect rule'.

The year 1857 was a historical landmark because this was when a rebellion of Sepoys (Indian soldiers in British service) broke out in Meerut, not far from Delhi. From there it developed and spread into a general insurrection in the north. Known alternatively as the First War of Independence or the Sepoy Mutiny, depending on one's point of view, this was a dangerous moment indeed for the British. The rebel-lion was finally and brutally suppressed in 1858, at which point the Mughal Empire – still nominally in existence – was abolished and the supposedly ruling emperor, Bahadur Shah Zafar, was sent into exile. India was taken directly under the Crown, meaning that India was now ruled by the British Parliament, and the EIC was dis-solved. In 1877, Victoria became Empress of India. This was the beginning of the years of the classic 'British Raj.'

Educational Policy

We need not dwell on details of British governance, but one issue merits our special attention because it has directly to do with the way Indian civilisation adjusted to – and was shaped by – British rule. Once domination had begun to be secured in the early nineteenth century, a major question facing the British was that of what kind of education to promote among their new subjects. In the late eighteenth century, the British authorities had been generally sympathetic to the idea that Indian customs should not be interfered with and that traditional forms of Indian education should be supported. This was in line with the views of those who came to be called 'Orientalists', of whom Sir William Jones (see Chapter 1) was a prime example. They maintained that India not only had an ancient connection with European civilisation, but also possessed a sophisticated literary culture and had, at least in the past, shown itself to be capable of great achievements. In the early decades of the nineteenth century, however, a reformist spirit, an amalgam of utilitarianism and evangelical disapproval of non-Christian ways, made its way into British attitudes. This had many manifestations, but the heart of the matter was education.

Thomas Babington Macaulay (1800–1859), a distinguished British historian and politician, came to India in 1834 where he served on the Governor General's Council. The then-serving Governor General was Lord William Bentinck, and in 1835 Macaulay submitted to him his famous 'Minute on Education', in which he addressed the critical issue of what was to be the language of education in British India. This was to prove to be a truly momentous document. Macaulay, a man of strong utilitarian proclivities, had little sympathy for the Orientalists' favourable view of Indian civilisation. It was agreed on all sides that the regional vernaculars (Bengali, Hindi, etc.) were an unsuitable vehicle for higher education, so the question was whether the language of instruction should be Persian and Sanskrit, on the one hand, or English on the other. It should be English, Macaulay argued, which would be the gateway to Western learning, about the superiority of which he had no doubts. On this point, he famously wrote:

> The question now before us is simply whether, when it is in our power to teach this language, we shall teach languages in which, by universal confession, there are no books on any subject which deserve to be compared to our own, whether, when we can teach European science, we shall teach systems which, by universal confession, whenever they differ from those of Europe differ for the worse, and whether, when we can patronise sound philosophy and true history, we shall countenance, at the public expense, medical doctrines which would disgrace an English farrier, astronomy which would move laughter in girls at an English boarding school, history abounding with kings thirty feet high

and reigns thirty thousand years long, and geography made of seas of treacle and seas of butter (from Trevelyan, 1883 p. 410).

Largely because of Macaulay's urgings, Western learning became the core of higher education in government schools (in urban centres and in post-primary school), and English the medium of instruction. Macaulay's 'Minute' was, as David Kopf (1979, p. 158) has pointed out, a death blow to the Orientalist movement within British officialdom in Bengal. Its powerful advocacy of the view that 'the only true passport to modernity for a culture like India's was the complete assimilation to British manners, customs and language' was to have an enormous impact on the future social, political and religious landscapes of the subcontinent.

Technology and the Velocity of Symbols

If this book has shown nothing else, it has surely established that there was never a time when Indian religion and society were not in a state of change. Still, the rapidity of change has varied as circumstances determine, and, during the period of British rule in India, religious change occurred very rapidly indeed. At first glance, however, this might not be obvious. An observer of Hindu religious practice in twenty-first century villages might well imagine that he or she had been transported back in time for, as far as one can tell, the calendrical celebrations and life-cycle rites of villagers are basically the same ones as those prevailing in the pre-British period. Then, too, there were weddings, funerals, celebrations of calendrical rites and all the rest. But a closer look reveals that the wider cultural context of religion has changed drastically, and, of all the changes, one of the most momentous was the increasing availability of printed religious content during the colonial period.

By now we are quite accustomed to being told that one of the main drivers of change in the late twentieth and early twenty-first century is a media revolution, which is indeed true. In our era, the changes are mainly the result of the enhanced density and velocity of information made possible by the Internet. But the emergence of the Internet is but the latest chapter of a much older story of the evolution of new forms of technology by which symbol-borne information is transmitted and circulated. Whatever else it is or is not, religion is a system of meanings – that is, a system of information – borne by symbols that can move slowly or swiftly, near or far. One of the most consequential effects of British rule in South Asia was precisely a revolution in the velocity by which information could be transmitted and the distances over which it could be carried. More than one factor was at work in this transformation: the building of railways; the introduction of electric telegraphy; and so on. But the most basic of the new factors was, of course, the introduction of the printing press, and it had a major effect on religious culture.

It was the Portuguese who installed the first printing press in South Asia in 1556 in Goa, and it appears that the Malabar coast was where, in 1578, the first material was printed in an Indian script (Tamil) in India itself (a document had been printed earlier, in 1554, in the Tamil script, but in Lisbon) (on these points, see Kesavan,1985; Wadley, 1995). More presses then followed, at first confined to the west coast and then spreading to the east coast and Sri Lanka. For the most part, they were utilised to produce religious tracts and Christian scriptures. In British India, the first press was installed in Madras in the 1760s, but the printing press did not come to Calcutta until one was installed in nearby Serampore by the Baptist missionary William Carey in 1798. After a somewhat slow start, the spread of the printing press in India accelerated over the course of the nineteenth century, and by century's end they were to be found everywhere in British India.

The introduction of print technology resulted in an explosion of publishing in vernacular languages. Generally underappreciated has been the role of the mission presses in this development, for missionaries were the pioneers in developing typefaces for Indian scripts. Newspapers, pamphlets and literature of every description began to appear in regional languages, which was a crucial development, for this made possible the emergence of, and then reinforced, regional and supra-regional identities that were to prove to be of lasting political consequence. In the religious sphere, and on the model of the Christian missionary press, the availability of print technology made possible the production of an enormous quantity of tracts and pamphlets on religious themes as well as mass reproduction of scripture. Among other effects of this was the ability of both existing sectarian traditions and new religious reform movements to communicate with and widen their constituencies, as will be seen in the next section of this chapter.

Although it was at a later stage in the British period, the mass production of printed images of Hindu gods and goddesses was another critical innovation in the religious domain (Smith, 1995; Inglis, 1995). The industry that produces these images was established in the late nineteenth and early twentieth century with the installation of chromolithographic presses in Bombay, Calcutta and Delhi, with many others to follow. These presses made possible a standardisation of visual imagery of Hindu deities, previously often shaped by regional traditions.

It should be emphasised that vision and seeing the images of deities have been major components of Hindu religious practice for centuries (on which see Eck, 1985). At a minimum, one visits a temple to see and be seen by the image-embodied deity (an activity known as 'taking *darshana*', the auspicious sight, of the deity). In consistency with this emphasis on seeing, religious poster art exploded once the technology used in its creation became available, and is a truly ubiquitous feature of popular religious practice today; indeed, to a visitor to India, it is likely to be the most visible and first-seen feature of Hinduism. Such images are cheap in price and available to virtually anyone. One sees them in temples, household shrines, on living-room walls, in places of business, even on the dashboard of taxicabs. Depending on the context, they are sometimes treated as objects of serious worship, sometimes not, but the sight of a shopkeepers or taxi drivers offering at least a stick of burning incense to these images is commonplace in Indian life.

Christians and Jews

Neither Christianity nor Judaism was brought to South Asia by Europeans, for by the time Europeans arrived on the scene both had long been well established on the subcontinent, although on a small scale. The Jews were never a significant element in the subcontinent's population, numbering only just over 20,000 in total at the time of independence. There are only around 5,000 today, the bulk of the remainder having migrated to Israel or to the UK, US or Canada. But Christianity, though never professed by large numbers, had a major impact on the subcontinent's culture and history.

Turning first to Judaism, the oldest Jewish community in South Asia is (or was) settled mainly in Kochi (formerly Cochin) in the state of Kerala (see Gamliel, 2018; Katz, 2000; 2013; Weil, 2006). The community's age is uncertain. Their traditions claim that they arrived at the time of the destruction of the Second Temple, but in fact the earliest actual evidence of their presence in the region is a Jewish woman's tombstone, dated 1269, and the earliest synagogue inscription is dated 1344 (Gamliel, 2018, pp. 45–7). It seems clear that Judaism was brought to this part of India by Jewish traders who plugged into local social and economic networks by means of marriage with local women. (For a fascinating account of the life and business of a Jewish trader who arrived in 1132, see Lambourn, 2018.) Although there were as many as 3,000 of them more than 800 years later at the time of India's independence, there are no more than a few dozen today. During their long sojourn in South Asia, they retained their Jewish identity, but their religious customs were significantly shaped by the Hindu context.

However, the community known as Bene Israel is the largest of the South Asian Jewish groups. Distributed mainly in Mumbai and environs, their traditional occupation is pressing oil. They claim to be descended from a small group of fourteen Jews (seven men and seven women), who were shipwrecked on the subcontinent's western coast many centuries ago, but this seems to be an example of a type of caste origin mythology common in South Asia. The first unambiguously datable written reference to their existence comes from the late eighteenth century, and the issue of when or how they became Jewish or acquired Jewish identity remains obscure.

The third major Jewish group is known as Baghdadi. These are Jewish latecomers to the subcontinent, who arrived as Arabic-speaking traders starting in the late eighteenth century, with close ties to the British EIC.

According to tradition, Christianity (on which see Raj and Dempsey, 2002; Thangaraj, 2006) was first brought to South Asia by Saint Thomas the Apostle, who visited the subcontinent in the first century CE and proselytised in what is now Kerala and Tamil Nadu. Tradition further avers that the San Thome Cathedral in Chennai was built (in the sixteenth century) on the site of his burial. Whether it is true or not that Saint Thomas evangelised in the subcontinent's south, the fact remains that a community of Syrian Orthodox Christians, who trace their spiritual descent to Saint Thomas, has existed in the south from at least the fourth century CE. At a later stage, Roman Catholicism was brought to the subcontinent and was energetically proselytised by the Portuguese. With Goa as a base, Dominicans and Franciscans undertook missions that resulted in the creation of a number of Catholic churches in the Malabar coastal region. The famous Jesuit missionary Saint Francis Xavier (1506–1552) arrived in Goa in 1542, having been sent to Asia on an evangelising mission by the pope. For three years, he pursued his mission in the south and Sri Lanka, with conversions resulting. Although he died in China, his final interment was in Goa at the Basilica of Bom Jesus.

The Catholic missionary effort produced two extraordinary figures. One was Roberto De Nobili (1577–1656), another Jesuit, whose approach was very different from that of other missionaries. He settled in Madurai, where he endeavoured to convert high-caste Hindus, who were and are normally quite resistant to the appeals of Christian missionaries. To do so, he learnt Sanskrit and Tamil and adopted the dress and manner of life of a Hindu renouncer. He also authored a number of works and hymns in Tamil, and has an honoured place in Tamil literary history. Another remarkable missionary, also Jesuit, was Constantine Joseph Beschi (1680–1742). He became extremely proficient in Tamil and wrote various works on Christianity in that language. In subsequent decades, Catholic missionaries also became deeply involved in promoting education and founded numerous schools in India that played a major role educating India's Westernised elites.

The Protestant missionary project came later. It began with the arrival of two German missionaries in the Danish trading enclave at Tranquebar in 1706, and others followed. However, a serious obstacle was the fact that the EIC did not allow missionaries on its territories, at least at first. They were in the business of business, not religion; the success of their endeavours depended on the tranquillity of the regions they governed, and on the assumption that Christian evangelism would antagonise both Hindus and Muslims they kept the missionaries at bay. This, however, did not sit well with Christian opinion in England, and the policy was ultimately rescinded in 1813.

A particularly important figure in the Protestant missionary movement was William Carey (1761–1834). He and other Baptist missionaries established their headquarters in Serampore, which, though near Calcutta, was held by the Danes when he arrived in 1793. In the tradition of De Nobili and Beschi, he was another missionary polyglot; he learnt several Indian languages and translated the *Ramayana* into English and the Bible into Bengali and other Indian languages. He was not, however, well disposed towards Indian cultural or religious traditions, nor were most of the Protestant missionaries that came after him. They were, simply put, of a very different mindset than Sir William Jones and like-minded Orientalists. This difference was to have consequences of very great importance, a point to which I return anon.

But while Christianity has pre-missionary roots in India, and while missionaries, both Catholic and Protestant, were successful to varying extents, it must be said that the Christian faith itself did not fare well in India, at least in terms of numbers (its impact was another matter), and this despite the fact that conversion was often coupled with economic incentives. At 28.7 million, Christians constitute a mere 2.3% of the current population of the Republic of India (2011 Census), with Catholics roughly half of the total, and with about 60% concentrated in the southern states of Andhra Pradesh (Telangana, which became a separate state in 2014, is undifferentiated from Andhra in the 2011 Census), Kerala and Tamil Nadu. Christians are a majority only in the tiny north-eastern states of Nagaland, Mizoram, Meghalaya and Arunachal Pradesh; they are also a significant part of the population in Goa, Andaman and Nicobar Islands and Kerala. The various forms of Christianity introduced by Europeans have evolved and adjusted to South Asian cultural contexts, and today typically use local languages and music in liturgy, although the Protestants lagged somewhat in this process of adaptation.

The Invention of Hinduism?

It is hardly possible to assess the religious scene in early nineteenth-century India without pushing our story well ahead, if only briefly, to the Republic of India's late twentieth and early twenty-first century concerns. This is because the historiography of this period has been deeply affected by political concerns of recent decades. At issue is the nature of what is called 'Hinduism', a matter that surfaces repeatedly in this book. As noted in Chapter 3, without the suffix there is no particular problem, for as an ethnographic term denoting the indigenous peoples and cultures of the subcontinent – which it was originally and remained for centuries – the term 'Hindu' is mostly unproblematic. But it is with the addition of the suffix and the claim that resulting word is the name of a particular 'religion' that the trouble begins. For if that is so, it becomes possible to say that adherence to the Hindu *religion* can define a *political* community and – more – it can be claimed that this is the 'majority community' of an Indian republic, or indeed of the South Asian subcontinent. This is an idea with a history; it emerged in the nineteenth century, played a major role in shaping the Indian independence movement, and is a major driver of contemporary politics in the Republic of India. The principal 'other' of the majoritarian claim is, of course, the Muslims and the object of the claim is to provide a foundation for the notion that Hindus, as a religious community, have a special entitlement to the Indian state.

This issue became the focus of intense scrutiny by historians in the late twentieth century because of a recrudescence of Hindu nationalism and the early stages of a crucial shift in the republic's politics that would bring Hindu nationalists into national power. The issue with which the historians wrestled was whether Hinduism was, in fact, a single, integrated, bounded religion (on the Semitic model) that had been the faith of the subcontinent's indigenes from ancient times, or whether it was merely a concept, a construct of the colonial period, an 'invented' tradition, that had no claim to be the foundation of any sort of 'majority community'. The historians favouring the 'invented tradition' alternative – most notably Romila Thapar (see, e.g., Thapar, 1985; also Frykenberg, 1989), widely regarded as the most distinguished of India's post-independence historians – argued that the indigenous peoples of South Asia did not use the term Hindu in *religious* self-description, and that the expression 'Hindu dharma', the expression closest to 'Hinduism', was rarely used at all. Rather, until quite recently the religious identity of 'Hindus', to the extent that it existed, was mostly sectarian in nature: Vaishnava, Shaiva and so on. And if this is so, then the whole idea of Hindus as a bounded religious community – or a community of any kind – is a purely modern idea, false to India's past, a mere construct and a dangerous one when politicised.

There is, in fact, a great deal of truth in these contentions. The English term 'Hinduism' itself does not appear in print until the early nineteenth century (Pennington, 2005, p. 60), and there is little doubt that the concept of Hinduism – by this name or not – as a world religion among other world religions (such as Islam or Christianity) is a modern idea that crystallised in the late eighteenth and early nineteenth centuries. To be clear, what is meant by this is not that the beliefs and practices in question are modern (although some of them are), but that the *idea* that they fit together as a unitary, integrated, bounded system – an 'ism' – is modern. As suggested in Chapter 3, Hinduism has always been better described as a religious culture than a 'religion', and this remains true to the present day. But does that mean that Hinduism, seen as a unity, is merely an invented *fiction*? Or did the unity exist all along, even if unnamed? And even if the idea of Hinduism was recently invented and never corresponded to any past reality, does that mean that the belief in such an entity on the part of contemporary Hindus is unfounded? It is indeed arguable that Hinduism, as we have come to understand it, was invented, but is it not possible that the invented concept gave rise to a religious reality?

This tangle of questions and issues – of moment, it must be stressed, not just to scholars but to the national life of the Republic of India – is much in need of ordering and examination in the light of historical data drawn from the era in which the alleged invention occurred. This has been done to conspicuously good effect by historian of religion Brian K. Pennington (2005), on whose work much that follows in this section is based. Pennington draws his material from the journal *Asiatick Researches* (first appearing in 1789 and house organ of the Asiatick Society, founded in 1784 in Calcutta by Sir William Jones), the *Missionary Papers* of the Church Missionary Society (founded by evangelical Anglican clergy and laity for the propagation of Christianity) and the *Samachar Chandrika* (a Bengali newspaper). He shows that the modern concept of Hinduism was indeed a product of India's colonial encounter with Britain. It was not, however, made of whole cloth; its component elements pre-existed the modern idea of Hinduism, as did some sense of its unity, assumptions I have stipulated in this book. Moreover, it was not – as some have maintained – merely a response to the needs of Orientalist scholarship, missionaries and imperial administrators for a religious label for those who were neither Muslim nor Christian. Rather, it emerged from a complicated tangle of shifting attitudes towards, and debates concerning, Indian religion that took place on both the British and Indian sides, and the result was hardly monolithic. In fact, it can be argued that more than one Hinduism was 'invented' during the period in question.

One element in the mix was the generally favourable construction of India's culture promoted by Sir William Jones and other Orientalists, who were mostly in the employ of the colonial state. They did indeed create their own vision of a Hindu religion, and at least at first it was part of a largely positive assessment of Indian culture. There was great admiration for the learning and philosophy they found in ancient literatures, and the profusion of gods, goddesses, myths and rituals was seen in romanticised terms as a sort of human parallel to the lush wonders of the subcontinent's tropical growth. But while their admiration for India was certainly genuine, it must be added that the glories of the India they loved were largely past glories, as they saw them, long since erased by decline. From the start, moreover, the Orientalist view was entwined with the purposes of the colonial state, and by the early nineteenth century admiration and sense of wonder began to give way to a less positive view that was more in line with the interests of the now-consolidating colonial order. Largely gone was the older admiration for the intellectual achievements of Indian civilisation, now corroded by the expanding influence of utilitarianism; in its stead was a growing sense of British moral and intellectual superiority as exemplified by Thomas Macaulay's famous 1835 'Minute' (see above). In the end, this was a 'Hinduism' that stood in the way of progress.

Emerging in parallel with these developments, and in interaction with them, was another version of 'Hinduism' constructed by Protestant missionaries, whose highly critical stance towards South Asian cultures had a major impact on British public opinion about India. In Britain itself, the missionary impulse was initially focused on what were seen at the benighted poor and labouring classes at home, but by the turn of the nineteenth century, British missionaries were confronting Hindu beliefs and practices on the ground in South Asia. The missionaries found much fault with what they saw, and the beliefs and practices of the Hindus became their bête noire; they cared less about Hinduism as an obstacle to progress than as the principal obstacle to the spread of the Christian message. A major target of the negativity was 'idol worship', which not only triggered the condemnation of image worship common to the Abrahamic monotheisms but also tapped into a deep vein of anti-Catholic bias. Various social customs also were singled out as examples of the moral deficiencies of the Hindus, and chief among these was *sati*, the immolation of widows on the funeral fires of their husbands, a practice that not only generated lurid images of its own but also fed into narratives about defective Indian manhood and cruelty to women.

Evangelical negativity was further energised by the actual experiences of British missionaries in India, for they found themselves in confrontation with numerous challenges and dangers, real and imagined. Illness, hostility and ridicule from the locals (as well as non-missionary Britons), communication difficulties resulting from poor language preparation – these and other trials made the experience of India anything but pleasant for many missionaries. Some were afflicted by mental illness, which gave rise to wild fantasies about dark forces and demonic spirits at work in the indigenous world, and these fantasies inevitably found their way into the missionary publications read by the British public at home.

The missionary reaction to local customs and their own afflictions became a key element in the context out of which a highly tendentious version of 'Hinduism' came into being. It must immediately be said that this highly negative view of Hindu religion and life was never shared by all Protestant missionaries, but it was certainly the outlook of many. This Hinduism was a religion suffused with demon-worship, widow-murder, human sacrifice and on and on. In an unlikely confluence, such negative imagery also provided a bridge between the evangelicals and utilitarians. In this perspective, concepts of Christianisation, rationalisation and modernisation blended in a single, harsh judgement.

But alongside these trends, yet another 'Hinduism' was being born. This was not the Hinduism of the anti-traditional Indian reformers of the nineteenth century, most of whom seem to have agreed in one respect or another with the critiques of their colonial critics, and to whom I turn shortly. Rather, it was the creation of educated Indians who respected their traditions and who sought ways of conceptualising Hinduism as a religious entity that could provide a unifying framework for existing Hindu traditions and at the same time serve as a religious foundation for a cohesive Hindu community. There were undoubtedly many engaged in this quest, but much of this intellectual activity was and will probably remain under the historians' radar. Pennington (2005, pp. 139–65), however, has found a window into such thinking and colloquy in the pages of the *Samachar Chandrika*, a nineteenth-century Bengali newspaper published from Calcutta beginning in 1822 and generally seen as the principal voice of well-off traditionalists in Bengal. Its main goal was to protect traditional beliefs and practices from the destructive effects of the criticisms of both Western and indigenous reformers.

One of the most striking features of the newspaper's approach to religion was its general disinclination to dwell on matters of doctrine. Instead of trying to cram Hinduism into some sort of monotheistic or quasi-monotheistic mould – as did some more prominent reformers – it placed the main emphasis on religious practice. Although the paper was quite progressive in some of its social and political views, in the sphere of religion it strongly opposed interference in traditional religious practices and even in such traditional social (or socio-religious) customs as the separation of castes. The immolation of widows, sati, was a major flashpoint in these debates, for there was hardly any Hindu custom more likely to inflame the indignation of British critics and Indian reformers. The practice was stoutly defended by the paper as firmly rooted in text and custom and accepted by the widows themselves. The *Chandrika* took the view that the criticism offered by rationalist reformers and missionaries of such practices were themselves a sign of the degraded kali yuga in which the world now finds itself. At the same time, the paper took a more positive view of the economic expansion and social progress of the period, rationalising the tension between this acknowledgement and Puranic pessimism by shifting focus to the potential of the new wealth of most of its readership to create a new kind of Hinduism with the accent on respect for tradition and the conservation of practice. The new wealth could be – and was – turned to such religiously laudatory purposes as temple construction and the support of lavish celebrations of festivals.

There was a deep tension in the paper's stance towards the colonial administration. On the one hand, such reforms as the abolition of widow immolation in 1829 were greeted with dark dismay. But, on the other hand, there was a real appreciation of such aspects of British rule as the British system of civil and criminal justice and such infrastructure improvements as roads and sewers. The paper's ambivalence on these issues – a reflection of feelings that were clearly quite widespread in the Bengali bourgeoisie of the period – was not hypocrisy but evidence of real struggle to interpret the events of the day in traditional Hindu terms.

The *Chandrika* did not respond directly to the evangelical attacks on Hinduism, preferring instead to elevate, in contrast, 'tolerance' to the status of a core Hindu virtue, which indeed remains as a trope central to the idea many Hindus have of their religion to this day. Contrasting vividly with the image of Hindu tolerance was what was viewed as Christian (or at least evangelical) single-minded proselytising that would stoop even to deception to undermine and destroy Hindu traditions. Much was made of what was viewed as a bait and switch tactic of missionary educational institutions, which were said to be less about education than conversion of young and malleable Hindus into Christianity. Such fears were reinforced by the fact that younger Bengalis were indeed beginning to look critically at Hindu traditions.

The *Samachar Chandrika* exemplified a crucial position in a wider debate that was the crucible in which the modern ideas of Hinduism were formed. It promoted respect for the sacred literature and ritual traditions of the past, but reset them in a new vision of a unified Hindu practice. The tricky issue of caste epitomised the new configuration, for elements of the old system, legitimised by ancient tradition, were packaged together with a purely modern social activism aimed at, among other things, alleviating economic deprivation. This approach to Hindu modernity would itself be subject to major changes, but in it we can see the first stirrings of a trend that assumed its mature form in the Hindu nationalism of the twentieth century.

The Invention of Caste?

Previous chapters have already referred to the system of social stratification known as the 'caste system', but without inquiring at any length about its nature. It is now time to say more, because the British era was critical not only in shaping Western ideas about caste but also in playing a role that shaped the reality of caste itself. It is often assumed that caste belongs to the realm of 'tradition', the implication being that the word describes an unchanging social order that has existed for centuries but has finally begun to erode in the face of modernity. In fact, however, caste is not a single social order – nor is it *just* a social order – it is many things at once, for its manifestations are quite various across the face of the subcontinent. Further, as far as we have the power to know, these manifestations have never been static, and the British period was a time of significantly accelerated change.

The word 'caste' comes from the Spanish/Portuguese term *casta* ('breed' or 'race'). (For good brief introductions to the caste system, see Jodhka, 2012 and Mines, 2009.) As the term is generally used, it refers to two quite different levels of cultural reality. One of these levels, the system of four varnas, we have already encountered in the early chapters of this book. Readers will recall that this is an idealisation of the social order that divides society into four interdependent and hereditary classes: Brahmans, Kshatriyas, Vaishyas and Shudras (with the lowly Chandalas being outside the system altogether). The varna system does indeed come close to being a stable and uniform Indic tradition. This is because it does not and never did describe social reality, which is always variegated and changing. It is, rather, a set of concepts about society that can applied to the actual flux and flow of social life differently in different periods or places.

But to illustrate how varna engages with social reality, I must turn to the second of our two levels. When social scientists use the term 'caste' in relation to India, they usually have in mind a social entity known in Hindi as jati, and that is the usage that I shall follow here. The varnas are broad social categories of subcontinental relevance; caste (i.e., jati) identity, however, emerges mainly in regional and local settings. A caste is a named, endogamous (i.e., in-marrying) social category, often associated with a traditional occupation, that tends to be concentrated in a given linguistic region. Not all castes have traditional occupations. A village community will typically be multi-caste, with some castes performing their traditional occupation, some not and some without a traditional occupation. Further, not all members of those that do have traditional occupations actually work in that occupation. A caste is not an actual group, for it cannot act in concert (although in modern times caste associations often act on behalf of castes), but it plays a crucial role in the social identity of members and in restricting marriage choice, and members of a caste are typically organised at the local level with caste councils exercising authority in caste-related matters. This is 'caste', properly speaking.

In this context, varna is best seen as a system for the classification of castes, a purely conceptual system, religiously sanctioned and anchored in ancient legal literature, that has all-India meaning, whereas caste has a close-to-the-ground social reality. As an example, in the Indian state of Rajasthan there is a caste known as Dadhich Brahman. Members of this group marry only among themselves, worship a common caste goddess, and take pride in their caste and the achievements of its members. However, this is not the only Brahman group in Rajasthan, for there are at least five other castes that enjoy varna status as Brahmans. Other regions have their own Brahman castes, such as the Iyer and Iyengar Brahmans of the Deep South. The varna category 'Brahman' thus provides a nominal identity, associated with priestcraft (though not all Brahmans are priests by any means) that transcends regional boundaries, and the other varna categories function in roughly equivalent ways.

The feature of caste that has most attracted the attention of observers is hierarchy, a phenomenon far more prevalent in rural communities than urban settings nowadays. Caste identities carry varying degrees of social honour, which means that castes coexisting in subregional or local communities typically form hierarchies. Rank in such hierarchies is often expressed in terms of the concepts of purity (high status) and pollution (low status). Purity and pollution can be considered ritual concepts because, in part, they have to do with who may or may not come into contact with images of deities or sacred places (such as the interiors of temples). These concepts are socially operationalised in the form of culturally-based judgements about the pollution or purity deemed to be inherent to certain traditional occupations. Thus, the Dalit sweeper, who removes human excrement from homes, is typically at the bottom of local hierarchies, and those who remove dead cows and eat beef are close to the bottom. In contrast, high rank is bestowed on Brahmans because of their association with priestcraft and religious knowledge (whether they are actually religious professionals or not). The concepts of purity and pollution are also socially manifested in certain restrictions contact and interaction between castes of different rank. Commensal restrictions are the most obvious example of this; circumstances vary, but as a general rule higher castes avoid eating with, and especially taking food from, the hands of members of lower castes lest they pollute themselves.

It should be borne in mind, however, that these local hierarchies have an economic and political foundation, with ritual categories being utilised as a means of expressing status that has its roots in relative degrees of local economic and political power. Thus, Brahmans, idealised as 'most pure', have high rank, but where Brahmans lack the economic wherewithal to command real respect, as in much of Rajasthan (the region this author knows best), their ritual superiority counts for less than it does elsewhere.

But how salient were caste groups in real social life? There is every reason to believe that the very high saliency of caste that we see in modern ethnographic literature is, in part, a product of British rule. Concerned as they were to establish a rational system of administration in the areas of India they ruled, the British insisted in fixing the social identities of their subjects. The *Census of India*, instituted in 1872, played a key role in this. As lived, social life does not shape itself into rigid categories, but such categories are precisely what census-takers require if they are to produce an intelligible account, in Western bureaucratic terms, of who is who in the social order. Caste was one of these categories and, by fixing its meaning and elevating its importance as a flag of social identity, the British in effect created caste as a fixed identity linked to the behavioural traits of the groups so identified (on these points, see especially Dirks, 2001). It would certainly be an exaggeration to proclaim that they 'invented' caste, for its foundations were present long before the British appeared on the scene, but caste as understood today is in part a product of British colonial rule.

But what does any of this have to do with religion? Is caste, as the question is sometimes put, 'part' of Hinduism? The answer, of course, is that it is and it is not. One must start with the simple fact that caste-like divisions are seen in other religious communities in South Asia, and this most notably includes Muslims. Moreover, to assert that caste is 'part' of Hinduism carries the hidden premise that there is a bounded entity – 'Hinduism' – of which caste could be, or not be, a 'part'. But all that said, and with the caveat that caste is certainly not purely religious, caste does indeed have important religious dimensions. As we know, the varna system was first described in religious texts and was associated with a divinely ordained division of labour. Furthermore, the traditional occupations of some castes have directly to do with ceremonial roles they take in rituals sponsored by the rich and powerful, with the role of the king sponsoring sacrifices performed by his Brahman priests serving as an ancient model. Moreover, the concepts of purity and pollution in terms of which hierarchy is often understood and expressed are ritual concepts. In addition to all of this, castes typically have their own caste deities. An example is provided by the Dadhich Brahmans just mentioned. Their caste deity is a goddess named Dadhimati, and her principal temple is located in an area of Rajasthan where large numbers of Dadhich Brahmans once lived. This temple serves as a physical epicentre for the caste – now largely dispersed to cities – where caste members come on pilgrimage in connection with certain life-cycle rites.

Religious Reform

As the example of the *Samachar Chandrika* has shown, the nineteenth century was a period of intense reflection on, and reaction to, the colonial experience for Indians, and religion was the arena for some of the most significant thinking on this subject. The social location of this intellectual activity was mostly among modernising elites, for of all the subcontinent's inhabitants they were the most exposed to the social and cultural dislocations resulting from the challenges of Western institutions and culture. These stirrings inevitably gave rise to reform movements, groups of like-minded individuals promoting reshaped versions of religious tradition. To some extent, this can be read as defensive, a reaction to a sense that an effort was needed to vindicate Indian traditions against the charge that they were irrational, filled with 'superstition' and conducive to social injustice, but this was not always so. Notably, whatever their ideology, these movements made highly creative use of print media and Western-style institutional structures and organisational formats as ways of preserving and propagating their messages. The reformist impulse was not confined to the Hindu world, for similar movements arose among non-Hindus as well, and in the remainder of this chapter I look briefly at some of the most consequential of these movements among Hindus, Sikhs and Muslims.

Religious Reform in Bengal

The first of the great Hindu reformers of the British period, often said to be the 'father' of the extraordinary intellectual movement known as the Bengal Renaissance (see Dasgupta, 2011; Kopf, 1979) was a Bengali polymath by the name of Ram Mohan Roy (1772–1833). Born into a well-off Brahman family, he was one of those lucky few who learnt multiple languages with apparent ease. In addition to Bengali, he mastered English, Persian, Arabic and Sanskrit (and Hebrew and Greek later in life). Because of his employment in the EIC's service, he became quite conversant with Western ways and acquired a rationalistic outlook, a reformist bent and a deep respect for Western science.

Although by background a Brahman, he reacted with disdain to what he regarded as irrational elements in Hinduism, but he also rejected Christianity, for he found the Christian belief in Christ's divinity unacceptably irrational. His religious reformism was deeply influenced by his admiration for Unitarianism and its monotheistic ways. In the social sphere, he was a liberal reformer. He was opposed to caste discrimination, child marriage and polygyny and was an implacable and bitter foe of the custom of sati. In fact, his was one of the voices that led to the British abolition of the practice in 1829. As a strong advocate of Western-style education and an admirer of the achievements of Western science, he provided ammunition for Macaulay's 'Minute on Education' (see above).

In 1828, Ram Mohan founded a Hindu reformist organisation at first called the Brahmo Sabha and later known as the Brahmo Samaj ('Spiritual Society'). The society was the first of the great Hindu reform organisations. The form of religion it promoted, strongly influenced by English Unitarianism, was highly intellectualised, devoid of image worship or other rituals, and based on what Ram Mohan took to be a form of monotheism that he found in the Upanishads. Belief in rebirth and *karma* were optional. He argued that, just as Christianity had become corrupted over the centuries by idolatry, saints, miracles, holy water and all the rest, the true Hinduism of the Upanishads had likewise been submerged in superstition and folly. In effect, Brahmoism was a Unitarian version of Vedanta. The society also supported a progressive programme of social reform along the lines of Ram Mohan's own views. After Ram Mohan's death in England, the society entered a period of desuetude. However, members of a prominent and well-off Bengali Brahman family bearing the name Tagore had earlier found their way into Ram Mohan's orbit, and the society was later revived by Debendranath Tagore (1817–1905), who was himself a major figure in liberal Bengali circles. Non-Indian readers are likely to be more familiar with the name of Debendranath's famous son, Rabindranath Tagore (1861–1941), a much celebrated poet, writer and artist and also renowned as a humanist reformer. He was the first non-European to receive (in 1913) the Nobel Prize for Literature.

For the most part, the subsequent history of the Samaj presents an unedifying spectacle of factionalism and secession, but from out of the fray emerged one figure of great importance named Keshab Chandra Sen (1838–1884) (see Stevens, 2018). A non-Brahman belonging to the Vaidya caste (practitioners of traditional medicine) and born into another prominent and wealthy Calcutta family, he was highly Westernised and deeply influenced by Unitarianism. He joined the Brahmo Samaj in 1857 – to the dismay of his highly orthoprax family – and rose rapidly within its ranks. He then embarked upon a career of advancing the Brahmo view of things in publications and lectures both within and beyond the borders of Bengal, including

England where he arrived in 1870. He was an ardent social reformer who opposed caste restrictions, the prohibition of widow remarriage, arranged marriage and child marriage. On the issue of child marriage, however, he apparently (and notoriously) changed his mind when he married off his daughter at the age of fourteen (the groom was fifteen). He was a religious eclectic. He admired Christianity, elements of which he incorporated into his teachings, and at one point in his life he apparently almost converted. He rejected image worship, but later in life his interest in Hindu traditions was revived under the influence of Ramakrishna Paramahamsa (see below).

The Brahmo Samaj was a pioneering venture in the sense that it was the first of the Hindu reform movements of the British period. With its general approbation of Western values and science, the Brahmo Samaj resonated with the outlook, religious and social, of a significant segment of Bengal's Westernising Hindu elite. It also found adherents beyond Bengal. When Bengali professionals sought employment in various other parts of British India, they took the Brahmo Samaj with them and achieved at least some success in attracting followers from among local educated elites. An important instance of this was the formation of a Brahmo Samaj offshoot in Lahore in 1863, but it was not notably successful in Punjab, where there was stiff opposition from conservative Hindus and the Arya Samaj (to be discussed below). The Brahmo Samaj was probably best suited to the Bengal of its birth, where it more easily found a social and cultural niche. Inevitably, the Brahmo Samaj languished and dwindled, and little was left of it but remnants by the early twentieth century. But this was not the end of the story, for a version of Brahmo Samaj lives on in the form of a sect known as Adi Dharm, which has a small following mainly in Punjab and Uttar Pradesh.

Reform Reset

Very different from the cerebral spiritualism of Brahmo Samaj (and the radical iconoclasm of Arya Samaj) was the outlook of Ramakrishna Paramahamsa, a religious figure of enormous charisma and a major factor in the religious history of nineteenth-century Bengal (see Sen, 2010). His extraordinary influence over Bengali intellectuals, the very cultural and social type most receptive to the ideas of Ram Mohan Roy, suggests the emergence of a reaction against what might have seemed to some to be an overly arid and culturally deracinated form of religion. For whatever else one might say about Ramakrishna, his religious life was profoundly shaped by the Bengali culture of his birth and upbringing.

He was born in 1836 into a penurious Brahman family in Hooghly District and given the name Gadadhar The village environment in which he spent his childhood could hardly have been more different from the Calcutta of Ram Mohan Roy and other intellectuals coming from a similar social background. He was never fond of school, and his education was basic, sufficient to give him literacy but little else, but the most important component of his education was not in school at all: it was his contact with a group of Hindu renouncers at a nearby resthouse for pilgrims, where apparently he spent much of his time. In 1852, Ramakrishna shifted to Calcutta, where he assisted his older brother Ramkumar, who at that time was operating a small Sanskrit school. When the school failed, the two brothers relocated to a temple for the goddess Kali at Dakshineshwar on the banks of the Ganga, where Ramkumar became the head priest. As we know, Kali is a fierce and fearsome form of the Great Goddess much venerated in Bengal. After his brother's death in 1856, Ramakrishna succeeded to his position as temple priest.

As a priest, Ramakrishna apparently spent more of his time in spiritual practice than in the performance of ceremonial duties. Kali was at the centre of his meditations and practice. He is said to have experienced trance-like, ecstatic experiences even as a child; these now continued, focused on the goddess whom he sometimes saw in visions. Upset at what they interpreted as symptoms of mental disturbance, his relatives arranged his marriage to a five-year-old girl from a nearby village, a marriage that was never to be consummated (although his wife joined him at the temple years later). (The issue of the nature of Ramakrishna's sexuality has generated extremely contentious debate; see Kripal, 1995; Tyagananda and Vrajaprana, 2010.) After his return to the Kali temple, Ramakrishna's visions and trances continued as before; often frenzied and spectacular, they were evidence to beholders of a kind of divine madness. His spiritual inclinations evolved and matured over time, and he even experimented with Islam and Christianity. In the end, his religious outlook was a universalistic and eclectic mixture of Tantric practice and devotionalism with a focus on worship of the Mother Goddess. The extent to which he was influenced by Advaita Vedanta is contested. He does seem to have adopted an unformalised non-dualism that he did not see as inconsistent with Tantrism, but it is far from clear that he was much taken with such philosophical concerns as logical consistency.

One might have thought that there was little basis for a bridge between the intellectualism of the Brahmo Samaj and the spirituality of someone like Ramakrishna. He was not only a polytheist and image-worshipper, but his polytheism was of the most exuberant sort. Given to intense emotional ties with the deities he worshipped, centrally Kali, and to visions and trances, the religious culture by which he was shaped was arguably the exact opposite of that of the early Bengal reformers. And yet he was a very compelling figure to many from the reformist milieu, and the most striking example of that was his relationship with Keshab Chandra Sen. They met in 1875, and Keshab became a link between Ramakrishna and prominent Brahmo-Samajists as well as the wider world of English-educated Bengalis.

Without a doubt, the most famous and consequential of Ramakrishna's followers was Swami Vivekananda (1863–1902), who was to become a crucial figure in shaping Western perceptions of Hinduism (see Sen, 2000). Vivekananda, whose original name was Narendranath Datta, was born in Calcutta as the son of a prominent lawyer belonging to the Kayastha caste (traditionally scribes and administrators). As was true of so many of his social background in the Calcutta of those days, he had a strong Western education and was deeply influenced by the Brahmo Samaj, to which he belonged as a young man. He apparently came into Ramakrishna's orbit during the early 1880s and began to shift away from his Brahmo outlook to a more traditional view of religion under Ramakrishna's influence. Sceptical at first, he ultimately came to accept the validity of image worship and the authenticity of Ramananda's spiritual experiences. He did not, however, embrace the traditional world-view completely, for he respected the achievements of Western science, admired Western political values, promoted India's economic development and opposed discrimination on the basis of caste.

In the immediate aftermath of Ramakrishna's death of throat cancer in 1886, his close followers, most prominently Vivekananda, created a new monastic community called the Ramakrishna Order to embody and promote the master's teachings. In 1893, Vivekananda famously travelled to America to represent Hinduism at the Parliament of Religions held in Chicago. This was followed later by a lecture tour of almost two years' duration, including trips to Britain, during which he founded (in 1896) the Vedanta Society (originally the Vedantic Society) of New York, which continues its mission today. His message was focused on a version of Vedanta strongly influenced by Shankara's Advaita position, and also on the idea that the 'Spiritual East' had much to teach the more materialistic West. His successes abroad were a cultural morale booster for many in India, for whom seeing Indian tradition admired and treated with respect in the West was a vindication and antidote to some of the humiliation of colonial rule. When Vivekananda returned to India in 1897 with a few Western followers in tow, he received a hero's welcome – although he had orthodox critics as well – and, in that same year, he founded the Ramakrishna Math (monastery) and Mission. Headquartered at Belur in Bengal, the mission became an international organisation dedicated to the propagation of Vedanta and the support of humanitarian causes. Vivekananda visited the West once more from 1899 to 1900, travelling in the US and various other countries. He died at Belur in 1902.

Quite apart from his importance as a key figure in the Bengal Renaissance, Vivekananda is also notable as the first of what ultimately became a succession of Indian spiritual ambassadors to the West. There were to be many similar emissaries in the future, especially to the post-1960s US.

Arya Samaj

Although Ram Mohan Roy and other Bengali reformers tend to play starring roles in discussions of nineteenth-century Indian reform movements, the Arya Samaj (meaning 'Society of Nobles' [*arya*]) had a social and political impact that was certainly very different but arguably at least as deep (see especially Jones, 1976). Its founder was Dayananda Saraswati (1824–1883). He was born to a wealthy and pious Brahman family in a small town in Kathiawar (in Gujarat), and his early years were spent in an atmosphere of religious seriousness and the study of religious texts. It is said that the first stirrings of his scepticism about traditional Hinduism arose because of an experience early in life. It seems that while staying awake the night long on the occasion of Mahashivratri (a Shaiva calendrical rite in which devotees are supposed to remain awake all night) he saw a mouse eating the offerings to Shiva. How, the young Dayananda wondered, could Shiva be such a powerful god if he could not even defend himself against a mouse?

Nonetheless, Dayananda opted for the religious life and left home in 1846 at the age of twenty-two to become a homeless renouncer. After twenty years of wandering about which we know little, he found himself at Mathura, where he became the disciple of a Punjabi renouncer named Swami Vijrajananda Saraswati. From him, Dayananda imbibed the doctrine that true and pure Hinduism was to be found in the Vedas alone, and this became the core idea in Dayananda's own teachings. True Vedic knowledge, he taught, had disappeared because of the subcontinental-level destruction caused by the *Mahabharata* war. A restoration of true Hinduism was possible, but would require the shedding of corrupt beliefs and practices that had accumulated in post-Vedic times. This included a dismissal of the vast bulk of smriti texts because all texts dating from after the *Mahabharata* war were corrupted by the demise of proper Veda study. When at variance with the Veda, all such texts should be repudiated. Rejected also was almost every aspect of day-to-day Hinduism: polytheism (the Vedic pantheon was recast as exhibiting alternative attributes of the same basic god), image worship, puja, pilgrimage, the religious authority of Brahmans, the casting of horoscopes and much more. Dayananda also condemned such traditional social customs as caste discrimination, child marriage and the prohibition of widow remarriage.

Dayananda was much less enamoured of Western values and scientific achievements than Ram Mohan Roy, and his teachings were devoid of the overt favouring of Western values and standards seen in the Brahmo movement in Bengal. Rather, his outlook was retrospective and revitalistic. Society and religion could be reformed, but not by plunging into a Westernising future; what was required was a return to the purity of the Vedic Age. In this idealised Vedic social order, religious authority would be conferred by merit, not by the accident of birth in the Brahman varna. Society would be open to social mobility on the basis of education, which is the path to an understanding of Veda and to leading virtuous and successful life.

These ideas became the doctrinal core of the Arya Samaj, which Dayananda founded in Bombay in 1875. However, the movement was most successful not in western India but in the north and especially Punjab. Owing to Dayananda's strong emphasis on literacy and education, its greatest appeal was to educated elites, especially among the trading castes (the Khatris, Aroras, Agrawals, etc.). To its adherents, it was both 'modern' and 'Hindu', but Hindu in the purest sense, devoid of the irrational supernaturalism and social injustices that had accumulated in post-Vedic times. The movement was firmly rooted when Dayananda died in 1883 in Ajmer, supposedly poisoned while visiting the court of the Maharaja of Jodhpur.

The Arya Samaj came into contact and conflict with the Brahmo Samaj in Punjab, where the Brahmos had established a beachhead. Dayananda had visited Punjab in 1877, and an Arya Samaj centre was then established at Lahore. The religious eclecticism of the Brahmos did not sit well with Dayananda's vision of a purified Hinduism, nor did what the Aryas (members of the Samaj) perceived as the Bengali Brahmos' elitist disdain for Punjabis. By stressing the cultural authenticity of his teachings so forcefully – the accent was always on the idea that Arya doctrine and practice are based on 'our own' Vedas – Dayananda made it possible for his followers to advocate and enact religious and social reforms while escaping, at least to some extent, the distrust and social obloquy that met the reforming efforts of others, such as the Brahmos, who were made to seem culturally uprooted in comparison.

In time, the Arya Samaj developed an austere and de-Brahmanised liturgy to match its back-to-the-Vedas ideology. The puja rite, the paradigmatic form for image worship, was discarded. In its stead, the Samaj dictated the performance of havan, the Vedic fire ritual, which is the main rite performed in Arya Samaj temples to this day. Also, the Samaj undertook to devise substitute versions of certain festivals deemed immoral or indecent. A major instance was the annual saturnalia called Holi; in its place, the Samaj instituted a sober version in which prayers were said, hymns sung and a havan performed.

It is one thing, however, to alter the way individuals or individual families conduct prayers or participate in calendrical rites, but quite another to push ritual reform into areas such as life-cycle ceremonies where ritual intersects with pre-existing social norms and obligations, and this is where the Aryas ran into significant snags. For one thing, these rites are bread-and-butter issues to the Brahman priests who conduct them and who thus have an economic stake in the ritual status quo. Furthermore, life-cycle rites involve cooperation between multiple families or branches of families, with the result that Aryas frequently found themselves in bitter conflict with non-Arya relatives about the conduct of funerals and marriages, to take the two most sensitive examples. For these reasons, steadfastness in Arya belief and practice sometimes led to social ostracism and boycott. The problem was particularly acute with respect to marriage, which meant that Aryas had to choose marriage partners for their children from a considerably narrowed pool of potential spouses. In turn, this required new ways of going about the search for marriage partners, most notably by matrimonial advertisements in newspapers, a practice the Arya Samaj seems to have pioneered.

The Arya Samaj advocated a social reform programme roughly the same as those of other reform movements of the era, but with its own special emphases. As did others, the Arya Samaj supported the remarriage of widows (often married and widowed as children before actually entering married life), and sponsored a number of showcase widow remarriages. They opposed child marriage. They rejected the system of castes (although they advocated a modified, merit-based varna system). They also opposed the seclusion of women in *parda*, promoted women's rights in general and played a vanguard role in supporting women's education. More generally, Aryas have always strongly supported education and created their own educational institutions as an antidote to missionary education, an effort undertaken by the Dayanand Anglo Vedic College Trust and Management Society (DAV for short), formed shortly after Dayananda's death.

But, the most innovative and socially radical of the Samaj's social policies was a programme of reconversion of non-Hindus to the supposed Hinduism of their ancestors. The idea of conversion itself was a novelty, for proselytising was not a part of traditional Hindu practice. The reconversions, which began in 1884, took the form of a ritual of 'purification' (*shuddhi*). The initial targets of reconversion were Muslims and Christians. The number of reconversions was scant, and a major difficulty, apparently unanticipated, was the problem of integrating converts into the caste-based Hindu social order, the converts having no caste location in Hindu society. In time, the reconversion project changed its emphasis from reconversion of Muslims and Christians to the full integration of members of the lowest castes into Hindu society. This effort was motivated by the recognition that these castes were particularly vulnerable to the appeal of Christian missionaries. Beginning in 1903, the Aryas were able to 'purify' over 36,000 members of the Punjabi Megh caste, a low caste whose traditional occupation was weaving.

Another issue of the period with which the Arya Samaj became deeply embroiled – one of lasting importance and truly great consequence that has played a key role in shaping the politics of the subcontinent to the present day – was that of cow protection (*gauraksha*). I return to this subject at the end of this chapter.

Reform among the Sikhs

In response to the challenge of colonial government and Western institutions, reformist trends similar to those already described also affected the Sikhs. The Sikh world had been seriously traumatised by the defeat and annexation of Punjab by the British in 1849, and, in the ruins of the Sikh Empire, Sikhism itself was losing its authority as a religious tradition, and significant numbers of Sikhs were drifting away. A big part of the problem was the proselytising activity of Christian missionaries, who were very active in Punjab and enjoyed imperial support. The mission schools were a major factor in Christian conversions, for English education came as part of a package with Bible classes. The Christians, however, were not the only contenders for Sikh converts, for the Brahmo Samaj also had some appeal to urban Punjabis.

The principal Sikh reaction to these developments was the Singh Sabha ('Sikh Assembly') movement, which originated in the 1870s (and on which see Oberoi, 1994). Created by Sikh intellectuals, the first Singh Sabha was established in Amritsar in 1873, with the purpose of advancing the Sikh community's interests generally. The formation of similar groups became a movement that rapidly took off, and 115 local Singh Sabhas were established between 1880 and 1900, mostly in Punjab. The factors encouraging the success of the movement included the commercialisation of agriculture and the resulting growth of new market towns, increasing levels of education, improved communications and the emergence of a print culture. These several trends favoured the mercantile elites whose aspirations the Singh Sabhas most clearly expressed.

The most dramatic effect of the advent of Singh Sabhas was that it opened the door to a fundamental transformation of the nature of Sikh identity. The original Amritsar Singh Sabha was dominated by the tolerant outlook of those known as Sanatan Sikhs (perhaps best rendered as 'Old-Time Sikhs'), whose stance on Sikhism was relatively inclusive and pluralistic. They tended to see Sikhism as a bundle of related but differing traditions associated with different communities with varying social customs and ritual practices, and they had no problem with a mixture of Sikh and Hindu practices in the religious lives of Sikhs. No central church or religious authority existed within Sikhism, so Sikhs – or at least Sikhs in the Sanatan tradition – gave little thought to issues of religious boundaries.

But from within the Singh Sabha movement, a very different view of the nature of Sikhism soon emerged. The promoters of this alternative vision were known as the Tat Khalsa ('True Khalsa'). Theirs was a puritanical and monolithic version of Sikhism, and they were bitterly opposed to what they saw as the contamination of Sikh life by the rituals and 'superstitions' of ordinary Hinduism. The contaminations included such practices as the worship of images, the veneration of village gods and goddesses, and pilgrimage to the tombs of Muslim saints. These practices were, in fact, quite widespread among the Sikhs of the day. The Tat Khalsa people were particularly outraged at the presence of images of Hindu deities in Sikh shrines, including the Golden Temple at Amritsar. Their concern over these ritual issues led to a general takeover of the management of Sikh shrines and temples by the Tat Khalsa.

Another major issue was the external symbols of Sikh identity. In practice, this led to a Tat Khalsa-approved dress code for Sikhs (for example, the *dhoti* was barred for men) and an insistence on distinctive Sikh rites of passage. The Tat Khalsa attached particular importance to the initiation ceremony. In the past, there had evolved various rites of initiation for Sikhs, and only one of these required upholding the Five Ks afterwards. The Tat Khalsa insisted that this latter rite alone was canonical for Sikhs, thus – in effect – making the upholding of the Five Ks definitive of Sikh identity for men. The Tat Khalsa also insisted that Punjabi be written in the Gurmukhi script as the distinctive language of the Sikh community.

Certain policies of the colonial government favoured the Tat Khalsa's recasting of Sikh identity. Beginning in the late nineteenth century, large numbers of Sikhs entered military service under the British and were warmly received because of their reputation as soldiers and because Sikh forces had kept faith with the British during the 1857 uprising. They were, however, integrated into the British army *as Sikhs*; recruits were not only made to undergo initiation but were also required to maintain the external symbols of Khalsa membership. The martial imagery of the Sikh soldier fitted seamlessly with similar Tat Khalsa views, and when soldiers returned to their villages they brought it with them. The result was propagation and reinforcement of Tat Khalsa creed. Government census-taking also played a role, compelling respondents to identify themselves as Sikh, Hindu or Muslim.

The story of the emergence of a new kind of Sikh identity is also entwined with the history of the Arya Samaj. Dayananda himself saw the Sikhs as simply another Hindu sect, and in his view Nanak had nothing of value to say because he knew nothing of the Vedas. As he saw it, if the Sikhs did not worship images of deities, their worship of the *Guru Granth Sahib* came to the same thing. But Dayananda notwithstanding, in the Arya Samaj's early days most of the Ayras of Punjab saw Sikhism as a movement that shared their desire to purify Hinduism. As a result, some Sikhs were able to become enthusiastic members of the Arya Samaj without feeling any particular strain. By the mid-1880s, however, the Aryas began to criticise Sikhism as having departed from the teachings of Nanak, as seen particularly in their worship of the *Guru Granth Sahib* and their apparent deification of Nanak himself. In time, these issues, and especially the criticism of Sikhism in Arya publications, brought Sikhs and militant Aryas into enmity.

In this situation, particularly during the 1890s, educated Sikhs found themselves in a dilemma. The Arya Samaj had lost its appeal, but what, then, was to be their place in a newly emerging Sikh world with its own unpalatable Tat Khalsa orthodoxies? And looming over all of this was the epochal question of whether Sikhism was 'part' of Hinduism or a separate religious community, an issue that generated fierce debates within the Sikh world during the closing years of the century. But by the early twentieth century, Sikhism was assuming a new form, and it is arguable that no religious community was more transformed by the cultural and social dislocations of the nineteenth century than the Sikhs. By means of their schools, their publications and their local associations, the Tat Khalsa had injected their concept of what it meant to be Sikh into the very culture of the Sikh community. The result was a situation in which Sikhs had come to understand themselves as a distinct group (as visualised by the Tat Khalsa) and to be so understood by others.

Aligarh, Deoband and Islamic Reform

There were two major late nineteenth-century reform movements among South Asian Muslims – the Deoband movement and the Aligarh movement – and both were educational projects. The Aligarh movement, originating in the city of Aligarh, was the creation of the strongly pro-British Sir Syed Ahmad Khan (1817–1898) who, in the aftermath of the 1857 rebellion, wished to repair Anglo-Indo relations. To this end, he promoted Western education for Muslims, hoping to prepare greater numbers of educated Muslims for recruitment into government service. In 1875, he established the Mohammedan Anglo-Oriental College, which was the movement's epicentre and subsequently became the highly acclaimed Aligarh Muslim University. He is most remembered, however, for his invention of the 'two-nation theory' of Hindu–Muslim relations, a concept that ultimately became rationale for the creation of Pakistan.

The Aligarh movement gave powerful impetus to the Westernisation of Indian Muslim elites, but from a religious standpoint the Deoband movement's importance was greater. When encountering the word Deoband, many readers will immediately think of Islamic militancy because certain militant groups in Pakistan and Afghanistan (including the Taliban) are linked to the Deobandis. Such groups are, however, not central to what the movement once was and is today.

It originated as an educational venture created in the 1860s by 'ulama ('Islamic religious scholars') in the aftermath of the 1857 uprising. (On the history of the movement, see Metcalf, 1982.) The basic idea was that the traditional Islamic learning would be transmitted by means of schools organised on a Western model but not supported by, or in any way linked to, the colonial government. These schools would have a fixed curriculum, library, classroom-style teaching, lectures, exams, admission by examination and so on. This, in fact, was a type of education that many of the Deoband founders had experienced themselves, though not in an Islamic setting or turned to Islamic purposes. Education along these new lines was a radical departure from the Islamic pedagogy of the past, in which instruction was usually undertaken by family members at home or in a mosque; in fact, the extraction of education from the familial setting was, in context, one of its most novel features.

The overall purpose of the project was the creation a new scholarly class whose influence in society – as teachers, preachers, writers, etc. – would aid in the preservation of Muslim culture and piety, perceived as being challenged by Christianity and Western culture. Although the curriculum would be devoid of

Western science or language, this was not a dogmatic proscription but a pragmatic measure designed to avoid duplication with government schools. In the event, however, it seems that few students studied secular subjects after leaving Deobandi schools.

The first school was established in 1867 at the town of Deoband, located some 93 miles north of Delhi in Saharanpur District. The town was a logical choice because it was a regional centre of Islamic culture, and some of its leading lights had been involved in previous reform efforts. In time, a network of loosely affiliated schools evolved, often drawing faculty directly from Deoband itself. At the heart of the curriculum was a reformist version of Islam taught both as a mode of thinking and a way of life. Its foundation was Islam of the Sunni branch and the Hanifi School of Islamic jurisprudence. The reformism of the Deobandis was aimed at purifying Islam of what they viewed as un-Islamic historical accretions. Although they strongly supported Sufism, the Sufism they favoured was detached from the centuries-old traditions of veneration of saints and pilgrimage to their tombs. They were particularly harsh critics of the Shi'a

Not only was the school's manner of instruction new, but it also drew upon novel means of support. In the past, scholar-teachers would have been supported by their own endowments and by the princely courts they served. But princely largesse had become ever-more problematic in post-Mughal India, so these new schools would depend, instead, on public donations provided by networks of donors, mostly on the basis of annual pledges.

Among the most consequential of the Deobandi innovations was the employment of Urdu instead of Persian as the language of instruction. Urdu is the same basic language as Hindi, but Urdu makes extensive use of Persian vocabulary and is written in the Indo-Persian script whereas Hindi draws more vocabulary from Sanskrit and employs the Devanagari script in which Sanskrit is written. Although Persian had hitherto been the language of government and high Islamic culture at the time the Deoband movement was taking shape, Urdu had played the role of a lingua franca in northern India and was widely known and used by educated people of the period. The students of Deoband were a cosmopolitan mix, speaking a wide variety of languages and dialects, but acquiring fluency in Urdu was the foundation of success in the Deobandi curriculum. These students then took Urdu with them to their places of origin in various parts of India and beyond, with the result that Urdu ultimately became a crucial medium of communication among the subcontinent's Muslims and an important factor in the emergence of a sense of trans-regional Islamic community in South Asia. The Deobandis were also highly proficient at using print technology as a proselytising medium, and the language they used was Urdu. Their publications included both translated religious texts and religious literature of their own.

The rapid spread of Deobandi schools was a measure of its enormous success. The ties that bound the schools together were less institutional than personal, for they were usually staffed by Deoband graduates. By 1880, there were a dozen or so schools, concentrated in what is today north-western Uttar Pradesh (but with one school in far-off Lucknow), and the growth continued in subsequent years; by the turn of the century, there were perhaps three times that many, and by the 1960s there were nearly 9,000 Deobandi schools in the subcontinent. These schools had a powerful impact on South Asian Islam. Despite the diverse ethnic backgrounds from which they came, Deobandi students left school carrying a common language and a shared sense of educational mission and purpose, and they took a similar Islamic religious subculture with them to every region of the subcontinent. This was surely one of the most successful educational reforms ever undertaken.

Although one might have thought that the creation of Pakistan would have been a project of the most religiously committed Muslims, the Deobandis and the 'ulama generally opposed it. They viewed the idea of a territorial Muslim state as a contravention of the Islamic tenet of universalism. It was, rather, the Western-educated Aligarh types who, inspired by the two-nation vision of Sir Syed Ahmad Khan and flying the flag of religion, pushed for a Pakistan. Still, the Deobandis' efforts contributed to a sense of shared community among the subcontinent's Muslims that was, if not a prerequisite, at least an element in the success of the Pakistan movement. I return to this topic in the next chapter.

Hindu Reaction: Cow Protection

The cow-protection movement was one of the most significant developments in the public culture of India in the late nineteenth and early twentieth centuries. Although the belief that the sacredness of the cow (and other bovines, though most importantly the cow) is both ancient and a pillar of Hinduism is simply taken for granted by many, it is actually quite problematic. Some, particularly Hindu nationalists, insist that beef-eating came to the subcontinent only with the Muslims. However, more exacting historical analysis (Jha, 2002) has shown that beef was indeed eaten in Vedic times. And as for the claim that eschewing beef is a pillar of Hinduism, many members of the lowest castes in Hindu society eat beef today, especially in the south, and they are certainly 'Hindus'. However, these observations are perhaps beside the point, for the fact remains that cows have indeed been venerated by Hindus in recent centuries, and even non-vegetarian Hindus of middle-ranking and upper castes do not eat beef. And leaving aside the fact that some low-caste Hindus eat beef, the fact that *Muslims do so* means that the claim of the cow's sacredness has the potential to be politically incendiary.

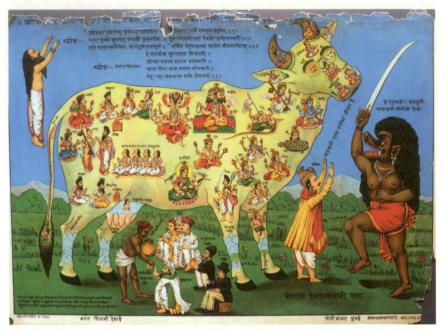

5.1 Kamadhenu: the cow as eighty-four deities, a 1912 depiction by famed artist Ravi Varma. The cow is being attacked by a demonic embodiment of the meat-eaters of the kaliyuga while 'Dharmraj' (Lord of Dharma) tries to protect her; 'Don't kill the cow who is everyone's life', he says. Her role as life-giver is dramatized by the portrayal of members of various communities being given her milk. From the private collection of Christopher Pinney, with thanks

But what do we mean by 'sacred' as the word pertains to the cow in Hindu India? There are two interrelated aspects to this question. First and foremost, the cow is an earthly embodiment of divinity. She is sometimes imaged as an embodiment of the goddess Lakshmi. As readers will recall, Lakshmi is Vishnu's consort and the goddess of wealth and abundance. She is more generally regarded as a cow-goddess named Kamadhenu (also Surabhi), the cow who grants all wishes. Each part of her is associated with a particular deity, and she, therefore, contains the Hindu pantheon within herself. In her persona as a goddess, the cow can be worshipped in the same way as an image of a deity might be. And more, given her divinity, the cow is not only ritually pure herself but also possesses the divine power to purify. Consumption of a mixture of five products of the cow – milk, dung, urine, clarified butter and curds – cleanses the consumer of internal ritual pollution, and doing so is part of a standard Brahmanical rite of absolution.

Because of the cow's embodiment of divinity, killing a cow is a major sin. The prohibition of beef-eating obviously follows from this, because to eat beef is to participate, at whatever remove, or even indirectly, in an act of deicide. Because Muslims are frequently butchers who deal in beef, and because Muslims of whatever profession eat beef and sometimes kill cattle in ritual, they are seen by many Hindus

– by no means all – as permanently stained by this sin. Along the same lines, anything else having to do with the death of cows is, by association with deicide, inauspicious or insalubrious, and this sense of things is socially expressed in the idiom of ritual pollution. As noted earlier in this chapter, ritual pollution is one of the marks (not the only one) of low status in the caste hierarchy. The handling of a cow's carcass or working in leather is seen as extremely polluting in many areas of India, and are the occupational specialties of the very lowest castes.

The other aspect of the cow's sacredness relates to her gender. As a goddess, the cow is a divine mother figure, a goddess who is seen as a giver and sustainer of life. At the centre of this symbolism is the cow as giver of milk. In South Asia, milk is generally viewed as the most nutritious and wholesome of all forms of nourishment, as are its derivatives – curds and ghi (clarified butter) in particular – and milk and milk products are used extensively in Hindu ritual. The saliency of the maternal symbolism of the cow – giver of milk, giver of life – is evidenced by the fact that, when queried about the taboo on eating beef, Hindus sometimes respond by asking if the questioner would be willing eat his or her own mother. Eating beef, therefore, not only participates in deicide but is also a form of matricide.

If, then, the ancient Vedic peoples ate beef, to point this out really has no bearing on the reality of the cow's sacredness to Hindus. And it is no help at all when it comes to understanding the role of the cow in the religious history of nineteenth-century India, for at this point the sacredness of the cow was a long-established fact of religion and culture for most Hindus. Also, because of the maternal symbolism inherent in Hindu cow-veneration, the treatment of cows was an issue capable of mobilising strong emotions based in the earliest experiences of childhood. Given the patriarchal nature of the Indian cultural context, the cow was easily imaged as a female body in need of protection by males. And this imagery readily lent itself to projection on to a larger social screen in which the bovine embodiment of the female vulnerability of mothers, sisters, daughters and indeed of 'Mother India' – the cow – was in need of protection by Hindu men, whose manhood was thereby on the line (Van der Veer, 1994, pp. 86–94). Thus, the inevitability of the cow as a flashpoint in Hindu–Muslim relations.

The cow-protection movement began in Punjab in the 1860s and was apparently initially mostly aimed at the beef-eating British (see Metcalf and Metcalf, 2012, pp. 151–3). But cow-protection agitation rapidly spread widely in British India, and by the 1880s was being promoted by numerous local cow-protection societies. The Arya Samaj soon became deeply involved. Although Dayananda himself was a passionate advocate of both vegetarianism and cow protection (the issues are not the same but are linked), the Arya Samaj initially took no position on either. However, Dayananda was one of the founders of the Gauraksha Sabha ('Society for Cow Protection'), and wrote a tract on the subject called *Gokarunanidhi* ('*Treasury of Cow-Compassion*') that was published in 1881. A faction of Aryas followed his lead into the vegetarian and cow-protection causes, which were then taken up by Arya Samaj publications as well, and in the end some Aryas became active proselytisers of cow protection among Hindus. As a result, it became impossible for the Arya Samaj to avoid the question of its official stance, which led to a serious split within the organisation between vegetarian and non-vegetarian branches. Ultimately, cow-protecting Aryas became one of the principal vectors for the spread of the cow-protection movement in nineteenth-century northern India. Dayananda himself encouraged Hindus to petition the colonial government to prohibit the slaughter of cows, and cow-protection societies staged marches and demonstrations in furtherance of this cause.

A major factor in the movement's spread was the fact that it matched the aspirations of the socially upwardly mobile seeking to emulate higher-caste culture. Another was that it provided a way for reformers to demonstrate their cultural bona fides in response to the criticisms of the orthodox. But, above all, it also provided a riposte to stereotypes of Hindu fecklessness and passivity; here were Hindus showing strength and courage in defence of their 'mother'.

The movement was not overtly anti-Muslim at first, but, by the 1890s, it had turned in the direction of lawsuits and violent agitations aimed mostly at Muslims, who butchered bovines, ate beef and sometimes sacrificed cows on such occasions as Eid al-Adha. A crucial point had been reached in 1888 when the North-Western Provincial High Court of Allahabad declared that the cow was not a 'sacred object' and, therefore, the killing of cows could not be held to be a religious affront to the Hindus. This decision obliged the British colonial government to protect Muslim butchers and ritual sacrificers of cows, with the result that colonial government found itself – of all things! – entangled in the issue of the sacredness of the cow. On the basis of the false belief that the court had ruled otherwise and that the government was failing to meet its alleged legal obligation to protect cows, Hindu–Muslim riots broke out in northern and western India in 1893. These riots took the lives of more than 100 people in these regions.

The geographic scope of the cow-protection riots demonstrates the power of new communications media, specifically the press and telegraph, in making mass movements possible. Because of its social and trans-regional spread, cow protection became a cause and a shared activity that shaped emerging ideas of nationhood, at least for some. The whole matter was exacerbated when the Muslims pushed back in the legal battles, which they were bound to do when the issue touched upon such symbolic issues as the right to sacrifice cows on Eid-al-Adha. Their pushback had the effect of further keeping these issues in the public eye. Also crucial was the fact that the cow-slaughter issue was far from a mere concern of religious or political elites, for it had the potential to mobilise the entire Hindu population of villages and other communities.

Cow-protection sentiment and agitations put the focus, for some, on the image of a national community defined by inclusions and exclusions. Hindus were included, as were Sikhs and Jains, but there was no room in such a vision for Muslims or Christians. It is hard to say what proportion of the Hindu population was swept up in the cow-protection movement, and the exclusionary view of national identity it fostered was certainly not then shared by all Hindus, nor is it now, nor will it ever be. Furthermore, the cow-protection movement was not the only factor encouraging the exclusionary view. Still, it was a major catalyst, and the sentiments awakened by the movement proved extraordinarily durable and persist to this day. In the near-term of the late nineteenth and early twentieth century, cow protection had an important impact on the development of the independence movement. While the uproars of the late nineteenth century ultimately subsided, cow protection was not forgotten and had the unfortunate legacy of inspiring suspicion among some Muslim leaders of the motives of some elements in the leadership of Indian National Congress.

6

Birth of a Secular State

Not even the remotest understanding of subcontinental politics today – national or international – can be had without taking the religious factor into account, nor can any comprehensive account of the state of South Asian religions today make much sense without considering the political factor. This is because religion is deeply intertwined with issues of group identity: social, political, national. The implications of this fact are two. Shared religious symbolism brings people together and gives rise to feelings of belongingness. But by virtue of this very fact, such symbols all too often also generate a sense of exclusion and otherness, and therein lie the seeds of distrust, fear and conflict. In this context, the distinctive systems of belief and practice described in previous chapters are reduced to social condensates, flaglike markers of social inclusion and exclusion.

This chapter traces the effects of the social and political two-sidedness of religious symbolism on the independence movement and on the religious politics of the Republic of India when newly created. Religion and religious difference were ubiquitous themes in the independence struggle. The Republic of India was created as a secular state, but Indian secularism has turned out to be significantly different from secularism as generally understood in the US and Western Europe, and it harbours awkward and potentially dangerous internal contradictions.

I begin with the independence movement when much of the groundwork for the best and worst of what came later was laid.

Independence

The Indian National Congress

The organisation that was most responsible for guiding India to independence was the Indian National Congress. It was not founded by an Indian but by a Briton named Allen Octavian Hume (1829–1912), a retired civil servant in the colonial government. His purpose was to create an organisation that could represent the interests of the English-educated elite in their relationship with the colonial government and seek ways of creating a more extensive role for members of this class in government. The first meeting took place in Bombay in 1885, and the fact that it took place so far away from Calcutta, still the imperial capital, attests to the fact that the class whose interests it served was indeed a national elite, despite the preponderance of upper-caste Hindus from the coastal cities in its membership. Although distinguished Muslims were invited to the gathering, few Muslims came; many, it appears, took the position that Muslims and Hindus, as two separate communities, could not be represented by a single organisation. From the start, however, the Congress was dedicated to the idea of an Indian national identity that transcended ties of religion, caste and region.

In this initial stage, the Congress was hardly a radical organisation; if anything, it most resembled a gentlemen's club, and its transformation into the mass movement it later became was decades away. Its birth was accompanied by declarations of loyalty to Queen Victoria. It did not pursue independence and was instead focused on the class interests of its membership, who sought increased representation in local governing councils and in the administration of British India. A major issue was access to membership in the Indian Civil Service. Recruitment was by a competitive examination held only in Britain, which meant that it was difficult for Indians to compete. The Congress advocated simultaneous exams in India and Britain. For the first two decades of its existence, the Congress was largely unengaged with issues of social reform, and its aspirations and programmes thus had little or no relevance to the overwhelming majority of the subcontinent's population.

But in the waning years of the nineteenth century, a fissure developed within the Congress that presaged the later trajectory of the independence movement. The split was between 'moderates' and a more radical faction from Bombay and Poona (now Pune) who associated themselves with the Maratha heritage of Shivaji. The latter, as readers will recall, resisted Mughal rule and on that account could serve as a symbol of militant resistance to the British colonial regime. The radical faction also utilised religion as a focus for patriotic sentiment by politicising the celebration of a festival of special importance in the Marathi-speaking region associated with the Hindu deity Ganesha. Quite obviously, the exaltation of a Hindu anti-Mughal rebel and the use of Hindu religious symbolism could hardly pass unnoticed by Muslims. Nor, in some Muslim eyes, was this to be the last ominous development in the evolution of the Congress movement.

But, in the meantime, social and political forces of great strength were being mobilised by events, and of these the most important was the partition of Bengal. At the turn of the century the province of Bengal was quite large, and in the interest of more efficient governance (at least ostensibly) the British viceroy, Lord Curzon (1859–1925), partitioned the province into eastern and western entities in 1905. The principal effect of the partition was to separate the Muslim majority east from the Hindu-majority west. An additional complication was that Orissa (now Odisha) and Bihar were added to the western section, which meant that Bengalis suddenly became an ethnic minority in the new western province. Whatever the merits of the administrative argument in its favour, and this is highly contestable, the partition of Bengal was a calamitous mistake. The immediate response to the partition was itself divided along religious lines, an ominous development and a harbinger of many troubles to come. The Muslims in the east were well enough satisfied with their new majority status (although they apparently did not support the partition at first). Less pleased were the aggrieved Bengali Hindus of the west, who now found their home region cut asunder and themselves reduced to minority status within it.

The partition gave rise to a furious anti-British political upheaval that soon spread to other areas of India. The Congress strongly opposed the partition, and the issue arguably rescued the Congress from desuetude. The most important manifestation of the anger was an India-wide campaign called *swadeshi*. This term means 'of one's own country', and the focus of the campaign was the boycott of British imports and a turn to Indian-made products instead. Not only would this hurt the British, most notably the Manchester-based textile industry, but it would also encourage the development of Indian national self-sufficiency. Inevitably, however, the swadeshi movement exploded in new directions. Movement leaders called for total boycott of British institutions and a refusal to pay taxes, which led to brutal repression and the arrest and deportation to Burma of two movement leaders. This was also a period in which terrorism and assassination began to emerge as tactics of resistance.

Religious difference was a highly visible feature of the turmoil from the beginning. This was perhaps inevitable, because the movement leadership was largely drawn from English-educated classes, and in Bengal – the starting point from which the conflagration spread to other areas of British India – the English-educated were mostly Hindu in contrast to the largely Muslim rural populations of the eastern section. Moreover, there was a strong element of Bengali chauvinism among the Hindus that drew its energy from religious symbolism. A widely read Bengali novel of the day was Bankim Chandra Chattopadhyay's *Anandamath* ('*Monastery of Bliss*'), first published in 1882. The author imagines a fraternity of religious renouncers in an eighteenth-century setting who engaged in violent resistance against the British. To them, Bengal (which becomes a stand-in for India) is the Mother Goddess, a goddess who is worshipped and defended by her renouncer sons. The novel's religious imagery proved to be a powerful source of inspiration for the struggle against British rule, and a song from the novel (*Bande Mataram*, set to music by none other than Rabindranath Tagore) was taken up by the nationalist movement as a musical rallying call. The song is actually a prayer that begins with 'Mother, I bow to thee!' and invokes the goddess as Durga, Lakshmi and the land itself. As Durga, she is sword-wielding, as are her defenders, whose 'swords flash out in twice seventy million hands'. The song was not necessarily an incitement to violence, but when coupled with the image of martial Durga it does seem to have served as an inspiration to terrorists. Here follows the *c.*1908 English translation by Shri Aurobindo:

Mother, I bow to thee!
Rich with thy hurrying streams,
Bright with thy orchard gleams,
Cool with thy winds of delight,
Dark fields waving, Mother of might,
Mother free.
Glory of moonlight dreams
Over thy branches and lordly streams, –
Clad in thy blossoming trees,
Mother, giver of ease,
Laughing low and sweet!
Mother, I kiss thy feet,
Speaker sweet and low!
Mother, to thee I bow.

Who hath said thou art weak in thy lands,
When the swords flash out in twice seventy million hands
And seventy million voices roar
Thy dreadful name from shore to shore?
With many strengths who art mighty and stored,
To thee I call, Mother and Lord!
Thou who savest, arise and save!
To her I cry who ever her foemen drave
Back from plain and sea
And shook herself free.

Thou art wisdom, thou art law,
Thou our heart, our soul, our breath,
Thou the love divine, the awe
In our hearts that conquers death.
Thine the strength that nerves the arm,
Thine the beauty, thine the charm.
Every image made divine
In our temples is but thine.

Thou art Durga, Lady and Queen,
With her hands that strike and her swords of sheen,
Thou art Lakshmi lotus-throned,
And the Muse a hundred-toned.
Pure and perfect without peer,
Mother, lend thine ear.

> Rich with thy hurrying streams,
> Bright with thy orchard gleams,
> Dark of hue, O candid-fair
> In thy soul, with jewelled hair
> And thy glorious smile divine,
> Loveliest of all earthly lands,
> Showering wealth from well-stored hands!
> Mother, mother mine!
> Mother sweet, I bow to thee,
> Mother great and free! (Aurobindo, c.1908)

The actual partition of Bengal was not to last long and was annulled in 1911. At that point, Lord Curzon had long been out of the picture, for he had resigned in the same year as the partition (for reasons unrelated to the partition uproar). His successor, Lord Minto, reacted to the partition-related disorders with repressive measures, but this was done against the background of promises of reform. The reform came in 1909, and mainly took the form of an enlargement of the legislative councils attached to the provincial governments and increased level of Indian participation in these bodies. These councils, which had been established in the early 1890s, were not true legislatures, having no control over the executive branch, but served as consultative assemblies. In addition to certain modest enhancements of their powers, they were now to be enlarged, allowing more Indians to serve, and those who served would have to be elected, albeit by indirect election.

The truly crucial innovation, however, was the establishment of separate electorates for Muslims. To understand the significance of this, we have to turn to the Muslim reaction to the partition and its aftermath. Coming, as it did, not long after the rise of the cow-protection movement, and considering the blatantly Hindu symbolism employed by many nationalist agitators, we cannot be surprised that many among the Muslim leadership were becoming nervous. This resulted in an important development in 1906; indeed, it might well be argued that this was the year of Pakistan's birth. Meeting in Dacca (now Dhaka) in December of that year, the Muhammadan Educational Conference, the core organisation of the Aligarh movement, voted to form an All-India Muslim League to represent the interests of the Muslims as a distinct community. The originators were hardly representative of the Muslim population as a whole; for the most part, they were a small, Western-educated gentry. But then and later, the Muslim League considered itself to represent all the subcontinent's Muslims.

Fearing Muslim exclusion from the legislative councils, the Muslim League looked with disfavour on the 1909 reforms while they were still in gestation, but they changed their minds when it emerged that the Muslims would have reserved seats with separate electorates. Whether this step was motivated by a divide-and-rule philosophy of governance is disputed, but it certainly had divisive implications, based as it was on the presumption that Muslims as a community had interests separate from those of the rest of the subcontinent's inhabitants and that these interests could be defended only by other Muslims. The issue was not the reserved seats for Muslims; it was the separate electorates. The problem is simple. If a reserved seat for Muslims is coupled with a mixed electorate, a candidate is likely to be pulled in the direction of moderation in deference to the wishes of all or most of his or her constituents. If, however, the electorate is Muslim-only, then the temptation will be strong for a candidate to stress the interests of the Muslim community alone.

Saintly Politics and the Run-Up to Independence

In 1915 and in the shadow of the First World War – in which Britain was supported by both the Congress and the Muslim League – a middle-aged lawyer named Mohandas Karamchand Gandhi (1869–1948) returned to India after a long sojourn abroad. Later acquiring the sobriquet Mahatma ('Great Soul/Spirit'), his presence was to exert a decisive influence on the political culture of the independence movement.

Gandhi was born in the town and princely state of Porbandar (Gujarat) to a family belonging to a Gujarati trading caste (Modh Baniya). His parents were Hindu. His mother belonged to Krishnaite sect (also strongly influenced by Islam) known as Pranami, but she was also very sympathetic to Jainism, which is a major strand in the religious culture of Gujarat. Young Gandhi was, therefore, exposed to both Vaishnava and Jain influences, and both traditions put great stress on the ethic of non-violence, a circumstance that was reflected in his deep commitment to non-violence in his later political career. Jain influence might also have had something to do with the important role fasting was to play in his later life, both as a spiritual practice and as a means of persuasion or moral coercion in his dealings with others. His education was adequate but unremarkable, and he was married at the age of thirteen (his bride was fourteen).

Having decided to become a lawyer, Gandhi shipped off to London at the age of eighteen to study for the bar. There, in what seems to have been a minor eruption of youthful identity experimentation, he took up Western gentlemen's clothing and dancing lessons, but quickly discovered the fruitlessness of this endeavour – he was what he was, and that was certainly not an English gentleman. In the end, his vegetarianism was his route to the social niche he found in London, which was that of spiritual seekers and non-conformist diet faddists. At the age of twenty-two, he was called to the bar, returned to India and embarked upon what he hoped would be the career of a Bombay barrister. But such was his shyness and lack of confidence that the need to cross-examine witnesses left him frozen and speechless. Defeated, he retreated to Gujarat where he prepared documents for lawyers more successful than he.

So matters stood when, in 1893, a well-off Muslim businessman in South Africa invited twenty-three-year-old Gandhi to become his lawyer. Gandhi accepted, and so began the crucial period in which the Gandhi the world knows, the Mahatma and leader of India's independence movement, was formed. The main cause of this transformation was his experience of discrimination and humiliation in South Africa because of his origins and colour. This seems to have unleashed a self-confidence in him that had lain quiescent for all his previous life. In consequence, after finishing the legal work he had been brought to do, Gandhi decided to stay in South Africa to help the Indians there in their fight for social and political justice.

It was in South Africa that Gandhi fashioned and honed the political tactic that made him famous. It was called *satyagraha* (grasping or holding on to truth, often rendered as 'truth force'), and was a tactic of non-violent resistance and conflict resolution designed to persuade opponents of the justice of one's cause. It was based on a practitioner's willingness to suffer pain and mistreatment without violent retaliation, thereby putting the oppressors in a situation in which they are compelled to recognise the injustice in which they are complicit. Ideally, the aim of the technique is not the total capitulation of the oppressor but a meeting of minds resulting in a resolution satisfactory to both. Needless to say, if undertaken in situations in which the oppressor possesses the means of inflicting violence and the will to do so, this is not, as it is sometimes alleged to be, a tactic for cowards.

It was also during his South African period that Gandhi began to exhibit the characteristics of a world renouncer, a trait that later became a key ingredient in his political persona and style of political action (dubbed 'saintly politics' by W. H. Morris-Jones [1964], although not in direct reference to Gandhi). In the background of Hindu religious culture, most notably in the Tantric tradition, is a physiological theory connecting control of sexuality with physical strength, well-being and spiritual growth. The basic idea is that vital energies in the body are dissipated and wasted in sexual intercourse but they can be channelled into personal power (spiritual and physical) if held in check. Whether directly influenced by these ideas or not (on which see Rudolph and Rudolph, 1967), Gandhi extolled both the health and spiritual benefits of sexual abstinence, and took a vow of chastity at the age of thirty-eight, in 1906. But sexuality was not the sole venue of his pursuit of self-control. The control of diet was also extremely important to him, as was the pursuit of an overall lifestyle of simplicity and self-denial.

To explore and promote the practical side of his evolving system of spiritual development, Gandhi established two utopian communities during his South Africa years. One was founded in 1904 near Durban and was called the Phoenix Settlement; the other, established in 1910 near Johannesburg, was called Tolstoy

Farm. Both were somewhat like Hindu ashrams (in this context meaning 'spiritual retreats'), especially Tolstoy Farm, and they were early prototypes of two ashrams that Gandhi would later establish in India.

Even before his return to India from South Africa, Gandhi had given much thought to the issues being engaged by the independence movement, but he did so in a manner consistent with his evolving spiritual ideals. In a famous essay published in 1909 ('Hind Swaraj') he analysed the real significance of the term *swaraj* (literally 'self-rule'). True self-rule would necessarily be more than a simple matter of independence from British rule. Indians would have to master themselves – the real meaning of 'self-rule' – which would enable an independent India to be a decent and just social order. The resulting society would be simple in structure and based on mutual trust and esteem between rulers and ruled, and would resemble the rule of Rama as depicted in the *Ramayana*. Given the near ubiquity of the Rama cult in India generally, and the embeddedness of the *Ramcharitmanas* in popular religious culture of the north and other versions of the *Ramayana* elsewhere, this was imagery profoundly meaningful to Hindus. It was also, however, a symbolism with which Muslims could hardly feel comfortable.

At the invitation of Gopal Krishna Gokhale (1866–1915), a major figure in the Congress, Gandhi returned to India in 1915. Gone was the shy aspiring barrister of his earlier years; he was now a substantial figure with a formidable reputation as a political organiser. He was a supporter of the British war effort and a moderate in the arena of political protest, and the first years after his return were spent in experimentation with satyagraha. However, the infamous and unconscionable 1919 British firing at a helpless festival crowd at Jallianwala Bagh in Amritsar, killing over 350 people and wounding many more, changed his mind. From this point forward, what faith he had in British justice was gone, and he now moved into the leadership of the Congress movement, becoming its dominant figure and the principal architect of India's quest for independence.

At the time of Gandhi's return, relations between the Congress and the Muslim League were quite good. They had actually had their annual meeting jointly in 1915 and 1916, and in the latter year they entered into a far-reaching political agreement called the Lucknow Pact (after the city in which they met that year). Among other things, the pact supported separate electorates for Muslims together with certain other electoral boosts. Among the negotiators on the League side was a Muslim lawyer from Bombay named Muhammad Ali Jinnah (1876–1948), who was active in the Muslim League and ultimately became one of the key players in the final drama of Indian independence. It was he, in fact, who was to become the principal strategist in the creation of Pakistan.

Not long after Gandhi's arrival, there arose a matter of considerable import for the future religious map of the subcontinent. A major issue for Muslims in the post-war period was that of the 'caliphate' (*khilafat*). The supreme leadership of the worldwide Muslim community was, at this point in history, held by the Ottoman sultans, and Turkey had sided with Germany in the war. Some Indian Muslims had objected to the use of Muslim soldiers against the Turks, and in response the British promised that they would respect the caliphate. After the war, caliphate supporters began active measures to pressure the British to honour their promise, and Gandhi and the Congress supported the caliphate movement. This period is sometimes looked back upon as an era of Hindu/Muslim comity that, if sustained, might have led to a very different post-independence India. Against this, however, is the fact that the caliphate movement referred to a context very different from the one that mattered most to the Congress nationalists; the caliphate advocates' goal was international, not national, and they saw themselves as representing a worldwide Islamic community. In any case, the issue died in 1924 when secularist reformer Mustafa Kemal Atatürk (1881–1938) abolished the Ottoman sultanate.

It was the Jallianwala Bagh atrocity that proved most crucial in shaping future events, for it led Gandhi and Congress, with the support of the caliphate supporters, to launch a major campaign of boycott and civil disobedience in 1920. They did so under the banner of a promise Gandhi had made of 'Swaraj in a single year'. This, the first of his major campaigns, got wildly out of hand and led to serious violence, which led Gandhi to close it down in 1922. As part of the fallout from the 1920 campaign, Gandhi himself was arrested and sentenced to six years in prison.

These events were the context of Jinnah's growing alienation from Congress. Although there were other points of disagreement, the most decisive factor was his basic distrust of Gandhi and the movement he started. To Jinnah, it all seemed like rabble-rousing, and he viewed the importance of religious symbolism in Gandhi's world-view as truly dangerous. It certainly did not help that Gandhi strongly supported cow protection, for it must be remembered that the havoc of the cow-protection riots of the late nineteenth century were still part of collective memory. Although Gandhi deplored the conflict between Muslims and Hindus that had arisen over the issue, he nevertheless proclaimed (in 1921) that the 'central fact of Hinduism' is 'Cow Protection'. To this he added, in an often-quoted passage:

> The cow is a poem of pity. One reads pity in the gentle animal. She is the 'mother' to millions of Indian mankind. Protection of the cow means protection of the whole dumb creation of God (from Jack, 1956, p. 170).

The pivotal separation of the Muslim League from the Congress occurred somewhat later, in 1928, when a report authored by Motilal Nehru (1861–1931, father of Jawaharlal Nehru) and other Congressites advocated an independent India with no reserved seats in the central government for Muslims. Of course, there were then and later many Muslims in the Congress movement, but this was a true and lasting divorce. Arguably, Pakistan was nearly inevitable from this point forwards.

Whether Jinnah's fears were fully justified or not, it is a fact that Gandhi's persona and political style were suffused with religious symbolism. Gandhi's most important achievement was transmuting Congress from an elite organisation into a mass movement. His persona as a renouncer and holy man was central to this extraordinary achievement. Wherever he went, he conducted daily prayer meetings. He founded two spiritual retreats in India. The first, Sabarmati Ashram, was established in the city of Ahmedabad. The second, Sevagram Ashram, was created near Wardha, in the deep interior of what is now the Indian state of Maharashtra, far from the tumult and distractions of city life. This ashram served as a venue for experiments with the simple, bucolic, pious life he so idealised. As a world renouncer, his material possessions were few and his diet exiguous and simple. In the end, he came to be treated as a semi-deity by the masses, for they sought his *darshana* ('auspicious sight'), just as if he were divine. But his holy-man charisma was coupled with a political agenda. Fixed in the public image of Gandhi was the spinning wheel at his side with which he was constantly creating cotton yarn to be used in the weaving of homespun cloth. This was both in keeping with the austerity and simplicity of the renouncer's lifestyle and a potent political symbol of swadeshi and boycott.

If Gandhi's initial non-cooperation movement was a failure, the second – the famous Salt March of 1930 – was a brilliant success. In those days, the British maintained a monopoly on the production and distribution of salt, from which they extracted taxes. The purpose of the Salt March was to defy the legal prohibition of the manufacture or distribution of salt by Indians, and the plan was that Gandhi would walk from his Sabarmati Ashram to the sea, where he would illegally manufacture salt from seawater. The march was a huge success; it grew as it progressed, and ultimately attracted international attention. There was frail-looking Gandhi with his staff (in fact, physically far tougher than he looked) traversing the nearly 250-mile route, and the ever-present press made sure that the world was witness to the brutal reception the marchers met when they finally arrived at the sea. These dramatic events were followed by a period of ever-growing civil unrest and disobedience, resulting in a British crackdown and mass arrests. The uproar drew in groups that had hitherto not been conspicuously involved in the Congress movement: women, Pathans from the north-west and South Indians. In general, however, Muslims stayed aloof, and in retrospection we can see that this was a portentous trend.

The Rise of Hindu Nationalism

But Muslim suspicion and Gandhi's holy-man persona notwithstanding, Gandhi was no Hindu nationalist. He was highly respectful of other religious traditions, his prayer meetings were quite ecumenical, and even though he extolled Rama's kingdom as the embodiment of justice in government his vision of Indian nationhood was universalist and inclusive. Hindu nationalism came from very different sources.

The year 1915 was momentous not only because of Gandhi's return to India but also because this was the year of the founding of an organisation called the Hindu Mahasabha ('Great Hindu Assembly'), which was to become the signature organisation of Hindu nationalists. It was a political umbrella association, formed as a loose aggregation of local Hindu groups, mainly in Punjab, Uttar Pradesh and Bihar. But if the organisation was new, its inspiration was much older, for in many ways it was a legacy of the cow-protection movement of the previous century, and the promotion of cow protection was one of its principal preoccupations. As we shall see, cow protection is in some ways the alpha and omega of Hindu nationalism as a social and political movement, for it is a fire that still burns to this very day. After a period of relative quiescence, the Hindu Mahasabha resurged in a reaction to anti-Hindu rioting by Muslims in some areas in the aftermath of Gandhi's tumultuous failed *satyagraha* of 1920. It was reorganised in 1923 under the flag of Hindu unity, strength, belligerency and opposition to *ahimsa* (i.e., non-violence), seen as a source of weakness, fecklessness and cowardice.

The issue of non-violence was, in fact, one of the Hindu nationalists' principal points of disagreement with Gandhi. In truth, there is plenty of room for principled dissent from Gandhi's interpretation of the 'Hindu' position. It must be remembered that Gandhi's own understanding of Hinduism was deeply influenced by the Vaishnava and Jain traditions favoured within his trading-caste Gujarati background, but – as we know – Hinduism is a bundle of traditions, and one can find within it martial strands that do indeed allow and even glorify warfare. It is difficult not to read the *Bhagavad Gita*, Gandhi's favourite Hindu text, as – among many other things – an exhortation to battle, although Gandhi did not read it this way. In any case, not everyone agreed with Gandhi's non-violent approach, and this included extremists within the Congress orbit (such as Bal Gangadhar Tilak [1856–1920]), who felt that violent means employed in a just cause, such as evicting the British from India, could certainly be defended on Hindu terms.

The most important of the Mahasabha's leaders was Vinaya Damodar Savarkar (1893–1966), who became its president in 1937, a position he occupied until 1943. He was born near Nashik in what is now the Indian state of Maharashtra to a family belonging to the Chitpavan Brahman caste. This caste, to which other Hindu nationalists of Maharashtrian background also belonged, had previously been deeply involved in the administration of the Maratha Empire, and had supplied its prime ministers (the Peshwas) from the early eighteenth century until its defeat in 1818. The Chitpavans were quick to take advantage of English education, and thus constituted a significant contingent among the region's educated elites, reformers and politicians. Many among them also saw themselves as legatees of the Maratha glories of the past, which translated in some cases into a radically anti-British and anti-Muslim revolutionary stance. Savarkar was one of these. While supposedly pursuing legal studies in Britain, he became involved in extremist politics and an advocate of violent revolution. His first book, a nationalist interpretation of the 1857 uprising, was banned by the British, and his later defence of assassination and other violent tactics led to his arrest in 1910 and subsequent transportation and imprisonment in the Andaman and Nicobar Islands. He was shifted to the Ratnagiri jail (in Maharashtra) in 1921, from which he was finally released in 1924.

It is fair to say that Savarkar became the chief theorist of Hindu nationalism. This might seem odd in light of the fact that he himself was apparently an atheist, but his understanding of the reality of Hinduism was actually more cultural and political than religious, an ethno-nationalism albeit with a strong religious coloration. His views were put forth in a book (Savarkar, 1969) written during the latter portion of his imprisonment and smuggled out of jail and first published in 1923. The book was entitled *Hindutva: Who is a Hindu?* The word Hindutva ('Hinduness'), popularised by Savarkar, stands for both an ideology and a cause, and the question put by the book's title obviously goes right to the heart of the conundrum of the relationship between India's national identity and religion by asking if a 'Hindu nationalism' is possible and, if so, what might it be.

His answer to this question was ethnicity-oriented and place-oriented rather than belief-oriented. Quite evidently, to hinge the whole matter on religious belief (or belief and practice) would lead nowhere because – as Savarkar knew, and readers of this book also know – the systems of belief and practice conventionally grouped under the Hindu rubric are far too disparate to form much of a foundation for political or any other kind of unity. But Hindutva, he said, is not the same thing as 'Hinduism,' for Hindutva is a national concept, not a religious concept. This being so, religious belief is mostly beside the point, an assertion that enables Savarkar not only to speak of the unity of those professing Hinduism in its vast variousness, but also to claim such outliers as Jains and Sikhs as part of the 'Hindu nation'.

But what is the Hindu nation? How is it to be 'imagined' (Anderson, 2006)? His response to this question is territorial and ethnic; it consists, writes Savarkar, of a people who share and love a bounteous and naturally fortified 'fatherland', which is the South Asian subcontinent. They are a 'race', both 'ancient' and 'homogenous', and possess a rich and shared cultural heritage. By race (Savarkar uses the term 'jati' or 'race jati'), he means common descent ('common blood'), which is the first criterion of Hindutva.

But there is another criterion, and it is ripe with potential for trouble. Hindus are also united by *reverence* for the Hindu fatherland. Here is where Savarkar brings in religion by the back door. Unlike the Hindus, he claims, adherents of the Semitic religions are united by ties that are neither racial nor national, but are purely religious in character. But not so the Hindus, for to them 'holy land' and 'fatherland' (he seems to prefer fatherland to motherland in the case of Hindutva) are one and the same.

India can be a fatherland to the Muslims but never a holy land, for they revere Mecca and their first loyalty can never be to India. Thus, Muslims (and Christians and Jews) can never belong to the Hindu nation. It was against this background that Savarkar supported Zionism as an expression of the diaspora Jews' desire to bring 'holy land' and 'motherland' together, an aspiration with which he totally sympathised.

Unity, he asserted, is the natural condition of those belonging to the Hindu community (as defined in Hindutva terms), and divisions within this community are to be resisted and eradicated as contrary to 'the ancient, the natural and the organic combination that already exists' (Savarkar, 1969, pp. 138–9). Among other things, this meant that caste distinctions should be done away with, and so Savarkar argued that customary restrictions on interdining and intermarriage between castes should be ended in the interest of Hindu unity of blood and culture. As can be seen, there was nothing orthodox or conservative about Savarkar's vision of Hindu nationhood. It was not really a religious nationalism as such, although it was linked with religion (i.e., 'holy land,' etc.), and it had little in common with – let us say – the fundamentally conservative concept of Hinduism we met in the pages of *Samachar Chandrika* in the previous chapter. His was a truly radical vision, and one that could hardly appeal – at least in Savarkar's formulation – to most traditional Hindus, as indeed it did not.

Another major development in the Hindu nationalist world of this period was the founding in 1925 of a militant organisation called the Rashtriya Swayamsevak Sangh ('National Assembly of Volunteers'), or RSS as it is generally known. Rooted in Maharashtrian political culture and historical memory, its purpose was to further the cause of the unity of the Hindu nation as conceived under the Hindutva rubric. It is significant that it was established on the day on which the Hindu festival of dashahra fell that year, because this festival celebrates Rama's victory over Ravana. As Rama once did, Hindus, too, could vanquish their enemies by means of violent struggle. Its founder was Keshav Baliram Hedgewar (1889–1940) – a Brahman but not a Chitpavan – who was a doctor from the city of Nagpur. He had first come into contact with radical revolutionaries while studying medicine in Calcutta, and his activism continued after his return to Nagpur. Having joined the extremists' wing of the Congress, he was involved in Gandhi's non-violent non-cooperation movement of 1920 with the result that he was sentenced to a year in prison. The entire affair led to his disillusionment with Gandhi and his methods. As tensions rose between Hindus and Muslims in Nagpur, Hedgewar began to formulate a new approach that was inspired by his reading of a handwritten manuscript of Savarkar's *Hindutva* in 1923.

Although Hedgewar was profoundly influenced by Savarkar's ideas throughout his political career, he had his own take on these ideas. How was it, he asked, that the Hindu nation was so easily subdued and ruled by foreigners? The answer, he came to believe, was at least in part psychological: it was a question of confidence, courage and a consciousness of Hindu unity. It was also a matter of physical strength and discipline. The goal of the RSS was a reawakening of Hindu awareness of collective identity and the cultivation of the martial mindset and physical prowess necessary to wrest India free from British rule. It was never a mass movement, nor was it designed to be. Rather, the goal was to recruit young Hindu males willing to engage in revolutionary activities into a paramilitary organisation. A major venue of recruitment was the traditional gymnasiums in which physical culture was seen as a form of worship of the chaste deity and patron god of wrestlers, Hanuman. And whatever else it was or was not, the RSS was deeply anti-Muslim.

Because the RSS originated in Nagpur, and also because it was conceptually linked to the heritage of Shivaji, it had and has to this day a special relationship with the Marathi-speaking region. However, it began to expand in the 1930s – at first to Sindh, Punjab and the United Provinces (now Uttar Pradesh), and then beyond – and by 1939 there were around 500 branches (roughly half in the Marathi-speaking zone) and a total membership of about 60,000 (Andersen and Damle, 1987, p. 38). A women's branch was also formed in 1936. During these years, the RSS stayed aloof from the politics of independence, concentrating instead on its militaristic training mission, providing escorts for Hindu pilgrims, and fighting on behalf Hindus' rights to hold religious processions in the vicinity of mosques. Although its ideology was inspired by Savarkar, he himself took a very dim view of the RSS's lack of political engagement.

After Hedgewar's death in 1940, he was succeeded by the much younger Madhav Sadashiv Golwalkar (1906–1973), also a non-Chitpavan Brahman. A seriously religious man, Golwalkar had at one point abandoned his legal practice and RSS activities in order to follow a guru in Bengal. Close to Hedgewar, he rose in the RSS apparatus during the late 1930s, which culminated in becoming his mentor's replacement. His temperament was ascetic and religious, and under his leadership the RSS remained aloof from politics and maintained its distance from the far more political Hindu Mahasabha during the war years. But this was by no means the end of the RSS story, as we shall see.

The Contenders

When India became independent at midnight on 15 August 1947, two countries came into existence, not one: India and Pakistan (Pakistan's independence was actually one day earlier). How this happened is a tangled tale, and need not detain us in detail, but to understand even the basics of contemporary religious politics in India certain essentials need to be mentioned.

Let us start in 1942, a year in which much of great importance for the subcontinent's future crystallised. When the Second World War had begun in 1939, the colonial government had joined the struggle without any consultation with Congress officeholders. Understandably outraged, the Congress had then withheld its support from the British on the premise that only a free India could legitimately enter the struggle. In 1942, the British offered Congress the pledge of independence at the end of the war, but with certain conditions unacceptable to Congress. As a result, Congress initiated a country-wide non-cooperation drive called the 'Quit India Movement'. In response, the British slapped the Congress leadership in jail, where they remained for the rest of the war, and brutally suppressed the movement. Adding to anti-British anger was the Great Bengal Famine of 1943. A result of the cessation of rice-imports from Japanese-occupied Burma compounded by the British policy of diverting grain to the cities and military, it was the cause of as many as a million deaths.

The Muslim League took no part in these upheavals, which left it free to cultivate British favour and pursue its own ideas about independence. An extremely important event had already occurred in 1940 in Lahore, where the Muslim League was holding its annual meeting. The assembly passed a resolution calling for the creation of an independent Pakistan, a goal based on the 'two nations' theory, a concept invented and promoted first by Sir Syed Ahmad Khan. This is the view that the subcontinent's Hindus and Muslims are not merely adherents of two different religions but in every significant sense two nationalities. Readers will surely note the similarity between this and the Hindutva concept of Hindu/Muslim relations. The term 'Pakistan' had been invented by one Chaudhry Rahmat Ali (1897–1951), who used it in 1933 in a tract advocating the creation of a separate state for the subcontinent's Muslims; it combined letters contained in the names (as they appear in Roman script) of five regions of northern India that, when blended into the word 'Pakistan', meant 'place' (*sthan*) of the 'pure' (*pak*).

A particularly eloquent advocate of the Pakistan resolution was Jinnah, and the speech he delivered at Lahore was an exemplary presentation of the two-nations theory (taken here from de Bary, 1988, pp. 228–31). The problem in India, he asserted, is 'international' rather than 'intercommunal'. Hinduism and Islam, he continued:

> are not religions in the strict sense of the word, but are, in fact, different and distinct social orders, and it is a dream that the Hindus and Muslims can ever evolve a common nationality …

This being so:

> To yoke together two such nations under a single state, one as a numerical minority and the other as a majority, must lead to growing discontent and final destruction of any fabric that may be built up for the government of such a state.

Thus, the necessity for a separate Pakistan.

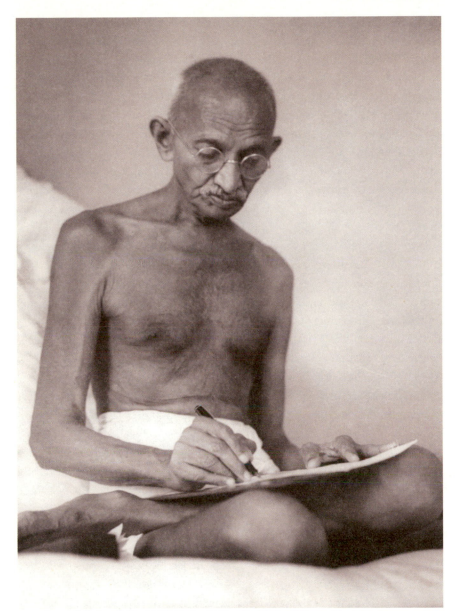

6.1 Gandhi in 1942. Photo: © Dinodia Photos / Alamy Stock Photo

In fact, huge obstacles stood in the way of the realisation of such a vision. The basic problem was that Hindus and Muslims had been living side-by-side in the same local communities and regions for centuries. How then could the egg be unscrambled? Moreover, it was far from true that all Muslims actually desired a partition of the subcontinent; indeed, the Deobandis and the Ulema generally were quite lukewarm to the idea. Pakistan was a dream of secularists. Furthermore, it is possible that Jinnah himself was not truly so inclined, and that he was

167

using the concept of Pakistan as a bludgeon to get better terms for the Muslims in a final settlement (such as reserved seats and electorates), at least at first. But in the end the goal of Pakistan held sway, and, in the final run-up to independence, the issue of what Pakistan would be was joined between Congress and the Muslim League under Jinnah's leadership. The Muslim League negotiated as the 'sole representative' of India's Muslims, a claim buttressed by the fact that the League had achieved a convincing electoral success in elections held in 1946.

At this point, the Congress was led by Jawaharlal Nehru (1889–1964), a Kashmiri Brahman who belonged to a prominent Allahabad family. Jawaharlal was formally schooled at Harrow and Cambridge University, followed by legal studies in London. After his return to India in 1912, he quickly lost interest in the practice of law and became deeply involved in the independence movement. His rise to leadership was rapid and, from the 1930s onwards, he was the principal architect of Congress policy. In the early 1940s, Gandhi chose him to be his successor to Congress leadership. Nehru was certainly not the sole architect of independent India, but his was the mind that had the decisive role in the republic's design.

Because of his family background and education, Nehru was, if not culturally deracinated, not well versed in the culture of the land of his birth. This was true to the extent that his magnum opus was entitled *The Discovery of India* (Nehru, 1946). Written during his imprisonment from 1942 to 1946 as a result of the Quit India movement, *Discovery* consists of a blend of autobiography, Indian history (beginning with the Indus valley civilisation) and cultural analysis. It is a deeply intelligent work, less a systematic treatment of these subjects than a meditation on the nature of India's nationhood from the standpoint of patriot fully engaged in the independence struggle. It is pervaded by Nehru's liberal and generous spirit, and in tone and substance stands in stark contrast to the visions of Savarkar and Jinnah.

The India Nehru discovered is a vast quiltwork of diverse peoples, and yet he came to see an underlying unity, however subtle and elusive:

> She was like some ancient palimpsest [he famously wrote] on which layer upon layer of thought and revery had been inscribed, and yet no succeeding layer had hidden or erased what had been written previously. All of these existed together in our conscious or subconscious selves, though we might not be aware of them, and they had gone to build up the complex and mysterious personality of India (Nehru, 1946, p. 47).

No one could argue, he wrote, that the Pathan of the north-west and the Tamil of the Deep South are the same in the stock from which they spring, or similar in outward aspects of their very different ways of life. But even so, there can be no mistaking the 'impress' of India on both, manifested in similar 'moral and mental qualities' (Nehru, 1946, p. 49). Among these traits are a tolerance of diversity itself and a genius for synthesis, which, in combination, have enabled numerous groups of outsiders to enter India and become thoroughly Indian.

But becoming Indian is not the same thing as becoming 'Hindu' in the religious sense of that word, for Nehru insists that no particular religion defines Indian nationality (Nehru, 1946, pp. 63–6). He points out that Jains and Buddhists are certainly not Hindu in the narrow sense – for they do not venerate the Vedas – yet nobody would argue that, in their outlook and values, they are anything but Indian. He also points out that Jews, Christians, Muslims and Parsis, who came to the subcontinent from elsewhere, have, while maintaining their non-Indic religious affiliations, become perfectly Indianised. And, furthermore, indigenous converts to non-Indic religions never ceased to be recognisably Indian.

End Game

The principal issue in the pre-independence debates was what was to become of two key provinces: Punjab and Bengal. Jinnah's main concern was that the Muslim majority districts of these two provinces (about 40% of each) not be separated off from the remaining districts in the final settlement; rather, he wanted the entire provinces to be absorbed by Pakistan. (For a study focused on Jinnah's aims, see Jalal, 1985.) An important consideration – not the only one – was that the large Hindu populations in the new Pakistan would serve as hostages, ensuring the fair treatment of Muslims in the rest of India. Against this, one might argue that they would also have presented an intractable problem of governance for Pakistan, but this issue never arose because Jinnah never got the Pakistan for which he had hoped.

In the end, and in the midst of chaos and unspeakable acts of violence, two entirely separate states emerged from erstwhile British India (the issue of the princely states would be settled later), and they have existed more or less at daggers drawn ever since. The new Pakistan consisted of two wings, East and West Pakistan. East Pakistan was eastern Bengal, not including Calcutta, which had long-term negative economic consequences for both the east and west. West Pakistan consisted of Balochistan, the North-West Frontier, Sindh and the western portion of Punjab.

It is often said that partition was a tragedy for the people of both India and Pakistan, which indeed it was. But one can take the tragic view of partition while acknowledging an unpleasant but important truth, which is that there can be no doubt that, had partition not occurred, the Republic of India would have faced even greater problems of governance than it actually faced in 1947. Under the no-partition scenario, Muslims would have constituted something like a quarter of the republic's population rather than roughly 11.5%. One can also speculate that governance problems might have been mitigated by the fact that there would have been none of the bitter memories left by partition, and some sort of federal structure for a larger Republic of India might have been possible. A weak centre, however, would never have been acceptable to Nehru, who wanted a strong central government that could execute the development of the country by means of economic planning

Punjab, where multitudes of Hindus, Muslims and Sikhs found themselves on the wrong side of a new international border, was the focus of much of the post-partition violence. The Sikhs, whose heartland had been cut in half by the partition, were particularly aggrieved. In the aftermath of the Second World War, there were large numbers of recently demobilised soldiers in Punjab whose military training added to the lethality of what would have been a very bloody business in any case. In western Punjab, Sikhs and Hindus fled in desperation towards the Indian border, while Muslims were doing the same thing on the Indian side. Columns and trainloads of refugees were attacked by vengeful bands on both sides of the border, bent on killing, rape and abduction of women. The number of resulting deaths is a contested matter; estimates range from hundreds of thousands to a million. Something on the order of twelve million people (ten million in Punjab, the rest in Bengal) were uprooted from their homes and livelihoods within the space of just a few months.

Left dangling was the issue of the princely states. Most of these were absorbed by India without serious incident over the course of the ensuing year, but there was one extremely troublesome holdout. This was Kashmir, a state bordering both India and Pakistan with a majority Muslim population but then ruled by a Hindu maharaja. The maharaja was paralysed by indecision about whether to join his kingdom to India or Pakistan but matters crystallised when the Pakistanis sent irregular troops into Kashmir in late 1947, at which point he acceded to India. The Indian army intervened, and in the aftermath of the resulting war (in 1948) Kashmir was divided by a UN-brokered 'line of control'. Pakistan was left with a sparsely populated and inaccessible zone now divided between Gilgit-Baltistan and a tiny sliver called Azad ('free') Jammu and Kashmir. The Indian side is the Indian state of Jammu and Kashmir.

The issue of Kashmir has never been settled and continues to smoulder and occasionally flame up to the present day. Internally, the state has been the venue of periodic unrest and insurgency, especially from the 1980s onward. Externally, Kashmir has been the cause of three wars between India and Pakistan (1947/48, 1965, 1999). Pakistan's case centres on the state's Muslim majority: as a Muslim majority area, it should have been part of Pakistan from the start, as it would have been were it not for the fact that it was not part of British India. For their part, the Congress never accepted the 'two nations' theory, which was the charter for Pakistan's existence. Furthermore, the Republic of India was to be a secular state. For the Congress, therefore, Pakistan had no particular claim on Kashmir on the basis of its Muslim majority, and Kashmir's very presence in the Indian union as a Muslim-majority state would validate India's own claim to secularity. A connected issue was Kashmir's unique constitutional position within the Indian union. The state of Jammu and Kashmir was guaranteed semi-autonomous status by Article 370 of the Indian Constitution, a concession that was supposed to be a temporary bridge to permanent inclusion within the republic. However, Kashmir's constituent assembly dissolved in 1957 without acting on the matter, with the result that the Article has become a permanent feature of the Constitution. An important consequence of this arrangement has been the barring of non-Kashmiris from property ownership in the state, a major factor in the preservation of the state's demographic integrity. Hindu nationalists excoriate the Article as an obstruction to India's unity.

On 30 January 1948, Gandhi was assassinated in Delhi while leading public prayers. His assassin was Nathuram Godse, a Chitpavan Brahman with an extensive background of RSS activities. Gandhi's enormous presence in the independence movement had left little room for the radical Hindu nationalists. But like a recessive gene, Hindu nationalism had been there all along, and now it had sprung back into high visibility. At the time of the assassination, Godse was no longer a formal member of the RSS, but he was strongly anti-Muslim and considered Gandhi a Muslim appeaser, a view shared by many others, especially among Hindu nationalists. With the first Kashmir war in progress, the Congress had decided not to pay money owed to Pakistan as its share of India's assets prior to partition. Gandhi opposed this position and went on a 'fast-unto-death' to get it reversed, which in fact was done in early January 1948. The assassination soon followed. Godse was caught, tried and hanged.

Because of Gandhi's assassination, Nehru temporarily banned the RSS and, although Hindu nationalists remained active, the extreme right wing would be excluded from the centre of Indian politics for decades to come.

Secular India

It was Nehru, not Gandhi, who had actually led India into independence. And however essential Gandhi's voice and saintly presence had been to the success of the nationalist cause, by 1948 he was completely out of step with the direction of events. Though Gandhi opposed it, partition was a fact. Such was his detachment from the views of movement colleagues that he believed that, with independence attained, the Congress had served its purpose and should be disbanded. And his concept of what independent India should be – a bucolic social order, based on manual labour with a minimum of machinery, devoid of soul-corroding competition, with power largely bestowed on self-governing villages – might be described as the exact opposite of Nehru's view.

Leading a Congress government, Nehru became independent India's first prime minister. He was definitely not a religious man, which was one of the many respects in which he differed from Gandhi. Although he might be described as 'culturally Hindu' but religiously agnostic, it is far from clear that he ever absorbed much of the religious culture of either popular or philosophical Hinduism. In addition, he had a healthy distrust of religion's potential to generate communal violence. Overall, his views on religion can be seen as part of a larger package, which was the world-view of a forward-looking, secular socialist who believed that Indian economic progress would require a strong, centralised state. Nehru believed that independent India should be a republic (i.e., with no residual connection to the British Crown) and a socialist democracy, with universal suffrage and freedom of expression and association. He also strongly supported the idea that the state should play a crucial role in the alleviation of social injustice. These ideals were embodied in the Indian Constitution, which was drafted by a committee under the direction of Dr Bhimrao Ambedkar and came into effect on 26 January 1950. (Ambedkar, as readers might recall from Chapter 2, belonged to a Dalit caste and led his caste fellows into Buddhism.) This date is celebrated as 'Republic Day' throughout the country.

The Republic of India was to be a 'secular' state, but – and oddly – the word secular did not appear in the Indian Constitution until the 42nd Amendment was enacted in 1976. Moreover, considerable ambiguity has always surrounded the question of what meaning the term has (or *could* have) under Indian conditions. Still, the very fact that a representation of the four-lion capital of an Ashokan pillar (with its Buddhist associations) was chosen as the official emblem of India testifies to the seriousness with which Nehru and others of his frame of mind took the idea that the republic was *not* and *never* to be identified with Hinduism.

Secularism in India

But what is secularism? At a minimum, and as understood in the West, it has three crucial elements (Copson, 2017). The first is the separation of religious institutions from those of the state and freedom of the political sphere from domination by any religious institutions – or, as was arguably the principal concern in the American case, the protection of religious institutions from the state. The second is freedom of conscience and belief; and the third is the absence of discrimination by the state against anyone because of religious beliefs or lack of same. Together these three elements represent an ideal that has never been perfectly realised by any state but is found in varying states of imperfection in many. France arguably comes very close to the realisation of secularism as an ideal type. In the aftermath of the Revolution, the state was entirely decoupled from the Catholic Church, and in the Third Republic (1870–1940) secularity (laïcité), as just defined, became the 'defining ideology of the state' (Copson, 2017, p. 24). All traces of religion or religious symbolism were removed from the operations of government, the educational system, the military and so on. Freedom of conscience and religious observance became state policy, there was no official recognition of any religion, and the principle was laid down that, when an individual citizen stands in the presence of the state, he or she bears no religious identity.

In the specific case of India, however, the issue of what form secularism must consider a cultural and historical context very different from that of France. We must start from the fact that in India the British colonial government confronted an extraordinarily complex ethnic and religious mixture. In coming to terms with this, the British sought social and political tranquillity, and had no interest in promoting any particular religion, although they did permit Christian missionaries to operate after an initial hiatus. While it is true that the British intervened in some religious matters (such as banning sati), for the most part they adopted a hands-off approach to the religious laws and customs of their Indian subjects.

Building on this legacy, but also departing from it in key respects, the post-independence Constitution established what is clearly a secular state, albeit with certain special characteristics. Tolerance is extended equally to all religions, and the state favours no religion. There is no state religion. In the Indian case, however, the wall between the state and religion is not, as in France, impermeable. The division between religious institutions and the state is invested with due importance, but the Indian system is concerned less about protecting the state from religion – or vice versa – than it is about keeping the peace between religious communities. Furthermore, and again in contrast to France, the state is friendly to religion and protects religion, but with the crucial proviso that it does so, in theory, without preference. The state may provide financial support to religious institutions (such as educational institutions), and the state may intervene in religious affairs in order to promote social justice (such as prohibiting the barring of members of low castes from temples) and tranquillity. And perhaps above all else – and also in contrast to France – a citizen can bear religious identity in dealings with the state under certain circumstances in the Indian system.

Citizenship and Religious Identity

This brings us to the arcane but crucial issue of the uniform civil code. In the case of India, a universal penal code has been in effect from British times, but the question of whether there should be a uniform civil code was and remains a highly contentious matter. In the days of the colonial state, personal law was treated as a special domain in which the religious norms and social customs of specific communities held sway, and this was the system inherited by the post-independence Republic of India. Although the British did codify the laws of different religious communities to some extent, this was largely for reasons of convenience and clarity; the British imposed no uniform civil code. This approach, however, was in direct contradiction to the liberal-democratic theory of citizenship embodied by the Indian Constitution and championed by Nehru and many others in the independence movement. For this reason, the Indian Constitution sets forth the *goal* of a uniform civil code (Article 44), under which all communities would be subject to the same laws in the personal sphere (i.e., in such matters as marriage, divorce, inheritance). This, however, proved to be an unrealisable goal (except in Goa, where there is indeed a uniform civil code), and the system that emerged is a sort of hybrid. Muslims are governed by Sharia law, as they were in British times. But the Hindu code was subjected to extensive legislative reforms in the form of four Hindu code bills that, with Nehru's support, were passed into law in the mid-1950s.

The apparent goal of Nehru and his supporters was to use codification of law as a means of unifying the country's Hindus (roughly 80% of the whole), which they saw as a stepping stone to true national unity and modernity. (On the issues involved and the evolving debates, see especially Williams, 2006.) The laws passed affected the domains of marriage, succession, guardianship of minors, and adoption, and covered by the laws were Hindus, Sikhs, Buddhists and Jains, all lumped together as 'Hindus'. But the new legal order was, of course, not extended to include the Muslims (along with Jews, Christians and Parsis); thus, the Hindu code bills were not an actual uniform civil code. It is arguable, in fact, that the linking of the goal of 'national unity' to 'Hindus' alone was an obstacle to national unity, for in fact it highlights the Muslims as 'other', thus energising a potent source of disunity. Furthermore, Nehru in effect chose to treat progressive, pro-reform opinion as representative of Hindu opinion generally. However, to those Hindus who opposed the bills – and they were many – it came to seem as if they were being forced to accept something resembling a uniform civil code, requiring changes in such matters as marriage, while the Muslims were being let off the hook and 'appeased'. This, it came to be said, was 'secularism' for Hindus alone. Nor was there uniform satisfaction on the Muslim side. Many progressive Muslims would have welcomed a rationalisation and modernisation of Muslim personal law, and Nehru's failure to do so marginalised progressive elements and seemed to reinforce the stereotype of the Muslims as a backward and benighted community.

The resulting situation has been the arena of endless contention and debate. On the face of it, leaving Muslims to their own legal devices might be said to have been an enlightened effort to acknowledge the cultural differences between the Muslims and other Indian communities were it not for the fact that the Muslims themselves were not and are not of one mind on the issue. Or it could be interpreted as nothing more than a pragmatic response to what would have been a formidable legislative challenge. But whatever one makes of these points, the result of the Hindu code bills was the aggravation of the problem of defining the rights of individuals vis-à-vis religion. The French system envisions rights as attributes of individuals as individuals, regardless of the communities to which they belong, but the Indian system allows group identities to have standing in the affairs of the state. The clearest example of this is positive discrimination on behalf of the impoverished and oppressed 'scheduled' castes and tribes, for whom the Constitution guaranteed reserved seats in legislatures, preferences in university admission and so on. But this is not a matter of religion. In the case of India's Muslims, the concession involves, and blatantly, granting to a particular religious community the right to bestow or withhold certain 'rights' according to that community's own traditional standards.

Quite evidently, the problem of balancing the claims of religious communities versus the rights of individuals qua individuals goes right to the heart of the question of how religion will fit into the national life of a country like India (see Gupta, 2017 for an illuminating discussion of the tensions between citizenship and other sources of identity in India). And this is an especially fraught issue in a historical period in which the concept of 'human rights' as rights borne by individuals *as individuals* holds sway. In the case of India, the tension was dramatically illustrated by a legal case that erupted in the 1980s and in which the relationship between the claims of a religious community and the rights bestowed by Indian citizenship was subjected to sharp scrutiny indeed.

Individual Rights and Religious Claims: Shah Bano

Shah Bano Begum was a Muslim woman, then in her sixties, from the central Indian city of Indore. (For a fine account of this entire affair and its aftermath, see Williams, 2006, pp. 125–54.) She had been divorced by her husband in 1978, and, in accord with Muslim law, was provided with no alimony. She, however, claimed an award in court, and the case had wound its way from her local court to the Supreme Court of India. In 1985, the Supreme Court unanimously upheld the judgement of the High Court of Madhya Pradesh that she was indeed entitled to alimony in order to avert her total destitution. Muslim reaction to the judgement was divided; progressives applauded it, but conservatives saw it as an assault on Islamic law as found in the Qur'an.

Now, at this point, Rajiv Gandhi (the eldest of Indira Gandhi's two sons and Nehru's grandson) had assumed the prime ministership on the crest of the wave of an enormous Congress victory in elections held in December 1984. Apparently undeterred by the fatal consequences of his mother's dabbling in religious politics with the Sikhs (to which we come in the next chapter), Rajiv began to play a similar game with the Muslims. Hoping to secure the votes of Muslims in future elections, Rajiv pushed an Act through Parliament – The Muslim Women (Protection of Rights on Divorce) Act of 1986 – that nullified the Supreme Court decision on the principle that such cases should be decided on the basis of Islamic law, which would have allowed Shah Bano only three months' maintenance. Just as Nehru took the views of pro-reform Hindus as representative of Hindu opinion in the 1950s, Rajiv Gandhi was now accepting the views of anti-reform Muslims as the average of Muslim opinion in the 1980s. Moreover, although he argued that 'secularism' required the protection of the rights of religious minorities, many believed that, unlike Nehru, he was not pushing the bill on behalf of some higher ideal but for reasons of political expediency.

In retrospect, this was a serious mistake. There was an immediate uproar from various groups on various grounds. Some argued that it inserted parliamentary power into an arena that more properly belongs to the courts, which on the face of it seems hard to dispute. Others pointed to the deprivation of Muslim women of rights enjoyed by other women in Indian society, which indeed was an effect of the Act. Also, the ensuing melee further entrenched the linkage of personal law with group identity for many Muslims, and the government's acceptance of conservative opinion as representative of Muslim opinion in general had the effect of marginalising Muslim progressives, a minority within an already divided Muslim community. Over the long term, the whole affair fostered the mythology that the Hindu community is generally 'progressive' by comparison with the Muslims, who are backward and 'against reform'.

But the most important of the results of the Act was Hindu backlash, and indeed the most telling criticism came from Hindu nationalists. To the Hindu nationalists (now represented by the BJP, of which more in the next chapter), this was appeasement of the Muslim community for political purposes. But more, the parliamentary intervention revealed Indian 'secularism' for the 'pseudo secularism' it is, as they saw it. Here, in their view, was secularity for Hindus alone vividly dramatised, while Muslims were allowed preferential treatment. There should be, they argued, a genuine uniform civil code, and creation of such a code has been a major demand of the Hindu nationalists ever since.

We find, therefore, that Indian secularism is indeed significantly different from the French version. We also see that the Indian version – not based on walling religion off from the state but on the pledge of equal treatment for all religions – harbours a potentially highly disruptive source of instability. This is an unresolved ambiguity about the rights of citizens as individuals versus the claims of a religious community to have collective rights superseding those of individuals. And as if this were not problem enough, the Hindu code bills produced a hybrid situation within what was already a hybrid secularity by creating an ersatz uniform civil code that was applied to only one religious community – the largest – among several. The Shah Bano case could conceivably have served as an off-ramp from the problem, but legislative intervention guaranteed that the case would further aggravate tensions between Hindu and Muslims and further fuel the sense of Hindu grievance so important to the appeal of Hindu nationalism. In the event, it led to an accentuation of the link between personal law and group identity and thus, in effect, established a new arena (personal law) for tensions between Hindus and Muslims.

7

Religion and the Struggle for National Identity

The Shah Bano affair laid bare a deep complication in the meaning of citizenship in the Republic of India, and Rajiv Gandhi's response certainly did nothing to resolve the problem. At the heart of the complication was and remains religion. The republic ended up with a faux uniform civil code, and the Shah Bano case had the unfortunate effect of reinforcing the idea that Muslims bear a significantly different status vis-à-vis the state because of their religion, an idea that was now enshrined in legislation. It is one thing to 'respect all religions', which on the face of it is surely a good idea, albeit a goal difficult to realise through policy. It is quite another to allow to religious groups what amounts to a sort of internal sovereignty. It is true that such a system (the millet system) seems to have worked well enough for the Ottomans, but whether it fits well with a modern, democratic polity is another matter altogether.

In India, the failure to create a uniform civil code and the enactment of the Hindu code bills in its place created an asymmetry that generated deep resentment among many Hindus who saw the arrangement as a form of appeasement to reactionary Muslim sentiment. The Hindu nationalist reaction to which this situation gave rise took the form of a renewed call for a uniform civil code, which was (or at least was perceived by many to be) an anti-Muslim demand flying the flag of 'fairness'. Given this context, many Muslims have come to see the defence of Muslim personal law as crucial to the maintenance of their identity and integrity as a community in the Indian republic.

On the other side of the coin of civic identity is national identity, and ambiguities on the one side are likely to be reflected on the other. If civic identity refers to the identity that persons bear in their relationship with the state, national identity refers to the self-conception of the community – usually called a 'nation' – of which the state is the political expression. As Benedict Anderson (2006) memorably put it, a nation is an 'imagined community'. But how is such a community to be imagined? And how is its relationship to the state to be conceived (on these issues, see especially Ra'anan, 1990)? In the case of true nation states such as Iceland or Finland, there is little mystery about the matter. In such cases – and they are not all that common – there is a fundamental congruence between state and national community in which state institutions foster and reinforce a sense of national belonging and in which a sense of national belonging is a source (not necessarily the only source) of legitimacy for the state. Much more complex is the situation of multicultural, multi-ethnic or multinational states. In such situations, shared ethnicity is not available as a unifying idea, but there are other possibilities. In the old Soviet Union, a multinational state par excellence, the symbolism of the Revolution and the sense of shared effort in the building of socialism served as the glue (although Stalin was compelled to resurrect the imagery of Mother Russia when facing defeat in the Second World War). In the United States, a civic religion focused on the founding documents, the shared memory of founding figures, democratic ideals, the rituals of participating in the institutions of democracy, the mythologies of open opportunity and so on provide common ground. This is a theme with many variations.

But what of India? This was a difficult problem indeed for the country's creators, but it was certainly surmountable. A great advantage was that India's regional linguistic and ethnic identities had never become national. As Sunil Khilnani (1999, p. 157) puts it:

> If India was weakly united, it was also weakly divided: there were no politically significant regional identities that could either obstruct unification or direct it – no subcontinental Prussia or Piedmont.

But what was the unifying principle to be? Here was the great difficulty. Given sheer ethnographic reality (as well as Nehru's secular proclivities), religion was obviously off the table, for roughly a quarter of the subcontinent's pre-independence population was Muslim. This left historical and cultural continuity as a possibility, and in his *Discovery* Nehru tried to tease out the threads of such continuity from the subcontinent's staggering historical and ethnographic complexity. The result – a shared history and a shared receptivity to diversity and talent for cultural synthesis – was hardly a very solid foundation for a convincing national idea. Nor, in fact, was it where Nehru's heart truly was when it came to building the nation. More promising, and a far better fit with Nehru's temperament, was to emphasise the future and what an independent India could be, and central to this vision were certain values Nehru held strongly and shared with most of his colleagues and a wide swath of elite opinion. High on this list, as we know, were democracy, equality, social justice and the amelioration of poverty by means of planned economic development within the framework of a strong state.

In post-independence India, these ideals came to be coupled with reverential memories of the independence struggle and its dominating figures – although some of whom, such as Gandhi, hardly shared Nehru's economic views – and the result was a plausible concept of nationhood. But for all the attractiveness of these ideals and images to modernisers such as Nehru himself, they were most powerful among educated and politically savvy, and not even all of them. The elites who shared this sense of the nation in common were distributed throughout the republic, and in that sense its appeal was national. But if its appeal was broad, it was not truly deep and, as the memory of the independence struggle and its heroes began to fade over time, a space began to open for some other form of national symbolism.

Waiting in the wings was religion. Now, it is surely true that religion is far more than politics by another name, but it is just as true that religion and politics can be natural allies, and this has certainly been a feature of India's religious history. The ancient Vedic sacrifice was, among many other things, a rite of legitimisation for rulers, and the pattern of ritual cooperation between king and priest – king depending on the priest's ceremonies for legitimacy, with priest dependent on the king's gifting for his subsistence – has been a lasting theme in Indian history. The building and patronage of temples and monasteries have played a similar legitimising role, and royal patronage has been a crucial factor in the spread of religions, as we have seen in the case of Buddhism and Jainism. But a fusion between polity and religion was certainly not a feature of modern India as Nehru conceived it.

During the republic's early years, Hindu nationalism was, if largely eclipsed by Nehruvian secularism, alive and well, but India was nonetheless very far indeed from becoming a confessional national community. A major obstacle was simple demographics. Religious minorities, who then comprised about 13% of the total population (with Muslims at about 10%), were a significant part of the republic's citizenship. In the absence of some as-yet uninvented formula of inclusion in a 'Hindu' polity, they would have to be left out of the national family. But also, the major available candidate for a Hindu nationalism was Savarkar's Hindutva, and Hindutva was hobbled by the difficulty of inherent limited appeal. The mobilising potential of religion is beyond doubt, but the problem was that Hindutva, at least in Savarkar's conception of it, was not really a religious idea. It was a form of ethno-nationalism, loosely tethered to some of the symbolism of Hinduism. And more, the Hindutva project was largely discredited in the eyes of the Indian people by Gandhi's assassination. The opprobrium of the assassination would fade with time, as would the memories of partition, but for Hindutva ever to succeed as a nationalist ideology it would have to find ways of tapping into the political voltage of religion at the grass roots. A pathway to this goal was found at last in the 1980s.

The decade of the 1980s was a truly fateful period for the Republic of India, for this is when latent fissures gave rise to open conflicts that were to shape India's future for decades to come, and religion was at the core of these disputes. One was the Shah Bano affair, which exposed a contradiction in the meaning of civic identity in the Republic of India. The other major issues of the 1980s, two in number, were challenges of a more directly national character. One involved the Sikhs and the republic's territorial integrity. The other brought India's national identity more directly into play. It involved Rama, the *Ramayana*, a TV series and the violent destruction of a mosque in northern India. The co-emergence of these events with each other and with the Shah Bano affair paved the way for the advent of a politically potent form of Hindu nationalism.

I turn first to the Sikhs.

Khalistan

The question of the place of Sikhism in India's national life was a problem from the republic's beginning. Currently, Sikhs constitute about 1.7% of the republic's population, and most live in the state of Punjab. When the tumult of partition subsided, almost all the Sikhs had ended up on the Indian side of the border in the Indian portion of the former Punjab province. From the start, there was a movement among some Sikhs to have their own Punjabi-speaking state carved out of what was left of the old Punjab, and this was duly done in 1965, with Punjab splitting from a new state called Haryana but sharing with Haryana the city of Chandigarh as its capital. But in time, it became clear that the demand for a Punjabi-speaking state was really a stalking horse for more radical demands. The dissatisfaction of many Sikhs with the shared-capital arrangement became the focus of agitation that escalated into a demand on the part of some zealots (financially supported by the large Sikh diaspora community) for an autonomous Punjab in which the Khalsa (see Chapter 4) would wield some sort of sovereignty or, as some true zealots demanded, an independent homeland, a 'Khalistan', for Sikhs. This movement gained impetus during the 1970s.

In the background of these events was a drama of party politics the fine points of which need not detain us. (A good account of the whole affair can be found in Talbot, 2000, pp. 265–73.) In broad strokes, a Sikh political party called the Akali Dal had spearheaded the drive for a language-based Punjab state, but in 1980 was defeated by Congress in the state assembly elections in Punjab. The defeat left leadership in the Sikh community in a highly fragmented state, and in the midst of the confusion, much of it having to do with parochial issues within the Sikh community, there arose a young firebrand Sikh activist named Jarnail Singh Bhindranwale (1947–1984). In the early 1980s, he embarked on a series of increasingly disruptive agitations on behalf of a range of Sikh grievances, and, in 1984, he and his followers had attempted to evade arrest by barricading themselves in the holiest shrine in the Golden Temple complex in Amritsar. He was not among those actually calling for Khalistan, for his main object appears to have been moral renewal among Sikhs, but his struggles certainly resonated deeply with the Khalistan cause. His choice of the Golden Temple as the place to make his stand was, of course, not fortuitous, for this is the most sacred of sacred places to the Sikhs, and the symbolic heart of Sikh identity.

Indira Gandhi herself, then India's prime minister, should be numbered among the authors of this unfortunate situation, for in the early stages she had encouraged Bhindranwale as a means of splitting the Akali Dal. In hindsight, this can surely be seen as an object lesson in the dangers of trying to achieve political goals by manipulating religious or ethnic sentiments in a polity such as India's.

With the Golden Temple occupation, matters were brought to a head. No government of India could possibly tolerate such a challenge to its sovereignty. In an operation named 'Operation Blue Star', the Indian army moved into the Golden Temple in June 1984. The attack, which included tanks, was not an easy one because the militants had brought heavy weapons with them. After fierce fighting with many casualties, the army prevailed and Bhindranwale was killed. There was also heavy loss of non-belligerent lives (the numbers are contested), aggravated by the fact that large numbers of pilgrims were present on the occasion of a major Sikh festival.

The outrage generated by the massacre and by the physical damage to Sikh holy places within the complex lent huge impetus to the Khalistan movement and the rise of militant groups supporting it. In October of the same year, Indira Gandhi was assassinated by two of her Sikh bodyguards. This unleashed a paroxysm of lethal anti-Sikh violence in Delhi, apparently with the connivance of some local Congress leaders, that left over 2,000 Sikhs dead. There then ensued a years-long period of often violent unrest in Punjab. The most spectacular incident was the 1985 mid-air bombing of an Air India flight over the Atlantic with the loss of 329 lives, but this was only the most internationally visible of the many and onerous trials of Punjab during the post-assassination years. The Khalistan agitation peaked in 1990, and thereafter secessionist energies dwindled and the Khalistan movement started to become a nightmare of the past. Khalistan sentiments, however, live on, apparently mostly in the Sikh diaspora. (In 2018, Canadian Prime Minister Justin Trudeau came under severe criticism while on a visit to India because of a careless dinner invitation to an alleged Sikh extremist, a Canadian citizen, while in Delhi.)

The Khalistan movement was a challenge to India on two interrelated levels. It was both a strategic threat and an intolerable challenge to India's national integration. Strategically, the loss of Punjab would have rendered north India indefensible. On the point of national integration, the entire episode posed a basic question, which was, very simply, whether the rights of a religious community qua community – a matter that India treats with notable tolerance – extends to the right of self-determination. Given the complications of Pakistani involvement, the Kashmir issue was not really a test case. The answer in the case of the Sikhs clearly had to be 'no'. The loss of Punjab would have been tantamount to a rip in the very fabric of India's independent nationhood. Who would have been next in line? In the Indian democratic system, a religious community does indeed have certain collective rights, but *not this right*. The national integrity of the Republic of India, within its established borders, trumps all else.

Rama and the Rise of Hindu Nationalism

For the better part of three decades after independence, Hindu nationalism was represented politically by a party called the Jan Sangh. Founded in 1951 and generally regarded as the political arm of the RSS, the Jan Sangh failed to achieve anything resembling national political success until the late 1970s. It and the right-wing movement it represented languished in general disrepute both because of Gandhi's assassination and the fact that Hindu nationalism was way out of step with the progressivism that animated Indian politics at its centre during the republic's early years.

The Jan Sangh's first real success on a national stage was in 1977, when it joined with other opposition parties to form a political coalition called the Janata Front (later to become the Janata Party). This was a hodgepodge, party-like entity created from ideologically disparate elements with the purpose of defeating Prime Minister Indira Gandhi and the Congress in general elections to be held that year. In coordination with yet other and lesser supporting parties, this rickety alliance achieved a decisive victory in the 1977 elections and installed an octogenarian Gujarati named Morarji Desai (1896–1995) as prime minister; he was India's first non-Congress figure to hold that office. These events occurred in the aftermath of, and in reaction to, a period of national 'emergency' declared by Indira Gandhi in June 1975 that lasted until March 1977. During this period, civil liberties were suspended, Indira's political opponents were imprisoned, and national elections set for 1976 were postponed. The postponed elections were held in 1977, and the Janata prevailed and formed a government. This government proved highly unstable and lasted a mere three years, with Congress and Indira Gandhi returning to power in elections held in 1980. In the aftermath of these events, the Jan Sangh left the collapsed Janata and reorganised as the Bharatiya Janata Party ('Indian People's Party'), usually called the BJP.

By this time, the wider Hindu nationalist movement had regained some of the impetus it had lost in the early post-independence period. The RSS had joined hands with various other groups, and in 1964 the RSS leadership created an offshoot umbrella organisation called the Vishva Hindu Parishad ('World Hindu Council', usually known simply as the VHP), which had the purpose of coordinating the promotion of Hindutva. Dominated by religious leaders, the VHP can be considered the ecclesiastical arm of the RSS. The cluster of organisations supported or created by the RSS, including the VHP, came to be called the Sangh Pariwar (the 'family' of associations), and these groups together became the organisational heart of the Hindu nationalist movement. They operate in a range of social and economic domains such as labour, agriculture, education and social service. In 2015, there were thirty-six such affiliated organisations (Andersen and Damle, 2018, pp. 23–42), some of greater significance than others. One of the most important is the all-male youth wing of the VHP known as the Bajrang Dal ('Party of Hanuman'). This organisation can be considered the activist arm of the VHP – itself an activist organisation – and it has become notorious for violent agitations on behalf of a right-wing religious agenda. As we know, Hanuman epitomises Rama devotion, so it is not by chance that he was symbolically attached to the cause of 'defending Hinduism', especially when the issue of Rama and Ayodhya became central to this defence, as will be seen anon. The VHP also has an activist women's wing called the Durga Vahini ('Durga's Army'), a name that draws on the imagery of the martial goddess.

Sunday Mornings with Rama

The Janata episode was the turning point on which a Hindu nationalist party with close links to the RSS emerged from the margins of Indian politics. But even so, Hindu nationalists had not yet found a solution to their fundamental problem, which was that of finding a way to become a mass movement, and their true ascent to national power still lay ahead. The central issue was the narrowness of their social base. During the years leading up to independence, Gandhi was the impediment. His extraordinary religious charisma had a mass appeal that pre-empted competing movements, and his assassination after independence left a stench that lingered around the Hindu nationalist movement. But a more fundamental and enduring problem for the Hindu nationalists, pre- and post-independence, was a caste and class issue. The foundation of their political support was mostly high-caste with an emphasis on urban middle-income traders, professionals and white-collar workers (Jaffrelot, 1996, p. 244), a reliable base but insufficient for a rise to national power. What was needed was a bridge outwards to other social groups, especially to middle and lower castes and classes, urban and rural, and to disadvantaged Hindus who would otherwise share class interests with the mostly equally disadvantaged Muslims.

A solution to this problem at last presented itself in the 1980s. It took the form of a symbolic issue, one centred on the widespread cult of Rama, that could connect Hindutva with the religious sentiments of large numbers of Hindus. And as an added benefit, this was an issue that could focus resentment on a ready-made group of scapegoats, the easily targeted and vulnerable Muslims. The stage was set for these events by – of all things – a television serialisation.

The use of moving images for the propagation of religious content already had a long history in India. Cinema became a major medium for the transmission of religious content in the early twentieth century. Films on religious themes (known as 'mythologicals' in the trade) are typically based on Puranic or Epic narratives, and have been a major part of the industry from its earliest days (Derné, 1995). In fact, the very first feature-length film produced in India, Phalke's *Raja Harishchandra* (1913), was a mythological. Typically, such films retell familiar stories, albeit spiced up with special effects, and filmmakers avoid deviation from well-known formulas because of the likelihood of adverse reactions from the conservative audiences attracted to explicitly religious films. The viewers of these films often treat the deities depicted on the screen as analogous to images in a shrine or temple and to be prayed to in a similar fashion. Because such films tend to attract audiences already attuned to the religious themes and symbols presented in them, their principal effect seems to be largely confined to reinforcement and further standardisation of familiar tropes.

The small screen of television, however, was a different matter, for the very scale on which it operated and the nature of the viewing experience made a qualitative difference in the effects of the content transmitted and, to some extent, in the content itself. After a slow start in India, television began to take off as a lively entertainment medium in the early 1980s. The notoriously stodgy national network, Doordarshan, had begun to liven up its offerings by introducing commercial advertising and utilising programming developed by independent studios, and audience size grew accordingly. The result was a liberation of moving visual imagery from cinema halls; such images could now be propagated simultaneously to audiences of – for all practical purposes – unlimited size.

Regarding religious content specifically, televised transmission had at least two significant consequences. One was that the vastness of audience size opened the door to an unprecedented standardisation of such imagery. Hindu belief and practice have always been regionally and socially varied. Now, however, there was at least the potential for 'national' versions of religious themes and images. The second effect, crucially important, has been noted by Philip Lutgendorf (1995, pp. 243–4) in reference to the TV serialisation of the *Ramayana*, to which I turn below. He points out that viewing this material was not just *seeing* something; it was *doing* something, and the social context of viewing was almost always a small group of one kind or another: a family, a group of neighbours, friends or whatever. The small size of the TV receiver and its screen lent itself perfectly to this sort of inwardly curving social context. Viewing was often accompanied by collective rites of worship, and, in the aftermath of each episode, viewers endlessly discussed with one another the acting, the costuming, the way the story was told, and on and on. These contextual factors guaranteed that, in contrast to film, televised religious matter could not only reach vastly bigger audiences but also could have a deeper emotional and cognitive impact.

It was, in fact, a TV serialisation of the *Ramayana*, which began in 1987, that broke the ice for televised religiosity in India. Over the decades, several film versions of the

Ramayana had already appeared, but never to such acclaim and with such a cultural impact as this televised version. The series was mostly the brainchild and creation of an already highly successful Mumbai filmmaker by the name of Ramanand Sagar, himself a fervent Rama devotee. The series was called simply *Ramayan* (the Hindi language drops Sanskrit's final 'a') and was presented on Sunday mornings by Doordarshan beginning in January 1987 and continuing to July 1988. Originally scheduled for fifty-two episodes, the series was so popular that it grew to a length of seventy-eight weekly episodes. As we know, one of the most beloved texts of the devotional Hinduism of the northern zone is the *Ramcharitmanas*, the Tulsidas version of the *Ramayana*. Although the serialisation did, to some extent, draw upon other regional versions, and although an oft-repeated theme in successive episodes was that of the *Ramayana* as a symbol of national unity, the *Ramcharitmanas* was its heart and soul. This is an important point. Whether intentionally or not, by mostly sidelining regional variants of the *Ramayana*, the series effectively 'nationalised' a regional version of the epic (Jaffrelot, 1996, p. 389). This fits well with parallel political developments, as will be seen.

The series came out at a time when India's Doordarshan, still hobbled with the mission of advancing national integration instead of providing mass entertainment, badly needed a boost to compete with the increasingly popular videocassette recordings of films. *Ramayan* was but one of several serialisations presented to reverse the trend. There is no doubt whatsoever that it was the most successful. Although the press reviews (in both the English-language and Hindi press) were highly critical of the hokeyness, crude production values and stilted acting of the series, its popularity steadily grew. Conservative estimates of its weekly viewership are in the 40–60 million range, but it must also be factored in that a significant part of the audience was in public places where TV sets had been stationed, and so the audience might well have peaked at something like 80–100 million (Lutgendorf, 1995, p. 223), which is extraordinary when one considers that in the India of the 1980s large numbers of people had no access to TV of any kind. Furthermore, non-Hindus also enjoyed the show in large numbers. It was widely observed that markets were semi-deserted on Sunday mornings when the show was on, and power failures were met with violent protests. The advertising revenue generated by the series broke all records at the time.

But of far greater significance than audience size was its cultural resonance with the viewing audience. Any analysis of Ramanand's *Ramayan* must take into account the performance traditions from which it emerged. From this standpoint, the series must be understood less as 'television' than as a spectacularly successful adaptation to television of traditional modes of storytelling (Lutgendorf, 1995, pp. 226–32). To some extent, it drew upon the widespread traditional practice of formal *Ramcharitmanas* recitation in daily or nightly instalments. In these text-based performances, the reciter presents a small section of the epic that he (rarely she) then expands into an improvised interpretation or sermon. Such performances are traditionally a major source of religious knowledge to their audiences. Another performance mode that *Ramayan* drew from is *ramlila* ('Rama's play'). A ramlila consists of re-enactments of important episodes of Rama's life. Such performances are part of the celebration of the major autumn festival of dashahra, when they culminate in the burning of a combustible image of Ravana in celebration of Rama's victory. Tableau, in which actors, dressed as characters in mythology, are displayed in scenes from sacred writings is another important traditional genre. In story-recitation, plays and tableaux, the human reciters or actors undergo consecration rituals and purifications in recognition of the fact that, in the context of these performances, they become embodiments of the divine beings they represent.

Against this background, we can see that those who criticised Ramanand Sagar's *Ramayan* as a corruption of a literary treasure – as many did – were completely missing the point. The overwhelming majority of viewers saw the series through the lens of familiar performance traditions that they had known from childhood, and, to most of them, the viewing experience was a religious experience in every sense that matters. In fact, it acquired many of the features of formal worship. It was, as noted above, an *activity*, not just a passive witnessing of something done by others, and it was an activity typically undertaken in a small group context. On the analogue of a temple visit, the Sunday morning viewing came to be seen as a form of *darshana*, the spiritually uplifting experience of seeing and being seen by a divine image. Television sets became shrines. They would be purified before the weekly show, and incense would be burnt during the performance. While many critics found the apparent worship of an electronic appliance outlandish and ridiculous, in fact it was the transposition of religious responses that had always been part of the performance genres from which *Ramayan* drew.

Given the size of the audience, the prolonged exposure to the audience of a year and a half, and the intensity of the viewing experience itself, Ramanand Sagar's *Ramayan* was a cultural event of historic magnitude. Among its many effects, it acted as a powerful accelerant of a Rama-mindedness that was already a major component of Hindu religious culture in northern India. The fact that Rama was the deity in question held a special significance. As seen in Chapter 3, Rama is above all a king; he is more than that, of course, but first and foremost he is a prince who became the king of Ayodhya. This is the reason that the most popular pictorial representation of Rama is a depiction of Rama's 'royal court' (*ram darbar*). But not only is Rama a king, he is also the greatest of all kings and the divine embodiment of just and benevolent rule. Gandhi himself pointed to ramrajya as the political embodiment of righteousness and a pattern for what a post-independence India should be. And small wonder that he should think so, for here is how Tulsidas describes Ayodhya when Rama ruled:

> In the whole of Rama's realm, there was no one who suffered from bodily
> pains, ill fortune or evil circumstance. Every man loved his neighbour
> and was contented with the state of life to which he had been born ...
> Men and women alike were devoted to Rama's worship and enjoyed all
> the blessedness of highest heaven. There was no premature death and no
> sickness even, but everyone was comely and sound of body. No one was
> in poverty, in sorrow or distress; no one ignorant or unlucky. All the men
> and women were unaffectedly good and pious, clever and intelligent.
> Everyone appreciated his neighbour and was himself learned and wise;
> everyone was grateful for kindnesses and guilelessly prudent (Book 7,
> *caupai* 19; from Growse, 1978, p. 642).
>
> The earth was suffused with the radiance of the moon; the sun gave us
> as much heat as required, and the clouds dropped rain whenever asked,
> in the days when Rama was king (Book 7, *doha* 23, from Growse, 1978,
> p. 644).

Given this as cultural background already long in place – the imagery of Rama's regal majesty, the glowing picture of life when he was king, all embedded in a story of which Hindu auditors never tire – and adding to this the tremendous amplification effect of modern television – Lord Rama became available as a political symbol of potentially very great power as a result of Ramanand Sagar's *Ramayan*. His imagery as a deity was the perfect confluence of the religious and the political, and the glossing over of the regional variations of Rama's story even suggested the possibility of his emergence as a sort of 'national deity', something that had never existed before. What was needed to unleash the power of this symbolism was a catalyst.

This brings us to the matter of Ayodhya.

Ayodhya and the Hindu Nationalist Surge

Rama's birthplace and capital was city named Ayodhya, and it is generally believed that the present-day town of Ayodhya (in central Uttar Pradesh) is that very city. The fact that the authenticity of the current Ayodhya is disputed by some modern historians hardly matters, for popular belief has its own ineluctable persistence, and Ayodhya is one of the most important pilgrimage destinations in the region for Hindus. It is also the site of one of the most contested patches of soil in all India.

The crux of the matter is that, until recently, there existed a mosque in Ayodhya that stood on what many Hindus believe to be the exact spot of Rama's birth (*janambhumi*). This, too, is a religious belief without historical foundation, but in such matters of passionate conviction the opinion of experts bears little weight, and the presence of the mosque on a place so sanctified was seen as profoundly unacceptable by Rama's devotees. The mosque is said to have been constructed on the orders of Babur in the early sixteenth century, and it, therefore, came to be known as the Babri Masjid ('Mosque of Babur'). Supposedly, a temple once stood on this site and was demolished by the Mughals in order to use the wreckage as material to build the mosque. This situation was a continuing irritant, bound to erupt in Hindu–Muslim conflict, which it periodically did. In the 1850s, the colonial authorities provided a platform outside the mosque for Hindu worship while allowing Muslims to conduct prayers within, and so matters sputtered along until the post-independence period.

The explosion that finally came was far from inevitable; it was the result of human agency motivated by political ambition. The run-up to the explosion began in 1984 and took the form of a campaign, orchestrated by the VHP to 'unlock' Rama's birthplace. The background of this demand was an early decision by the post-independence government to close the mosque to any worship by either community – this was the 'lock'. But then, in December 1949, Hindu radicals associated with an offshoot of the Hindu Mahasabha entered the mosque in the dead of night and installed images of Rama and Sita there. The appearance of the images was seen as divine miracle by the credulous, a belief that the perpetrators did nothing to dispel. Secularist Nehru wanted the images to be removed from the mosque, but a local government official (said to have been a Hindu nationalist sympathiser) refused to do this, arguing that to do so would itself incite serious violence. In the end, the public (Hindu and Muslim) continued to be barred from the mosque, but the images remained and Hindu priests were allowed to worship them once per day.

So matters stood in 1984, when the VHP began its agitation to open the doors to Rama's birthplace. (For an excellent account of the entire Ayodhya affair, see Jaffrelot, 1996, pp. 363–4; 369–410.) To dramatise the issue, a procession consisting mostly of Hindu holy men was organised to make its way from Sita's alleged birthplace (Sitamarhi, a town and district in the Indian state of Bihar) to Ayodhya, and from there via Lucknow to Delhi. The procession was accompanied by truck-borne images of Rama and Sita and a flag declaring 'Victory to Mother India'. This campaign fizzled when the somewhat unprepossessing procession reached Delhi, where the Ayodhya issue was completely sidetracked in the midst of the convulsions resulting from Indira Gandhi's assassination. But the issue continued to smoulder and the VHP continued to apply steady political pressure. In the end, a judge in Faizabad yielded to VHP demands and, in February 1986, ordered that the mosque be opened to the public. The actual 'unlocking', which took place immediately after the judgement, was of sufficient national importance to merit the presence of a Doordarshan film crew, and the result was Muslim protests and communal violence in various parts of northern India. From this point forwards, the goal of the Hindu nationalists shifted to the demolition of the mosque and its replacement by a Rama temple, a demand that became a major element in the political programme of the BJP.

The VHP's next move was culturally quite clever. In the summer of 1989, and in anticipation of forthcoming elections, it organised a nationwide campaign in which local communities – villages, towns, neighbourhoods – would enshrine and worship consecrated bricks with the name 'Ram' stamped on them in Devanagari script. Worshippers would be asked to make donations to support construction of the Rama temple at Ayodhya, in exchange for which they would be given certificates. The funds and the sanctified bricks would then be taken in procession to Ayodhya, there to be used in constructing a temple to stand in place of the mosque (at this point, still standing). This proved to be an extraordinarily effective use of sacred symbolism as a political mobilisation tool, and the resulting processions had widespread incendiary effects including riots that took hundreds of lives. The culmination of these events was the Uttar Pradesh government's authorisation in late 1989 of a *shilanyas* (foundation-stone laying ceremony) for the new temple, which duly took place on a spot in front of the mosque.

The point of all these activities was to create a national cult of Rama with Ayodhya as its physical and ritual centre (Jaffrelot, 1996, pp. 398–403). The Rama to be the focus of this cult was, however, rather different from the Rama of traditional iconography; this was a muscular, warrior Rama, portrayed in VHP propaganda with his bow drawn, as it is typically not in more traditional depictions. No such national cult ever emerged, but the Ayodhya agitations were themselves a potent source of energy for the Hindu right wing and also had the ongoing effect of unleashing serious anti-Muslim violence.

In the 1989 elections, Congress – deeply stained by a corruption scandal – was replaced by a fragile coalition government led by a party called Janata Dal. The Janata Dal is not to be confused with the Janata Party that governed India briefly during the late 1970s; it was a party formed out of bits and pieces including a remnant of the old Janata Party. It was created to oppose Congress, and it was supported, though not joined in government, by the BJP. The BJP itself was rapidly gaining popular support, largely because of the Ayodhya issue, which was now on the boil. At this point, a new source of national turmoil appeared on a completely different front. In September 1990, V. P. Singh, the prime minister, decided to implement a policy greatly expanding the scope of a system of reservations in government service and educational institutions. These reservations were originally intended to provide a leg up to the most downtrodden groups in society; now these benefits would be extended to groups that were called Other Backward Classes (OBCs). Leaving aside the pros and cons of this policy, its implementation was seen, and not unreasonably, as penalising members of higher castes, and this resulted in widespread violence including self-immolations by university students.

7.1 A gigantic image of Hanuman appearing in downtown Jaipur in the aftermath of Advani's 'chariot trip'. The writing on the flag says 'Victory to Sita and Ram'; below is 'Let's go to Ayodhya—we'll build a temple at that very place!

The Hindu nationalists chose this moment to reset and revive the Ayodhya issue. The leader of this new phase was a BJP leader and activist named Lal Kishan Advani (1927–). He organised what he called a *rath yatra* ('chariot journey'; in ritual contexts, the expression refers to a formal procession, as when an image of a deity is taken on a journey around the precincts of a temple). The journey, which began in September 1990, was intended to wind its way from Somnath (in Gujarat, a symbolically significant location also associated with temple destruction by Muslims) through ten states, terminating in Ayodhya, where it was to arrive at the end of October; its purpose was to rouse an army of 'volunteers' (*kar sevaks*) to build a Rama temple there. Accompanied by large numbers of Hindu nationalist activists, Advani rode in Rama-like majesty in a vehicle fitted out to look like an ancient chariot. The procession frequently left Hindu–Muslim violence in its wake as it wound its way through north Indian villages and towns, and tension rose high as the procession neared Ayodhya. Advani himself was arrested in Bihar and there were many other arrests in Uttar Pradesh, but a large contingent of his followers made it to Ayodhya where, on 30 October, they were met with a police firing that left perhaps twenty dead (the figure is disputed). In the aftermath, the VHP organised public ceremonies honouring those volunteers who succeeded in reaching Ayodhya and carried the ashes of the 'martyrs' of Ayodhya in processions around the entire country. The result was further agitation and rioting.

Then, in November 1990, the BJP withdrew its outside support of the Janata Dal government, which led to new elections in 1991. In the 1991 elections, Congress was led initially by Rajiv Gandhi (Indira's eldest son), who was assassinated during the campaign. The result, partly influenced by a sympathetic reaction to Rajiv's assassination, was a return of Congress to power as the leading party of a coalition. However, the most significant consequence of the election was an extraordinary increase in the strength of the BJP, which now had 22% of seats in the Lok Sabha, the lower house of the Indian Parliament. The BJP also won the state elections in Uttar Pradesh, where it formed a government. BJP strength, however, was not truly national, for it was concentrated in the Hindi-speaking belt in the north and in the state of Gujarat, but was weak in the south.

The culmination of these developments occurred on 2 December 1992, when VHP operatives organised an invasion of Ayodhya by Hindu nationalist activists determined to destroy the Babri mosque. In contrast to 1990, this time there was no significant police resistance (indeed, the Uttar Pradesh government has been accused of complicity in the demolition), and the mob tore the mosque down to the ground. The images were then installed in a makeshift shrine, which continues to function as a place of worship to the present day and attracts multitudes of pilgrims. Although the central government took immediate action by dismissing the BJP governments in Uttar Pradesh and three other northern states, and by banning the VHP and other

Hindu nationalist organisations that played a direct role in the demolition, there ensued severe rioting in several major cities – in Delhi, Ahmedabad, Surat and most notably Mumbai – resulting in thousands of deaths.

The success of the BJP in the 1991 elections can be traced largely – though not entirely – to a widening of the BJP's electoral base resulting from the Ayodhya movement, especially within the rapidly growing urban middle class, which was the tide that carried the rise of the BJP. However, the chains of cause and effect were quite complex. (On these points, see Jaffrelot, 1996, pp. 424–36; also Hansen, 1999.) Clearly, the Ayodhya affair enabled Hindu nationalism to make significant headway in villages, at least in the north, and purely religious motivations were certainly important in this context. The movement also had a significant appeal to women, large numbers of whom were active as movement volunteers; for many women, the movement offered a rare opportunity to acquire political identity as actors in public spaces. A major source of recruits to the movement was male, urban, Hindu youth, mostly poorly educated and only marginally employable. Although many were no doubt attracted mainly by the sheer excitement of it all, their imaginations were fired by the heroic, muscular imagery of Rama promoted by the VHP; here was a figure with which young men whose day-to-day lives were mostly grim and dreary could indeed admire and strive to emulate.

Generally speaking, however, religious sentiments were blended with, and often superseded by, other motivations among BJP voters. For example, a major motivating factor, especially among upper-caste youth, was the BJP's opposition (albeit lukewarm) to the enlargement of reservations. In addition to reservation resentments, BJP voters were commonly influenced by apprehensions about the rising power of hitherto suppressed groups, corruption issues, a concern for social discipline and government efficiency, a desire for pro-growth economic policy, and (especially among military retirees) a hard line on national defence.

But all of that said, there can be no doubt that religious symbolism was the catalyst that brought the entire complex package of motivations together. The occurrences preceding the destruction of the Babri mosque and the demolition itself together constituted a truly tectonic episode in the evolution of India's modern state. It is true that, in defiance of VHP hopes, a national cult of Rama with Ayodhya as its Vatican never came into existence, not then and not subsequently. But without the push of the Ayodhya movement, it is hard indeed to see how the BJP could ever have widened its base of support to the extent that it did. In its original formulation, Hindutva lacked breadth of appeal, for there was little in it for rural and lower-caste populations. And although it did have the capacity to mobilise the ardent support of some elements of Indian society, it lacked the motivating energy that religious symbolism can uniquely supply. By coupling Hindutva with the widespread cult of Rama, the Ayodhya uproar provided Hindutva with the capacity to mobilise a religious passion it did not itself possess. The resulting widening of its appeal could never approach universality, for – even leaving religious minorities out of the reckoning – the variegation of India's population will always mitigate universalities of any sort. But it was enough to set in motion a deep transformation of India's politics. When the mosque came down, as Ian Talbot puts it: 'Nehru's vision of a secular India tumbled along with the domed structures' (Talbot, 2016, p. 247).

The 'Hinduism' that enabled Hindu nationalism to enter the Indian mainstream bore little resemblance to the abstract and bloodless distillate favoured by the Brahmos, nor did it look much like Dayananda's revivalist 'back to the Vedas' version. Nor, and more to the point, did it have much in common with Hindutva, at least as Savarkar conceived it. Rather, to the extent that it resembled any of the Hinduisms that emerged in the nineteenth century, it was the version that appeared in the pages of the *Samachar Chandrika* that we met in Chapter 5 – respectful of the entire range of sacred literature and tradition, less focused on abstract belief than religious practice, and comfortable with modern media and modern forms of social mobilisation and activism.

Rise to Power

We must not get side tracked in the complexities of India's subsequent electoral history; what is important is the trend. In broad strokes, national elections in 1998 enabled the BJP to form a coalition government led by the then-elderly prime minister Atal Bihari Vajpayee (1924–2018). It quickly fell, but not before India's testing of nuclear weapons in May ('Vajpayee's Viagra', as some opposition humourist put it), closely followed by Pakistan's response in kind. A more stable BJP-led coalition then came to power following national elections held in 1999. But then, led by Sonia Gandhi (Rajiv Gandhi's widow) and with the crucial support of low-caste groups, Congress was returned to power in the 2004 elections as the leading party of a coalition government under the prime ministership of Manmohan Singh (1932–), a distinguished economist. There then ensued several years of extraordinary economic gains for India, fuelled by economic liberalisation policies initiated in 1991. During these years, the BJP was on the sidelines but never out of the game, and was returned to power decisively in 2014 with an absolute majority in the Lok Sabha and with Narendra Modi (1950–) as prime minister. This was the first time any single party had commanded a parliamentary majority since the 1980s.

Modi is a man of ascetic temperament and obvious political acumen. Of lower-caste origin, his involvement with the RSS began in his early twenties. He first emerged into national political prominence as chief minister of Gujarat, which position he held from 2001 to 2014. Although he is often credited with Gujarat's extraordinary economic progress during those years, he has also been much criticised for an incident and its aftermath that occurred in 2002 in the town of Godhra (on the whole affair, see Basu, 2015, pp. 162–200). There, a carriage on a passenger train containing Hindu pilgrims returning from a ceremony at Ayodhya was consumed by a fire, resulting in fifty-nine deaths. The causes of the fire are disputed. It was quite possibly caused by an electrical malfunction, but a large section of the Hindu population of Gujarat came to believe that it was set by a Muslim mob. The result was a three-day, statewide pogrom against Muslims that led to at least 1,000 Muslim deaths, and the violence was at a level not seen since the eruptions of the partition era. Modi was thought by many to have sat on his hands during the violence. In fact, it does seem that some government officials were complicit in the violence, although Modi himself was exonerated by an investigating commission. In any case, the BJP and Modi handily won statewide elections held later that year, a pattern repeated in two subsequent elections. These political successes, combined with Gujarat's economic growth during this period, made Modi the obvious BJP choice for the prime ministership in 2014, an election in which the BJP victory was secured as a result of Modi's image and campaigning skills and Congress corruption and fecklessness.

The 2014 election has to be considered a truly decisive event in India's post-independence history, for it marked the point at which a trend in the republic's political life – the growing influence of Hindu nationalism – crystallised into a permanent reality. Let us quickly add, however, that it can never be an unchallenged reality. It must be remembered that electoral outcomes in India will always be influenced by many issues other than ethno-religious ones, most importantly economic issues. And it must also be borne in mind that, even though the appeal of Hindutva has been significantly broadened, its constituency is inherently limited by demographic and political counterforces. Religious minorities constitute approximately 20% of India's population today, and many Muslims and Hindus, especially lower-caste Hindus, have powerfully convergent economic and class interests. Furthermore, attempts to universalise any Hindutva version of Hinduism must inevitably stall in the face of the deep regionality of Hindu traditions as they are actually lived. But even with these caveats in mind, it seems unlikely that, whatever the electoral success or failure of the BJP, India can ever return to the secularism pursued by Nehru and his like-minded supporters. For constitutional reasons, India cannot have a national religion. But it does appear that a religious concept that – as many would say – did not even exist until the modern era has now become a permanent factor in the political life of the Republic of India and is moving ineluctably from the margins to the centre of India's national identity.

Epilogue: Some Loose Ends

At the time this epilogue is being written (summer 2019) it has become clear that the BJP victory of 2014 was no flash in the pan, for Modi and the BJP scored a landslide victory in national elections held in spring 2019 and are now more firmly ensconced in power than ever. This was not seen as inevitable, because the number of BJP chief ministers of states had fallen from fifteen to twelve as a result of state-level elections held in 2018, and the three losses were in states generally thought to be BJP redoubts (Chhattisgarh, Madhya Pradesh and Rajasthan). Furthermore, India's economy had failed to measure up to the expectations raised by Modi's 2014 victory. Nonetheless, when the votes were counted in May, the magnitude of the BJP victory was even greater than that of 2014. The BJP emerged with 303 seats out of 545 in the Lok Sabha, with the Indian National Congress lagging badly with only 52.

Religion was only one among many factors behind the outcome. National security played a major role. In February, a Muslim suicide bomber had attacked a military bus in Kashmir, killing over forty-five paramilitary security personnel. This resulted in a surge of national feeling, and Modi received high marks for his subsequent aggressive response, which was to order airstrikes in Pakistan. Money, of which the BJP seemed to have an inexhaustible supply, also played a role. Modi's own personal charisma was a major factor, especially in contrast with weak leadership on the Congress side. Modi and the BJP were able to cultivate and capitalise on resentments against established elites, of which Congress-leader Rahul Gandhi was a perfect embodiment. But exerting a steady pull was always the religious factor, which was especially important in the grassroots voter mobilisation undertaken by local affiliates of Hindu nationalist organisations. It is highly revealing that out of the 303 post-election BJP members of the Lok Sabha only one is a Muslim.

While the BJP has engaged a broad range of non-Hindutva issues since coming to power in 2014, most notably those related to economic development, it and—under the umbrella of its overt or tacit approval—its non-governmental allies have also pursued traditional Hindutva policy goals, albeit with varying levels of energy and commitment. Of some of these matters there is relatively little to say. The BJP continues to advocate a uniform civil code, but, although the Supreme Court outlawed 'triple *talak*' (in which a husband can divorce his wife by uttering or writing the word 'talak', meaning 'divorce', three times) in 2017, the more general issue languishes. Propelled by demographic anxieties, the old Arya Samajist program of reconversion of Muslims and Christians to Hinduism, now called 'coming home' (*ghar wapsi*), has been revived by the VHP and RSS, and significant successes have been claimed, but it is hard to imagine that this program—or any like it—could ever have a significant impact on the county's demographics. Far more consequential have been actions and policies related to four major issues: Kashmir; school textbooks and curricula; the Ayodhya problem; and cow protection.

Of these four, the most potentially dangerous is the BJP government's abrogation of Article 370 of the Constitution, which took place in early August 2019, just when this book was in final preparation.

As explained in chapter 6, Article 370 of the Indian Constitution guarantees semi-autonomous status for Jammu and Kashmir, India's only Muslim-majority state. The repeal of Article 370 has long been a Hindu nationalist goal because it was seen as compromising India's national unity and also because of the irksome barring of non-Kashmiris from owning property in the state, a prohibition that ceases with the abrogation. The BJP promised to revoke Article 370 as part of its 2014 election manifesto, but efforts to do so were blocked by a ruling of the of the High Court of Jammu and Kashmir in October 2015 and a similar ruling by the Supreme Court in April 2018. The same promise was made in the 2019 election manifesto, and this time the BJP government simply shoved the matter through by means of a presidential order, with debatable constitutional validity. The people of Kashmir were not consulted in any meaningful way. Not only was Article 370 revoked, but the state was made into a union territory, meaning that significant governmental powers would be shifted to New Delhi; indeed, the state of Jammu and Kashmir simply ceased to exist. The consequences of the abrogation, domestic and international, are only just beginning to play out. There will definitely be dismay and resistance from within the region and outrage from Pakistan side. A challenge to the legality of the abrogation is certain. But where the matter will end, we cannot tell at present. All that is certain is that life teaches us that some of the repercussions will turn out to have been unintended by and unwelcome to the authors of this risky and undemocratic measure.

The remaining three issues are of long-standing and continuing import, and it is to these that we now turn.

Textbooks

Under the aegis of the BJP, there has been a concerted effort to 'saffronise' (i.e., Hinduise) the textbooks used in schools. (An excellent account of the saffronisation effort up to the year 2005 can found in Guichard, 2010.) The books in question are primarily those employed in history and the humanities, and the goal is to present what Hindu nationalists view as a more 'balanced' view of India's culture and past – reflecting what they call 'Indian values' – than has been presented in the books vetted in the past by committees of leading professional scholars. One set of issues revolves around the growing practice of presenting incidents recounted in Hindu sacred literature as India's actual history. Another involves the way Islam and Muslims are portrayed in Indian history.

While there have been efforts to produce such textbooks at the federal level, the most important changes so far have been at the state level, which is where most textbooks used in Indian schools originate. A good example is the educational transformations that took place in the state of Rajasthan, under BJP rule from 2013 to 2018, as described in an article by Alex Traub (2018) in the *New York Review of Books*. He recounts a visit to an eighth-grade class at a school for Muslims in Udaipur in which a *Muslim* teacher presented her *100% Muslim class* with the question: 'Was there anything positive about the Mughals?' The view of history presented in this class, and as promoted in textbooks published by the government of Rajasthan, is one in which India's ancient glories were destroyed by Muslim rule. This is a historiography that vilifies Muslim rulers and elevates regional Hindu heroes to a higher level of importance than Mughal emperors. It portrays the Indus valley civilisation as Indo-Aryan (a view already encountered in Chapter 1), thus indigenising the origins of Vedic culture, and characterises the Vedic period as the onset of a glorious epoch in which India was uniformly prosperous, well-governed, and in which everyone followed a uniform and vegetarianised 'Hinduism', glories that came to an end with the conquests of temple-smashing Muslim invaders. This is a historiography that also deprecates the non-Hindu nationalist versions of Indian history – whatever their authorship – as a colonial legacy originally foisted on Indians as a way of devaluing Indians and their past achievements, all the more easily to dominate them.

While most professional historians have strenuously objected to these assertions, their voices may be increasingly muted as the higher echelons of Indian universities become increasingly saffronised. At the federal level, such matters are the purview of the Ministry of Human Resource Development (HRD). After 2014, the RSS exerted pressure on the ministry to reset the Indian educational system to reflect Hindu nationalist goals in curricula at the national level, and an RSS activist was named head of the ministry in 2016 (Andersen and Damle, 2018, p. 69). This suggests that, in the aftermath of the extraordinary BJP victory in 2019, an intensification of educational saffronising lies ahead.

Ayodhya and Family Fissure

The lingering Ayodhya issue has been and will continue to be a source of difficulty for the BJP. Since the demolition of the Babri mosque, the situation at Ayodhya has remained in a kind of suspended animation. Although temple advocates have initiated the carving of stonework for the future temple, actual temple construction has not yet begun, with the question of the site's ownership languishing in court. In 2010, the Allahabad High Court ruled that the disputed land be divided into three parts: two to Hindu groups (with the temple-activists gaining the site of the shrine) and one to the Muslims. The decision satisfied nobody, and the matter then moved to the Supreme Court, where a judgement is still awaited. But whatever the court's decision, the temple's most passionate supporters are certain to press forward with their demand for a temple on what they regard as the site of Lord Rama's birth.

We have seen that the energies generated by the Ayodhya controversy played a key part in propelling the BJP into national power. Since the late 1990s, however, the Ayodhya dispute has lost a great deal of its former national immediacy and usefulness to the BJP. When Modi and the BJP came to power in 2014, they campaigned not primarily on such concerns as building a temple at Ayodhya but on issues of economic development (Modi's supposed strength) and corruption, and Ayodhya remained largely on a backburner in the 2019 election as well. Furthermore, the cultural makeup of both the BJP and RSS has undergone a change as they draw membership increasingly from India's growing middle class whose views on Hindutva tend towards moderation. Indeed, the BJP has even tried to gain what support it can from non-Hindu groups. All of this has led to a soft-pedalling of such explosive religious issues as Ayodhya. Religious strife is antithetical to effective governance and economic development, and actually to move ahead with the construction of a temple would be a reckless and incendiary act.

Moreover, it needs to be stressed that the RSS and BJP have never understood Hindutva in the narrowest religious sense (on these points, see Andersen and Damle, 2018, pp. 77–91), or at least this has been so at the leadership level, and have never advocated Hinduism as a state religion. The RSS rarely used overtly religious symbolism until the years of the Ayodhya flare-up, and it and most of its affiliates in the Sangh Pariwar have downplayed such symbolism since then, but with the conspicuous exception of the VHP. And if Savarkar's original idea of Hindutva excluded Muslims and Christians on the grounds that their 'holy land' was not India, the RSS and BJP have come to favour a more consistently cultural version of Hindutva that retains the concept of India as a land that must be in some sense 'sacred' to all Hindus but does not insist that such reverence requires that one be religiously Hindu. It needs to be stressed that, from the very start, Hindutva was mostly about patriotism and unity, not religion as such. This is shown especially by the hostility of Hindutva advocates to caste distinctions and, above all, to untouchability, as impediments to national integration.

This more generous construction of Hindutva implies that Muslims and Christians can qualify as belonging to the 'Hindu nation', which is a major departure indeed from Savarkar's original idea. As the descendants of converts, they were once part of Hindu society and continue to partake of attitudes and values that they share with all indigenous Indians; they, too, can be 'sons of the soil'. In conformity with this idea, the RSS opened its membership to non-Hindus in 1979 (although large numbers have not joined), and in 2002 the RSS leadership encouraged a subsidiary (not an affiliate) organisation called the Muslim Rashtriya Manch ('Muslim National Forum') to be formed to work among Muslims.

However, this is an outlook far stronger at the leadership level than at the grassroots of the RSS and BJP and is not shared by the entire Sangh Pariwar, in particular not by the VHP with its deep ecclesiastical roots. The very fact that the VHP is reviving the old reconversion movement is obviously premised on the idea that loyalty to India requires that one be religiously Hindu.

The fissure between these two views of Hindutva is highlighted by the Ayodhya issue. The goals of the activists who tore the mosque down was the construction of a temple in its place, and that remains their goal. If, to many, the temple issue is something best left dangling, to the right-wing elements of the Sangh Pariwar, especially the VHP, it retains its saliency and they continue to press and challenge the central government to authorise construction of the temple, although the radical elements of the Sangh Pariwar appear to have abandoned the tactic of street-level violence, at least for the present. The BJP has responded to the problem with an affirmation of the goal of building the temple coupled with vagueness about when and how it will be done. Their difficulty is simple: any attempt to build a temple at Ayodhya without Muslim compliance runs the risk of major civil strife. While this might not deter VHP firebrands, it is not necessarily in the best interests of the BJP.

But at the same time, the BJP cannot afford to alienate the Sangh Pariwar's right wing, for, after all, Hindu religious symbolism retains its power to generate a sense of Hindu community that transcends caste, class and regional boundaries, a fact the BJP cannot ignore. Within the BJP and RSS senior leadership are moderates who would be willing to compromise by allowing both a temple and a mosque at the site, who would prefer the courts to decide the issue of title to the land, and who – we must surmise – would be well satisfied if the whole issue would simply go away. But even if the wiser heads of the BJP might wish it to be otherwise, the party remains tethered to the radical elements of the Sangh Pariwar and vulnerable to challenge from the Pariwar's right wing. Indeed, the VHP organised a major pro-temple rally in Delhi in early December 2018 that drew an estimated 50,000 participants (BBC, 2018), which suggests that the issue is coming to a boil once again. The construction of a temple at Ayodhya remains on the BJP agenda to the present day, and the question of when and how it will be built cannot be evaded indefinitely. The magnitude of the 2019 BJP victory will almost certainly encourage increased pro-temple pressure from the right wing of the Sangh Pariwar. It is quite possible that the abrogation of Article 370 of the Constitution in 2019 is a harbinger of a renewed effort to get the temple built.

[On 9th November 2019, as this book was being prepared for press, the Supreme Court of India ruled on the Ayodhya dispute. On the basis of a report from the Archaeological Survey of India that there was evidence of an earlier structure that was 'not Islamic' below the ruins of the Babri Masjid, the Court ruled that the disputed land be given to a trust to build a temple, and that an alternative 5 acres of land be given the Muslims for the construction of a mosque. We may expect temple construction to begin soon.]

Cow-Protection Redux

If there are any doubts about the contemporary relevance of the religious as opposed to the cultural construction of Hindu nationalism, they should be dispelled by the recent recrudescence of cow protection.

Hardly any issue in the public domain draws more directly on deeply embedded religious sentiments of large numbers of Hindus, and no issue has greater power to pit Hindus against Muslims on a matter of religious belief. As we saw earlier in this book, cow protection was deeply intertwined with the emergence of anti-Muslim feeling among Hindus (not yet Hindu nationalism) in the late nineteenth century. And while there was no single cause to the chain of events leading to partition, Muslim suspicions of Hindu intentions were certainly quickened by their recollection of cow-protection turbulence, and Gandhi's own self-professed attachment to the cause of cow protection was hardly reassuring in this context. Now, more than a century since the late nineteenth-century explosions, a serious problem of cow-protection violence has, once again, emerged in northern India, promoted primarily by elements on the extreme right wing of the Hindu nationalist movement. Muslims are the targets, and rampant vigilantism is the name of the game.

In assessing the implications of this development, I should begin by reiterating that a significant part of the Indian population eats beef. A National Sample Survey Office report states that currently about 80 million Indians eat beef or buffalo meat (reported in Gittinger, 2017). For the most part, beef is consumed by the poor because of its low cost. Muslims and Christians, of course, are not barred from beef-eating by religious prohibition, but it must also be noted that significant numbers of low-caste Hindus, for whom the religious proscription is ambiguous at best, also eat beef. Obviously, therefore, the prohibition of cow slaughter must have a disproportionate impact on the poor. Cow protection has additional economic implications. In 2017, the Modi government established a ban on transportation for slaughter, and this has been a blow to the economically important meat and leather industries. Also, fearing attack by Hindu radicals if they sell their non-productive cattle, farmers have been releasing them into the countryside; as a result, the farmers lose the income and the stray cattle have become a threat to crops and grazing land. In addition, beef and buffalo meat is a significant source of export income for India.

Article 48 of the Indian Constitution directs the state to prohibit the slaughter of cows and other milk-producing or draught bovines, but this is a directive only and lacks the force of law. However, the Congress party supported cow protection in the post-independence period with the result that most states in India have laws against cow slaughter of some kind, but these vary widely in content and enforcement has often been desultory. The non-prohibiting states are Kerala and the north-eastern states, the latter being Christian majority and on the fringes of the Indic world. The BJP leadership has not sought a nationwide prohibition, which would require a constitutional change, but in the wake of the BJP victories of 2014 several states strengthened these laws. However, the hardest line on this matter has been taken, not by the BJP or RSS, but by the VHP, which has embarked on a crusade for stronger enforcement of state laws (Andersen and Damle, 2018, pp. 189–90). An additional element in the mix was the creation in 2012 of an organisation called the Bharatiya Gau Raksha Dal ('Indian Cow Protection Organisation'), which has operated mainly in Punjab, Haryana, Uttar Pradesh, Bihar, Odisha, Madhya Pradesh and Rajasthan (Gittinger, 2017).

The result of this rise in cow-protection activism has been an upsurge of vigilantism and violence, usually conducted with impunity. There have been many such incidents, the usual targets being Muslim butchers and truckers hauling cattle to market. The most famous case was the Dadri 'beef lynching', which occurred in 2015 in Dadri, about 50 miles east of Delhi in Uttar Pradesh (*The Hindu*, 2016). At the centre of the incident was one Mohammad Akhlaq, a fifty-two-year old Muslim man who was accused by one of his neighbours of stealing and slaughtering a calf. Soon the word spread that Akhlaq and his family had sacrificed and eaten a female calf on Eid-ul-Adha, and a mob attacked and entered his house where they discovered meat of some kind in the refrigerator. Although the family insisted that it was mutton, the crowd leapt to the conclusion that it was beef. The mob then attacked Akhlaq and one of his sons with bricks and knives, and Akhlaq died of his wounds. The police made a number of arrests in the case, but the arrests themselves gave rise to further rioting. Akhlaq's family eventually received substantial financial compensation from the Uttar Pradesh government and were shifted to Delhi for their own safety. The family eventually requested that inquiries into the case be stopped. The meat in the fridge was ultimately determined to be mutton.

This case became a major cause célèbre and focus of nationwide discussion. Although Prime Minister Modi declared the incident unfortunate, and although he further declared that Hindus and Muslims should join in the fight against poverty instead of fighting each other, this would seem to posit a false symmetry of blame that clearly applies poorly to any case of vigilante justice. In any event, harassment and attacks on Muslims suspected of beef eating, purveying or trafficking continue at the time of this writing.

One cannot hold the BJP government directly responsible for such crimes. Prime Minister Modi has condemned them, if belatedly and under pressure, and he has also encouraged state governments to punish vigilantes. In truth, the protection of cows has been less important to the RSS and BJP than to the Pariwar's right wing, because of the BJP's economic-development agenda and desire to promote a moderate image of Hindu nationalism for political reasons. The violence has sparked public revulsion, heightened by a growing realisation that vigilantism is frequently a cover for criminality in the form of extortion or theft. In addition, the BJP wants to avoid alienation of lower-caste, beef-eating Hindus, especially in south India, and hopes to make inroads among Christians and even Muslims. But while preferring a light touch on this issue, the BJP and RSS have not stood in the way of VHP activism, and many critics argue that the Modi government has created an atmosphere of tolerance (if not active encouragement) for vigilante criminality. In a recent article on the problem, journalists Annie Gowan and Manas Sharma (2018) cite statistics showing that there has been a 'spike' in religious hate crimes since 2014, mostly involving Hindus attacking Muslims and mostly in the BJP stronghold states of Uttar Pradesh, Bihar and Jharkhand.

As does the lingering temple issue, cow-protection agitation presents the RSS and BJP with a serious problem. The moderate leadership of these organisations would probably be quite happy to allow the BJP to drift ever closer to an ethno-civic conception of the nation, with religious identities, strictly speaking, receding in the rear-view mirror. But for the present, it is hard to see how Hindu nationalism can ever truly break free of religion's embrace. It was the religious fervour of the Ayodhya issue that elevated the BJP to national power, and such sentiments remain widespread both at the grassroots level of the BJP and RSS and, especially, among the organisations on the right wing of the Sangh Pariwar. Here we find deep scepticism about whether Muslims and Christians can ever be loyal to India, and, in the current atmosphere, issues like the temple and cow-protection disputes will, among the true believers, continue to push Muslims and Christians to the outer boundaries of the imagined national community.

References

Andersen, W. K. and Damle, S. D. (1987) *The Brotherhood in Saffron: The Rashtriya Swayamsevak Sangh and Hindu Revivalism*, Boulder, CO: Westview Press

Andersen, W. K. and Damle, S. D. (2018) *The RSS: A View from the Inside*, Gurgaon: Penguin/ Viking

Anderson, B. (2006) *Imagined Communities: Reflections on the Origin and Spread of Nationalism*, rev. edn, London: Verso

Asher, C. B. and Talbot, C. (2006) *India before Europe*, Cambridge: Cambridge University Press

Aurobindo, S. (*c.*1909) English translation of Chattopadhyay's 'Bande Mataram' (online). Available from URL: www.poemhunter.com/poem/bande-mataram (accessed May 2019)

Babb, L. A. (1986) *Redemptive Encounters: Three Modern Styles in the Hindu Tradition*, Berkeley, CA: University of California Press

Babb, L. A. (1996) *Absent Lord: Ascetics and Kings in a Jain Ritual Culture*, Berkeley, CA: University of California Press

Babb, L. A. (2004) *Alchemies of Violence: Myths of Identity and the Life of Trade in Western India*, New Delhi: Sage Publications

Babb, L. A. (2015) *Understanding Jainism*, Edinburgh: Dunedin Academic Press

Basham, A. L. (1968) *The Wonder That Was India: A Survey of the History and Culture of the India Sub-Continent before the Coming of the Muslims*, 3rd rev. edn, New York: Taplinger

Basu, A. (2015) *Violent Conjunctures in Democratic India*, New York, NY: Cambridge University Press

BBC (2018) 'Ayodhya: Thousands rally in Delhi over disputed religious site,' BBC World News, 9 December (online). Available from URL: www.bbc.com/news/world-asia-india-46499737 (accessed December 2018)

Berkwitz, S. C. (2010) *South Asian Buddhism: A Survey*, London: Routledge

Biardeau, M. (1989) *Hinduism: The Anthropology of a Civilization*, trans. R. Nice, Delhi: Oxford University Press

Brass, P. R. (1999) 'Secularism out of its place', in Das, V., Gupta, D. and Uberoi, P. (eds) (1999) *Tradition, Pluralism and Identity: In Honour of T. N. Madan*, New Delhi: Sage, pp. 359–79

Brockington, J. L. (1981) *The Sacred Thread: Hinduism in its Continuity and Diversity*, Edinburgh: Edinburgh University Press

Bronkhorst, J. (1998) *The Two Sources of Indian Asceticism*, Delhi: Motilal Banarsidass

Bronkhorst, J. (2011a) *Buddhism in the Shadow of Brahmanism*, Leiden: Brill

Bronkhorst, J. (2011b) *Karma*, Honolulu, HI: University of Hawai'i Press

Bryant, K. E. (ed.) and Hawley, J. S. (trans.) (2015) *Sur's Ocean: Poems from the Early Tradition*, Cambridge, MA: Harvard University Press

Burchett, P. E. (2019) *A Genealogy of Devotion: Bhakti, Yoga, and Sufism in North India*, New York, NY: Columbia University Press.

Cantwell, C. (2010) *Buddhism: The Basics*, London: Routledge

Carrithers, M. (1983) *The Buddha*, Oxford: Oxford University Press

Church, C. D. (1971) 'The puranic myth of the four yugas', *Purana*, Vol. 13, No. 2, pp. 151–9

Cole, W. O. (2004) *Understanding Sikhism*, Edinburgh: Dunedin Academic Press

Conze, E. (trans.) (1959) *Buddhist Scriptures*, London: Penguin

Copson, A. (2017) *Secularism: Politics, Religion, and Freedom*, Oxford: Oxford University Press

Cort, J. E. (2001) *Jains in the World: Religious Values and Ideology in India*, New York, NY: Oxford University Press.

Cort, J. E. (2010) *Framing the Jina: Narratives of Icons and Idols in Jain History*, Oxford: Oxford University Press

Dasgupta, S. (2011) *Awakening: The Story of the Bengal Renaissance*, Noida: Random House

Davis, R. H. (1991) *Ritual in an Oscillating Universe*, Princeton, NJ: Princeton University Press

de Bary, W. T. (1988) *Sources of Indian Tradition*, Vol. 2 (2nd edn, edited and revised by S. Hay), New York, NY: Columbia University Press

Derné, Steve (1995) 'Market forces at work: Religious themes in commercial Hindi films', in Babb, L. A. and Wadley, S. S. (eds) (1995) *Media and the Transformation of Religion in South Asia*, Philadelphia, PA: University of Pennsylvania Press, pp. 191–216

Deutsch, E. (trans. and commentary) (1968) *The Bhagavad Gita: Translated, with Introduction and Critical Essays by Eliot Deutsch*, New York, NY: Holt, Rinehart and Winston

Dirks, N. (2001) *Castes of Mind: Colonialism and the Making of Modern India*, Princeton: Princeton University Press

Doniger, W. (2009) *The Hindus: An Alternative History*, New York: Penguin

Doniger O'Flaherty, W. (1973) *Asceticism and Eroticism in the Mythology of Siva*, London: Oxford University Press

Doniger O'Flaherty, W. (1975) *Hindu Myths*, London: Penguin

Doniger O'Flaherty, W. (1976) *The Origins of Evil in Hindu Mythology*, Berkeley, CA: University of California Press

Doniger O'Flaherty, W. (trans. and commentary) (1981) *The Rig Veda: An Anthology*, London: Penguin

Dumont, L. (1970) *Homo Hierarchicus: An Essay on the Caste System* (trans. by M. Sainsbury), Chicago, IL: University of Chicago Press

Dundas, P. (2002) *The Jains*, 2nd edn, London and New York, NY: Routledge

Eaton, R. M. (1993) *The Rise of Islam and the Bengal Frontier, 1204–1760*, Berkeley, CA: University of California Press

Eck, D. L. (1985) *Darsan: Seeing the Divine Image in India*, 2nd edn, Chambersburg, PA: Anima Books

Elias, J. J. (1999) *Islam*, Upper Saddle River, NJ: Prentice Hall

Esposito, J. L. (2011) *Islam: The Straight Path*, 4th edn, Oxford: Oxford University Press

Flood, G. (1996) *An Introduction to Hinduism*, Cambridge: Cambridge University Press

Flueckiger, J. B. (2015) *Everyday Hinduism*, Chichester: John Wiley & Sons

Frykenberg, R. E. (1989) 'The emergence of modern "Hinduism" as a concept and as an institution: A reappraisal with special reference to South India', in Sontheimer, G. D. and Kulke, H. (eds) (1989) *Hinduism Reconsidered*, New Delhi: Manohar, pp. 29–49

Gamliel, O. (2018) 'Textual networks and transregional encounters: Jewish networks in Kerala 900s-1600s', *Social Orbit*, Vol. 4, No. 1, pp. 41–73

Gittinger, J. L. (2017) 'The rhetoric of violence, religion, and purity in India's cow protection movement', *Journal of Religion and Violence*; doi: 10.5840/jrv201751540

Gold, D. (1987) *The Lord as Guru: Hindi Sants in the Northern Indian Tradition*, Oxford: Oxford University Press.

Gold, D. (1994) 'The Dadu-*panth*: A religious order in its Rajasthan context', in Schomer, K., *et al.* (eds) (1994) *The Idea of Rajasthan: Explorations in Regional Identity, Vol. II, Institutions*, Columbia, MO: South Asia Publications, pp. 242–64

Gombrich, R. F. (1998) *Buddhist Precept and Practice: Traditional Buddhism in the Rural Highlands of Ceylon* (reprint of 1991 edn originally published by Oxford University Press),

Delhi: Motilal Banarsidass

Gowan, A. and Sharma, M (2018) 'Rising Hate Crime in India', *Washington Post*, 31 October (online). Available from URL: https://wapo.st/india-hate-crimes?tid=ss_mail (accessed November 2018)

Growse, F. S. (trans.) (1978) *The Ramayana of Tulasi Dasa* (edited and revised by R. C. Prasad), Delhi: Motilal Banarsidass

Guichard, S. (2010) *The Construction of History and Nationalism in India: Textbooks, Controversies and Politics*, London: Routledge

Gupta, D. (2017) *From 'People' to 'Citizen': Democracy's Must Take Road*, New Delhi: Social Science Press

Hansen, T. B. (1999) *The Saffron Wave: Democracy and Hindu Nationalism in Modern India*, Princeton, NJ: Princeton University Press

Hawley, J. S. (1984) *Sur Das: Poet, Singer, Saint*, Seattle, WA: University of Washington Press

Hawley, J. S. (2005) *Three Bhakti Voices: Mirabai, Surdas, and Kabir in Their Time and Ours*, New Delhi: Oxford University Press

Hawley, J. S. and Juergensmeyer, M. (eds. and trans.) (1988) *Songs of the Saints of India*, New York, NY: Oxford University Press

Heim, M. (2004) *Theories of the Gift in South Asia: Hindu, Buddhist, and Jain Reflections on Dana*, New York, NY and London: Routledge

Heim, M. (2018) *Voice of the Buddha: Buddhaghosa on the Immeasurable Words*, Oxford: Oxford University Press

Hess, L. and Singh, S. (1983) *The Bijak of Kabir*, San Francisco, CA: North Point Press

Hiltebeitel, A. (1978) 'The Indus Valley "proto-Siva", reexamined through reflections on the goddess, the buffalo, and the symbolism of vahanas', *Anthropos*, Vol. 73, pp. 767–97

Hindu, The (2016) 'The Dadri lynching: how events unfolded', *The Hindi*, 28 March (online). Available from URL: www.thehindu.com/specials/in-depth/the-dadri-lynching-how-events-unfolded/article7719414.ece (accessed December 2018)

Hopkins, T. J. (1971) *The Hindu Religious Tradition*, Belmont, CA: Wadsworth

Inglis, S. R. (1995) 'Suitable for framing: The work of a modern master', in Babb, L. A. and Wadley, S. S. (eds) (1995) *Media and the Transformation of Religion in South Asia*, Philadelphia, PA: University of Pennsylvania Press, pp. 51–75

Jack, H. A. (ed.) (1956) *The Gandhi Reader: A Sourcebook of His Life and Writings*, New York, NY: AMS Press

Jaffrelot, C. (1996) *The Hindu Nationalist Movement in India*, New York, NY: Columbia University Press

Jain, K. C. (2010) *History of Jainism* (three vols), New Delhi: D. K. Printworld

Jaini, P. S. (1974) 'On the sarvajnatva (omniscience) of Mahavira and the Buddha', in Jaini, P. S. (ed.) (2001) *Collected Papers on Buddhist Studies*, Delhi: Motilal Banarsidass, pp. 97–121

Jaini, P. S. (1979) *The Jaina Path of Purification*, Berkeley, CA: University of California Press

Jalal, Ayesha (1985) *The Sole Spokesman: Jinnah, the Muslim League and the Demand for Pakistan*, Cambridge: Cambridge University Press

Jha, K. N. (2002) *The Myth of the Holy Cow*, New York, NY: Verso

Jodhka, S. S. (2012) *Caste*, New Delhi: Oxford University Press

Johnson, E. H. (trans.) (1978) *Asvaghosa's Buddhacarita or Acts of the Buddha* (reprint of 1936 original), Delhi: Motilal Banarsidass

Jones, K. W. (1976) *Arya Dharm: Hindu Consciousness in 19th-Century Punjab*, Berkeley, CA: University of California Press

Juergensmeyer, M. (1987) 'The Radhasoami revival of the Sant tradition', in Schomer, K. and McLeod, W. H. (eds) *The Sants: Studies in a Devotional Tradition of India*, Berkeley, CA and Delhi: Berkeley Religious Studies Series and Motilal Banarsidass (co-publishers), pp. 359–55

Juergensmeyer, M. (1991) *Radhasoami Reality: The Logic of a Modern Faith*, Princeton, NJ: Princeton University Press

Katz, N. (2000) *Who Are the Jews of India?*, Berkeley, CA: University of California Press

Katz, N. (2013) 'South Asian Judaisms: Practicing tradition today', in Pechikis, K. and Raj, S. J. (eds) (2013) *South Asian Religions: Tradition and Today*, London: Routledge, pp. 143–58

Keay, J. (2000) *India: A History*, New York, NY: Atlantic Monthly Press

Kelting, W. (2001) *Singing to the Jinas: Jain Laywomen, Mandal Singing, and the Negotiations of Jain Devotion*, Oxford: Oxford University Press

Kenoyer, J. M. (1998) *Ancient Cities of the Indus Valley Civilization*, Karachi: Oxford University Press

Kesavan, B. S. (1985) *History of Printing and Publishing in India: A Story of Cultural Re-awakening*, Vol. I, New Delhi: National Book Trust

Khilnani, S. (1999) *The Idea of India* (first paperback edn), New York, NY: Farrar, Straus and Giroux

Kinsley, D. R. (2000) *The Sword and the Flute: Kali and Krsna, Dark Visions of the Terrible and Sublime in Hindu Mythology*, 2nd edn, Berkeley, CA: University of California Press

Klostermaier, K. K. (1994) *A Survey of Hinduism*, 2nd edn, Albany, NY: State University of New York Press

Klostermaier, K. K. (1998) *A Short Introduction to Hinduism*, Oxford: Oneworld Publications

Knipe, D. M. (1991) *Hinduism: Experiments in the Sacred*, San Francisco, CA: HarperSanFrancisco

Kopf, D. (1979) *The Brahmo Samaj and the Shaping of the Indian Mind*, Princeton, NJ: Princeton University Press

Kramrisch, S. (1981) *The Presence of Siva*, Princeton, NJ: Princeton University Press

Kripal, J. J. (1995) *Kali's Child: The Mystical and the Erotic in the Life and Teachings of Ramakrishna*, 2nd edn, Chicago, IL: University of Chicago Press

Laidlaw, J. (1995) *Riches and Renunciation: Religion and Economy among the Jains*, Oxford: Oxford University Press

Lal, K. S. (1973) *Growth of Muslim Population in Medieval India (AD 1000–1800)*, Delhi: Research Publications

Lambourn, E. (2018) *Abraham's Luggage: A Social Life of Things in the Medieval Indian Ocean World*, Cambridge: Cambridge University Press

Lawrence, B. B. (1987) 'The Sant movement and North Indian Sufis', in Schomer, K. and McLeod, W. H. (eds) (1987) *The Sants: Studies in a Devotional Tradition of India*, Berkeley, CA and Delhi: Berkeley Religious Studies Series and Motilal Banarsidass (co-publishers), pp. 359–73

Lorenzen, D. N. (1987) 'The Kabir-panth and social protest', in Schomer, K. and McLeod, W. H. (eds) (1987) *The Sants: Studies in a Devotional Tradition of India*, Berkeley, CA and Delhi: Berkeley Religious Studies Series and Motilal Banarsidass (co-publishers), pp. 281–303

Lorenzen, D. N. (1999) 'Who invented Hinduism?', *Comparative Studies in Society and History: An International Quarterly*, Vol. 41, No. 4, pp. 630–59

Lorenzen, D. N. (2004) 'Bhakti', in Mittal, S. and Thursby, G. (eds) (2004) *The Hindu World*, London: Routledge, pp. 185–209

Lutgendorf, P. (1991) *The Life of a Text: Performing the Ramcaritmanas of Tulsidas*, Berkeley, CA: University of California Press

Lutgendorf, P. (1995) 'All in the (Raghu) family: A video epic in cultural context', in Babb, L. A. and Wadley, S. S. (eds) (1995) *Media and the Transformation of Religion in South Asia*, Philadelphia, PA: University of Pennsylvania Press, pp. 217–53

Lutgendorf, P. (2007) *Hanuman's Tale: The Message of a Divine Monkey*, Oxford: Oxford University Press

McLeod, W. H. (1968) *Guru Nanak and the Sikh Religion*, Oxford: Oxford University Press

McLeod, W. H. (1976) *The Evolution of the Sikh Community: Five Essays*, Oxford, Oxford University Press

McLeod, W. H. (1987) 'The development of the Sikh Panth', in Schomer, K. and McLeod, W. H. (eds) (1987) *The Sants: Studies in a Devotional Tradition of India*, Berkeley, CA and Delhi: Berkeley Religious Studies Series and Motilal Banarsidass (co-publishers), pp. 227–49

Madan, T. N. (1987) 'Secularism in its place', *Journal of Asian Studies*, Vol. 46, No. 4, pp. 747–59

Majmudar, A. (trans. and commentary) (2018) *Godsong: A Verse Translation of the Bhagavad-Gita, with Commentary*, New York, NY: Alfred A. Knopf

Marriott, M. (1955) 'Little communities in an indigenous civilization', in Marriott, M. (ed.) (1955) *Village India: Studies in the Little Community*, Chicago, IL: University of Chicago Press, pp. 171–222

Marriott, M. (1976) 'Hindu transactions: Diversity without dualism', in Kapferer, B. (ed.) (1976) *Transaction and Meaning: Directions in the Anthropology of Exchange and Symbolic Behavior*, Philadelphia, PA: Ishi Publishers, pp. 109–42

Metcalf, B. D. (1982) *Islamic Revival in British India: Deoband, 1860–1900*, Princeton, NJ: Princeton University Press

Metcalf, B. D. and Metcalf, T. R. (2012) *A Concise History of Modern India*, 3rd edn, Cambridge: Cambridge University Press

Michaels, A. (2004) *Hinduism: Past and Present* (trans. by Harshav, B.), Princeton, NJ: Princeton University Press

Michaels, A. (2016) *Homo Ritualis: Hindu Ritual and its Significance for Ritual Theory*, Oxford: Oxford University Press

Mines, D. P. (2009) *Caste in India*, Ann Arbor, MI: Association for Asian Studies

Morris-Jones, W. H. (1964) *The Government and Politics of India*, London: Hutchinson University Library

Nandy, A. (1985) 'An anti-secularist manifesto', *Seminar*, Vol. 314, pp. 14–24

Narayan, R. K. (1977) *The Ramayana: A Shortened Modern Prose Version of the Indian Epic (Suggested by the Tamil Version of Kamban)*, London: Penguin

Narayan, R. K. (1978) *The Mahabharata: A Shortened Modern Prose Version of the Indian Epic*, New York, NY: Viking

Nasr, S. H. (2003) *Islam: Religion, History, and Civilization*, New York, NY: HarperSanFrancisco

Nehru, J. (1946) *The Discovery of India*, New York, NY: John Day

Oberoi, H. (1994) *The Construction of Religious Boundaries: Culture, Identity and Diversity in the Sikh Tradition*, Delhi: Oxford University Press

Olivelle, P. (1993) *The Asrama System: The History and Hermeneutics of a Religious Institution*, Oxford: Oxford University Press

Olivelle, P. (trans. and commentary) (1996) *Upanisads*, Oxford: Oxford University Press

Olivelle, P. (trans. and commentary) (2004) *The Law Code of Manu*, Oxford: Oxford University Press

Olivelle, P. (trans. and commentary) (2008) *Life of the Buddha by Asvaghosa*, New York, NY: New York University Press

Omvedt, G. (2003) *Buddhism in India: Challenging Brahmanism and Caste*, New Delhi: Sage

Padoux, A. (2017) *The Hindu Tantric World: An Overview*, Chicago, IL: University of Chicago Press

Parpola, A. (2015) *The Roots of Hinduism: The Early Aryans and the Indus Civilization*, Oxford, Oxford University Press

Parry, J. (1994) *Death in Banaras*, Cambridge: Cambridge University Press

Patton, L. L. (trans. and commentary) (2008) *The Bhagavad Gita*, London: Penguin

Pennington, B. K. (2005) *Was Hinduism Invented? Britons, Indians, and the Colonial Construction of Religion*, New York, NY: Oxford University Press

Pinch, W. R. (2006) *Warrior Ascetics and Indian Empires*, Cambridge: Cambridge University Press

Pinney, C. (2004) *'Photos of the Gods': The Printed Image and Political Struggle in India*, London: Reaktion Books

Possehl, G. L. (2002) *The Indus Civilization: A Contemporary Perspective*, Walnut Creek, CA: AltaMira

Ra'anan, U. (1990) 'The nation-state fallacy', in Montville, J. V. (ed.) (1990) *Conflict and Peacemaking in Multiethnic Societies*, Lexington, MA: Lexington Books, pp. 5–20

Rahula, W. (1974) *What the Buddha Taught*, 2nd and enlarged edn, New York, NY: Grove Press

Raj, S. J. and Dempsey, C. G. (eds) (2002) *Popular Christianity in India: Riting between the Lines*, Albany, NY: State University of New York Press

Richman, P. (ed.) (1991) *Many Ramayanas: The Diversity of a Narrative Tradition in South Asia*, Berkeley, CA: University of California Press

Robinson, A. (2015) *The Indus: Lost Civilizations*, London: Reaktion Books

Rodrigues, H. (2006) *Introducing Hinduism*, New York, NY: Routledge

Rudolph, L. I. and Rudolph, S. H. (1967) *The Modernity of Tradition*: Political *Development in India*, Chicago, IL: University of Chicago Press

Sahgal, S. (1994) 'Spread of Jinism in North India between circa 200 BC and circa AD 300', in Bhattacharyya, N. N. (ed.) (1994) *Jainism and Prakrit in Ancient and Medieval India: Essays for Prof. Jagdish Chandra Jain*, New Delhi: Manohar, pp. 205–32

Sangave, V. A. (1980) *Jaina Community: A Social Survey*, Bombay: Popular Prakashan

Savarkar, V. D. (1969) *Hindutva: Who Is a Hindu*, 5th edn, Bombay: Veer Savarkar Prakashan

Schmidt-Leukel, P. (2006) *Understanding Buddhism*, Edinburgh: Dunedin Academic Press

Schomer, K. and McLeod, W. H. (eds) (1987) *The Sants: Studies in a Devotional Tradition of India*, Berkeley, CA and Delhi: Berkeley Religious Studies Series and Motilal Banarsidass (co-publishers)

Sen, A. P. (2000) *Swami Vivekananda*, New Delhi: Oxford University Press

Sen, A. P. (2010) *Ramakrishna Paramahamsa: The Sadhaka of Dakshineswar*, New Delhi: Penguin Viking

Seneviratne, H. L. (1999) *The Work of Kings: The New Buddhism in Sri Lanka*, Chicago, IL: University of Chicago Press

Shanta, N. (1997) *The Unknown Pilgrims: The Voice of the Sadhvis: The History, Spirituality and Life of Jaina Women Ascetics*, Delhi: Sri Satguru Publications

Singh, P. (2006) 'Sikh Dharm', in Mittal, S. and Thursby, G. (eds) *Religions of South Asia: An Introduction*, London: Routledge, pp. 131–48

Smith, H. D. (1995) 'Impact of "god posters" on Hindus and their devotional traditions', in Babb, L. A. and Wadley, S. S. (eds) (1995) *Media and the Transformation of Religion in South Asia*, Philadelphia, PA: University of Pennsylvania Press, pp. 24–50

Smith, W. C. (1957) *Islam in Modern History*, Princeton, NJ: Princeton University Press

Srinivas, M. N. (1965) *Religion and Society among the Coorgs of South India* (reprint of 1952 original), London: Asia Publishing House

Stevens, J. A. (2018) *Keshab: Bengal's Forgotten Prophet*, Oxford: Oxford University Press

Talbot, I. (2000) *India and Pakistan: Inventing the Nation*, London: Arnold

Talbot, I. (2016) *A History of Modern South Asia: Politics, States, Diasporas*, New Haven, CT: Yale University Press

Thangaraj, M. T. (2006) 'Indian Christian tradition', in Mittal, S. and Thursby, G. (eds) *Religions of South Asia: An Introduction*, London: Routledge, pp. 185–98

Thapar, R. (1985) 'Syndicated moksha', *Seminar*, Vol. 313 (September), pp. 14–22

Traub, A. (2018) 'India's dangerous new curriculum', *New York Review of Books*, 6 December, pp. 41–3

Trautmann, T. R. (2005) 'Introduction', in Trautmann, T. (ed.) (2005) *The Aryan Debate*, New Delhi, Oxford University Press, pp. xiii–xliii

Trautmann, T. R. (2011) *India: Brief History of a Civilization*, Oxford: Oxford University Press

Trevelyan, G. O. (ed.) (1883) *Life and Letters of Lord Macaulay*, Vol. I, 2nd edn, London: Longmans, Green

Tyagananda, S. and Vrajaprana, P. (2010) *Interpreting Ramakrishna: Kali's Child Revisited*, Delhi: Motilal Banarsidass

Vallely, A. (2002) *Guardians of the Transcendent: An Ethnography of a Jain Ascetic Community*, Toronto: University of Toronto Press

Van der Veer, P. (1994) *Religious Nationalism: Hindus and Muslims in India*, Berkeley, CA: University of California Press

Vaudeville, C. (1974) *Kabir*, Oxford: Oxford University Press

Vaudeville, C. (1987) 'Sant mat: Santism as a universal path to sanctity', in Schomer, K. and McLeod, W. H. (eds) (1987) *The Sants: Studies in a Devotional Tradition of India*, Berkeley, CA and Delhi: Berkeley Religious Studies Series and Motilal Banarsidass (co-publishers), pp. 21–40

Vinayasagar, Mahopadhyaya (ed. and Hindi trans; English trans by Lath, M.) (1984) *Kalpasutra*, Jaipur: Prakrit Bharati

Wadley, S. S. (1995) 'Printed images: Introduction', in Babb, L. A. and Wadley, S. S. (eds) (1995) *Media and the Transformation of Religion in South Asia*, Philadelphia, PA: University of Pennsylvania Press, pp. 21–3

Wasson, R. G. (1971) *Soma: The Divine Mushroom of Immortality*, New York, NY: Harcourt, Brace, Jovanovich

Weber, Max (1958; orig. 1922–23) 'The social psychology of the world religions', in Gerth, H. H. and Mills, C. W. (eds and trans.) (1958) *From Max Weber: Essays in Sociology*, New York, NY: Oxford/Galaxy, pp. 267–301

Weil, S. (2006) 'Indian Judaic tradition', in Mittal, S. and Thursby, G. (eds) (2006) *Religions of South Asia: An Introduction*, London: Routledge, pp. 169–83

Whaling, F. (2009) *Understanding Hinduism*, Edinburgh: Dunedin Academic Press

Wiley, K. L. (2004) *Historical Dictionary of Jainism*, Lanham, MD: Scarecrow Press

Williams, R. V. (2006) *Postcolonial Politics and Personal Laws: Colonial Legal Legacies and the Indian State*, New Delhi: Oxford University Press

Witzel, M. (1997) 'The development of the Vedic canon and its schools: The social and political milieu', in Witzel, M. (ed.) *Inside the Texts, Beyond the Texts: New Appoaches to the Study of the Vedas*, Cambridge, MA: Department of Sanskrit and Indian Studies (Harvard University), pp. 257–345

Zelliot, E. (2001) *From Untouchable to Dalit: Essays on the Ambedkar Movement*, 3rd edn, New Delhi: Manohar

Zimmer, H. (1946) *Myth and Symbols in Indian Art and Civilization*, Princeton, NJ: Princeton University Press

Glossary

Advaita Vedanta (Advaita Vedānta) – monist school of Hindu philosophy associated with Shankara

Agni – Vedic god of fire

ahimsa (*ahiṃsā*) – non-harm, non-violence

anatman (*anātman*) – the Buddhist doctrine of no-self or soul

Aranyakas (Āraṇyaka) – forest books; a layer of material in the Vedas preceding the Upanishads

arhat – worthy of worship; one who has achieved enlightenment

Arjuna – one of the five Pandavas; his mentoring by Krishna is described in the *Bhagavad Gita*

Ashoka (Aśoka) – Mauryan emperor; patron of Buddhism

ashrama (*āśrama*) – the four *ashramas* are the idealised stages of life of twice-born men; the term can also denote a spiritual retreat.

atman (*ātman*) – self or soul

avatara (*avatāra*) – 'descent' of a deity; normally used in connection with Vishnu

Ayodhya – the city of Rama's birth and his later kingship; also a city in Uttar Pradesh believed to be the original Ayodhya

Babri Masjid – mosque at Ayodhya said to have been built on the exact spot of Rama's birth

Bajrang Dal – 'Party of Hanuman'; a Hindu nationalist activist group

Bhagavad Gita (*Bhagavad Gītā*) – a portion of the *Mahabharata* in which Krishna mentors warrior Arjuna and reveals himself to be the Supreme Being

bhakti – devotion

Bharatiya Janata Party (BJP) – Hindu nationalist political party

Brahma (Brahmā) – an important (but not major) Hindu deity; the deity responsible for the world's creation

brahman – the unitary reality underlying the diversity of the experienced world

Brahman (Brāhmaṇ) – the varṇa of priests and teachers

Brahmanas (Brāhmaṇa) – in the Vedas, the layer of material succeeding the Samhitas and dealing particularly with sacrificial rituals

Chandala (Caṇḍāla) – the ancient social category of those excluded from the four-varna system; the ancient equivalent of today's Dalits

Congress Party – see Indian National Congress

Dalit – 'downtrodden'; formerly called untouchables

dana (*dāna*) – alms, charitable gift; merit-generating gift

darbar (*darbār*) – royal court; royal audience

darshana (*darśana*) – auspicious seeing of a deity or august personage

dashahra (*daśahrā*) – an autumn Hindu festival celebrating the victory of Rama over Ravana

deva – a god

Devanagari (*devanāgarī*) – script used in writing Sanskrit, Hindi and other Indic languages

devi (*devī*) – a goddess

dharma – sacred duty, law, religion; also, the Buddha's teachings

Dharmashastras (Dharmaśāstra) – treatises on dharma

dhoti (*dhoti*) – lower body garment worn by men and consisting of a single piece of cloth

Digambara – sky clad; the branch of Jainism whose highest-ranking monks wear no clothing

doab – the tongue of land between two converging rivers, esp. between the Ganga and Yamuna

Doordarshan – India's government-run television network

Dravidian – the language family to which the major languages of South India belong

Durga (Durgā) – a warlike form of the goddess

Eid al-Adha – the Islamic 'festival of sacrifice' in which animals are sacrificed in commemoration of Ibrahim's willingness to sacrifice his son to God

'Five Ks' – five symbols worn by all-male members of the Sikh Khalsa

Ganesha (Gaṇeśa) – the elephant-headed son of Shiva and Pavarti

guru – teacher, religious mentor

Guru Granth Sahib (*Guru Granth Sāhib*) – sacred scripture of Sikhism

Hanuman (Hanumān) – monkey-like deity who assisted Rama in the recovery of Sita

havan – fire sacrifice

Hindu Mahasabha – Hindu nationalist organisation founded in 1915

Hindutva – term used by V. D. Savarkar to denote Hindu/Indian national identity; also the title of his book on the subject

homa – fire sacrifice

Indian National Congress (INC) – the organisation that brought independence to India and subsequently became a major political party

Jan Sangh – the Hindu nationalist party that was the precursor of the Bharatiya Janata Party (BJP)

janambhumi (*janambhūmi*) – place of birth

Jat (Jāṭ) – agricultural caste of north-western India

jati (*jāti*) – 'birth group'; caste

Jina – conqueror; a synonym of Tirthankara

jiva (jīva) – 'life'; in Jain teachings, the individual self or soul

jivan mukti (*jīvan mukti*) – liberation while still living

jnana (jñāna) – knowledge

Kali (Kālī) – ferocious form of the goddess

kali yuga – current degraded era of world-time

karma – action that affects the subsequent destiny of the actor; in Jainism, a form of matter that adheres to the soul

kar sevak – volunteer worker

kevalajnana (kevalajñāna) – omniscience

Khalsa (Khālsā) – the reformed and martialised Sikh community instituted by Guru Gobind Singh in 1699

Khatri (Khatrī) – trading caste of northern India concentrated in Punjab

khilafat (*khilāfat*) – the caliphate

Krishna (Kṛṣṇa) – Vishnu's eighth avatara and mentor to Arjuna in the *Bhagavad Gita*

Kshatriya (Kṣatriya) – the varna of rulers and warriors

Lakshmi (Lakṣmī) – the goddess of prosperity and consort of Vishnu

linga (*liṅga*) – phallic object in which form Shiva is usually worshipped

Lok Sabha – people's assembly; the lower house of the Indian Parliament

Mahabharata (Mahābhārata) – one of the two great Hindu Epics; it describes the war between the Pandavas and their cousins the Kauravas

Mahayana (Mahāyāna) – greater vehicle; one of the major branches of Buddhism

moksha (*mokṣa*) – liberation

Nath Yogi (Nāth Yogī) – a type of Shaiva ascetic

nawab – governor of a Mughal province

nirguna (*nirguṇa*) – without attributes (opp. *saguna*)

nirvana (*nirvāṇa*) – extinction; in Buddhist teachings, the end of one's existence in samsara

Other Backward Classes (OBCs) – castes higher in status than Dalits but also deemed worthy of government reservations

Pandavas (Pāṇḍavas) – the five sons of Pandu who fought a war against their cousins as depicted in the *Mahabharata*

panth – path; sect or religious community

parda (*pardā*) – curtain; the seclusion of women

Parvati (Pārvatī) – consort of Shiva

phala – fruit; the fruits of our karmas (i.e., actions)

prasada (*prasāda*) – offering made to a deity in puja and then returned to the offerer

puja (*pūjā*) – homage; a Hindu rite of worship

Puranas (Purāṇas) – antiquities; religious compendia, conventionally eighteen in number, containing a vast range of stories of the Hindu deities and other material

ramrajya (*rāmrājya*) – rule of Rama; just rule

Rajput (Rājpūt) – sons of kings; martial community of northern India

Rama, also Ram (Rāma) – Vishnu's seventh avatara; prince and king of Ayodhya

Ramayana (Rāmāyaṇa) – epic poem telling the story of Rama and his defeat of the demon Ravana

Ramcharitmanas (Rāmcaritmānas) – Holy Lake of the Deeds of Rama; a version of the *Ramayana* composed in the Avadhi dialect of Hindi by the great poet Tulsidas

Rashtriya Swayamsevak Sangh (RSS) – the right-wing Hindu nationalist organisation

saguna (*saguṇa*) – with attributes (opp. *nirguna*)

Samhitas (Saṃhitā) – collections; the oldest strata of the four Vedas

Samkhya (Sāṃkhya) – dualist school of philosophy and philosophical background of the *Bhagavad Gita*

samnyasa (*saṃnyāsa*) – world renunciation

samsara (*saṃsāra*) – rebirth; the world of rebirth

Sangh Pariwar – the 'family' of right-wing Hindu nationalist organisations

sangha (*saṅgha*) – society, association; in Buddhism, the community of monks and nuns

Sanskritisation – emulation of customs and norms of higher castes as a means of achieving upward social mobility

sant – often glossed as 'saint'; a spiritually realised person

sant mat – the teachings of the Sants, here referring to the nirguna Sants of central and northern India

Sarasvati (Sarasvatī) – consort of Brahma; the goddess of learning, music and the arts generally

sati (*satī*) – a virtuous woman; a woman who immolates herself with her husband's body

satyagraha (*satyāgraha*) – grasping or holding to truth, often rendered as 'truth force'; Gandhi's distinctive method of non-violent resistance and persuasion

Shaiva (Śaiva) – devotee of Shiva

shakti (*śakti*) – power, energy; goddesses (who personify power)

Shakta (*śākta*) – *devotee of the goddess*

Shankara (Śaṅkara) – eighth-century philosopher and Hindu revivalist who systematised the Advaita Vedanta

Shi'a – Islamic sect whose adherents believe that the khilafat should have passed to Ali, Muhammad's son-in-law and his descendants

Shiva (Śiva) – a major Hindu deity; sometimes said to be the god of 'destruction'

Shivaji (Śivājī) – seventeenth-century Maratha warrior-king

Shramana (Śramaṇa) – exerter or striver; a non-Vedic ascetic

shruti (*śruti*) – heard; revealed knowledge; the Vedas

Shudra (Śūdra) – lowest of the varnas whose function is to 'serve' the top three varnas

Sita (Sītā) – wife of Rama

smriti (*smṛti*) – remembered; scripture authored, not revealed

stupa (*stupā*) – dome-like structure in which relics of the Buddha are kept

Sunni (Sunnī) – Islamic mainstream that accepts the legitimacy of the first four caliphs

Svetambara (Śvetāmbara) – white-clad; the branch of Jainism whose mendicants wear white clothing

swadeshi – (*svadeśī*) – of one's own country; the use of products originating within India as promoted by Indian nationalists

swaraj (svarāj) – self-rule

tapas – ascetic practice

Theravada (Theravāda) – teachings of the elders; the oldest branch of Buddhism, prevailing in Sri Lanka and South-east Asia today

Tirthankara (Tīrthaṅkara) – in Jainism, one who establishes a 'ford' (as in a ford across a river); an omniscient teacher; synonymous with Jina

Trimurti (Trimūrti) – the Hindu triform consisting of Brahma, Vishnu and Shiva

Twice-Born – males of the top three varnas who undergo an initiation regarded as a second birth

'ulama (*'ulamā*) – Islamic jurists and theologians

Upanishads (Upaniṣad) – the most recent and philosophical of the four strata of Vedic texts

Vaishnava (Vaiṣṇava) – devotee of Vishnu

Vaiśya – third in rank of the four varnas; associated mainly with trade and banking

varna (*varṇa*) – a hereditary class, viz. Brahman, Kshatriya, Vaishya, Shudra

varnashrama (*varṇāśrama*) *dharma* – a framework of statuses determining the duties of twice-born males based on varna (class) and ashrama (stage of life)

Veda – a category of sacred and originally oral literature including the Samhitas, Brahmanas, Aranyakas and Upanishads

Vedanta (Vedānta) – end of the Vedas; schools of philosophy based on the Upanishads of which the most famous is Shankara's Advaita Vedanta

Vishnu (Viṣṇu) – a major Hindu deity who intervenes in the affairs of world in the form of avataras (descents), the most famous of which are Rama and Krishna

Vishva Hindu Parishad (VHP) – World Hindu Council; considered to be the ecclesiastical arm of the Rashtriya Swayamsevak Sangh (RSS)

yoga – contemplative discipline

yogi (*yogi*) – practitioner of yoga

yoni – womb; vulva

yuga – era; any of the four successive ages (four yugas) of the world

Suggested Further Reading

In what follows, I provide suggestions for further reading about some of the principal topics covered in this book. It is by no means comprehensive, but it might be helpful as a starting point for further exploration of some key matters. Many are works cited (and in some cases suggested) in the text; others are not.

There is an abundance of good general histories of India. One of the best is Keay (2000); much less detailed but perfect for one or two sit-downs is Trautmann (2011). A highly accessible work on the Indus valley is Robinson (2015), but further inquiry should include Kenoyer (1998), Possehl (2002) and especially Parpola (2015).

Translations of Vedic hymns can be found in Doniger O'Flaherty (1981), and Olivelle (1996) provides translations of the principal Upanishads. The evolution of Hindu traditions from their earliest beginnings is treated in such general works as Brockington (1981), Flood (1996), Hopkins (1971), Klostermaier (1994; 1998), Michaels (2004), Rodrigues (2006) and Whaling (2009). In a refreshing variation from conventional surveys, Doniger (same author as Doniger O'Flaherty) (2009) emphasises the normally unmentioned contributions of women and low castes. Doniger O'Flaherty (1975) has translated Puranic and Epic material dealing with major figures in the Hindu pantheon, and for a translation of *The Laws of Manu*, see Olivelle (2004). Famed novelist R. K. Narayan has authored wonderful retellings of the Mahabharata and Ramayana (Narayan, 1977; 1978). Tantrism is a hard subject to explain, but Padoux (2017) has notably succeeded in doing so. There have been many translations of the *Bhagavad Gita*, and among the best is Patton (2008), but also see Majmudar (2018) for a very readable and deeply felt verse translation. Readers interested in an ethnographically oriented introduction to Hindu traditions as they exist today could start with Flueckiger (2015).

Turning to the dissenting traditions, the Buddha's teachings are treated in three fine introductions for the general reader – Cantwell (2010), Carrithers (1983) and Rahula (1974) – and the story of the historical development of Buddhism in its South Asian context is lucidly told by Berkwitz (2010). No introduction to the complexities of formal Jain teachings has ever surpassed Jaini (1979) for clarity and scholarly authority; a more historically oriented study, also deservedly a classic, is Dundas (2002). Descriptions of mendicant lifestyles among Jains are provided by

Shanta (1997) and Vallely (2002), and descriptions of contemporary lay Jain life can be found in Cort (2001), Kelting (2001), Laidlaw (1995), and Babb (2015); Babb (1996; 2004) treats Jainism and caste.

General works on Islam are many, and among the most accessible are Elias (1999), Esposito (2011) and Nasr (2003). A very good treatment of Islam's South Asian career can be found in Asher and Talbot (2006), and conversion issues are laid out in detail in Eaton (1993, and extensively cited in this book). The post-Islamic career of non-Muslim traditions presents a highly varied scholarly landscape. Readers will find relevant material in the general works on Hinduism cited above, and the most important figures among the northern poet-saints are introduced along with samples of their verse in Hawley and Juergensmeyer (1988). On Mirabai and Surdas specifically, see Hawley (1984; 2005), and see Lutgendorf (1991) on Tulsidas and the *Ramcharitmanas*. Fine translations of Surdas's *Sursagar* can be found in Bryant and Hawley (2015). On the nirguna sants, Gold (1987) presents a good overview, and Schomer and McLeod's (1987) edited volume provides an array of essays on specific sant-related topics. On Kabir specifically, Vaudeville (1974) and Hess and Singh (1983) are good introductions, and the works of W. H. McLeod (1968; 1976) are standard starting points for the study of Sikhism. A concise survey of Sikhism's history, teachings and practice can be found between the covers of a single book in Cole (2004).

There is certainly no shortage of general works on modern Indian history, but Metcalf and Metcalf (2012) and Talbot (2016) are noteworthy for their accessibility and manageable length; Talbot's book widens the aperture to include Pakistan and Bangladesh and follows the story well into the twenty-first century. No inquiry into the disputatious matter of the invention of Hinduism can overlook Pennington's (2005) study. The literature on nineteenth-century religious reforms abounds in hagiography, but Kopf (1979), Jones (1976) and Oberoi (1994) are good guides to Bengali reform, Arya Samaj and the Singh Sabha movement, respectively. Barbara Metcalf's (1982) study of Deoband is indispensable for an understanding of Islamic reform in South Asia.

The story of India's independence movement and the subcontinent's partition has been told and retold, but Metcalf and Metcalf (2012) pull the many threads of the tale together with particular clarity. Talbot (2000) emphasises the historical and cultural context from which emerged the national ideas that gave birth to the Republic of India and the Islamic Republic of Pakistan. For a fascinating study of the independence movement as depicted in printed imagery, see Pinney (2004). The rise of the RSS is treated in Andersen and Damle (1987). On Jinnah's role in the events surrounding independence, see Jalal (1985).

A sense of the debates in the 1980s about the nature of India's secularism can be gained from reading Madan (1987), Brass (1999) and Nandy (1985). The Shah Bano affair and the issues at stake are thoroughly dissected by Williams (2006). A fine account of Ramanand Sagar's *Ramayan* and its cultural significance is Lutgendorf (1995), and by far the best single analysis of the Ayodhya affair and its political significance is to be found in Jaffrelot (1996). Andersen and Damle (2018) have written a well-informed account of how matters stand with the BJP and RSS today, and Basu (2015) has traced and analysed anti-minority violence in the Indian republic.

Index